W9-DAH-627

Freud's Theory of Culture

Freud's Theory of Culture

Eros, Loss, and Politics

Abraham Drassinower

CABRINI COLLEGE LIBRARY
610 KING OF PRUSSIA ROAD
RADNOR, PA 19087

ROWMAN & LITTLEFIELD PUBLISHERS, INC.
Lanham • Boulder • New York • Oxford

#50477298

ROWMAN & LITTLEFIELD PUBLISHERS, INC.

Published in the United States of America
by Rowman & Littlefield Publishers, Inc.
A Member of the Rowman & Littlefield Publishing Group
4501 Forbes Boulevard, Suite 200, Lanham, Maryland 20706
www.rowmanlittlefield.com

P.O. Box 317, Oxford, OX2 9RU, United Kingdom

Copyright © 2003 by Rowman & Littlefield Publishers, Inc.

All rights reserved. No part of this publication may be reproduced, stored
in a retrieval system, or transmitted in any form or by any means, electronic,
mechanical, photocopying, recording, or otherwise, without the prior permission
of the publisher.

British Library Cataloguing in Publication Information Available

Library of Congress Cataloging-in-Publication Data

Freud's theory of culture : Eros, loss, and politics / Abraham Drassinower.
  p. cm.
  Includes bibliographical references and index.
  ISBN 0-7425-2261-X (cloth : alk. paper) — ISBN 0-7425-2262-8 (pbk. : alk.paper)
    1. Psychoanalysis and culture. 2. Freud, Sigmund, 1856–1939. I. Title.
  BF175.4.C84D723 2003
  150.19'52—dc21

                                                                    2002012735

Printed in the United States of America

♾™ The paper used in this publication meets the minimum requirements of
American National Standard for Information Sciences—Permanence of Paper
for Printed Library Materials, ANSI/NISO Z39.48-1992.

For Catherine

In Parting—Not how one soul comes close to another but how it moves away shows me their kinship and how much they belong together.

—Friedrich Nietzsche

Contents

Acknowledgments

No one writes a book on his own. I would like to thank Alkis Kontos for his guidance; Zev Friedman and Gad Horowitz for their insight and support; and William Connolly, Fred Dallmayr, and Arnold Weinrib for their encouragement. William Robinson helped me understand the virtues of saying what comes to mind. Catherine Davis continues to insist that we are at our best when we find our generosity. I am grateful for it all.

Edward Andrew, Ronnie Beiner, Norman Doige, David Dyzenhaus, Terry Heinrichs, Mark Lippincott, Loralea Michaelis, Melissa Orlie, and Alice Ormiston commented on parts or on all of the manuscript. Victoria Blond, Mary Newberry, and Andrea Slane assisted me in the transition from manuscript to book, as did Mary Carpenter, Janice Braunstein, Laura Roberts, and Chris Thillen of Rowman & Littlefield. The project was completed with the assistance of the Social Sciences and Research Council of Canada and the Connaught Foundation at the University of Toronto.

Introduction

We are living in a specially remarkable period. We find to our astonishment that progress has allied itself with barbarism.

—Sigmund Freud, *Moses and Monotheism: Three Essays*

This book is a dialogue with Freud about unhappiness—and about whether a tragic sense of life must of necessity ally itself with the actual rather than the possible, with things as they are rather than with things as they can be. I will argue that Freud's theory of culture positions itself between the demands for action and the claims of a truly human wisdom. It lays bare the dynamics whereby, in refusing the ontological predicaments of loss and death, we deliver ourselves over to the ravages of a history both distant from life and intent upon destroying it.

My central claim is that what is generally (mis)taken as Freud's pessimism is, on the contrary, the very standpoint from which he envisions an alternative to the cultural 'malaise' he describes. Freud's theory of culture is a deeply critical theory about how human beings fall short of who they can be by refusing to be the mortal beings that they are. To mistake Freud's attentiveness to loss and death is therefore to forgo the opportunity to develop a language of critique that, neither optimistic nor pessimistic, opposes to things as they are the lessons, in Northrop Frye's phrase, of an "educated imagination." It is this opportunity that I seek to seize.

Contrary to prevailing images of Freud as a predominantly psychological thinker, my purpose is to display a deep affinity between Freud's theory of culture and the Western tradition of political philosophy. I develop

1

this affinity through an examination of the related roles of loss, death, authority, and intersubjectivity in Freud's theory of culture. This examination grounds an approach to Freud that, by way of comparisons with Hobbes and Hegel, grasps Freud's relation to political life not in terms of a diagnostic imposition of psychoanalytic categories, but rather in terms of an analysis of shared themes that animate both psychoanalysis and political thought. By providing an account of things as they are as well as a vision of an alternative configuration of cultural life, Freud's theory of culture expressly addresses questions pertinent to the formation of individual-society relations, to the entanglements of politics and pedagogy, and to the encounter between power, knowledge, and historical change. Freud's stature as a participant in the Western tradition of political philosophy has been vastly underestimated.

My reflection recalls that highly problematic tradition of Freud interpretation that finds in psychoanalysis not so much a therapeutic technique as much as a philosophy of culture. In North America, Herbert Marcuse, Norman O. Brown, and Philip Rieff are still its most illustrious representatives.[1] Unlike Marcuse and Brown, however, I do not attempt to enlist Freud in the service of utopian aspirations that, when all is said and done, Freud clearly discounted. Yet unlike Rieff, I do not see Freud as adopting a stance of stoical toleration toward the discontents of culture. For Freud plainly regarded those discontents as increasingly intolerable; and culture itself, if left unaltered, as likely fated to self-destruction.[2] Thus I seek neither to historicize the perennial cleavages Freud disclosed, nor to overlook the sense of urgency that both enlivened and haunted Freud's concerns. Rather, I want to set forth Freud's unique intertwining of a profound vision of the necessity of unhappiness and a trenchant critique of a culture that, in seeking to deny that unhappiness, renders it intolerable.

Of those three great architects of Freud as a theorist of culture, I am closest to Marcuse: not the well-known Marcuse who entertained thoughts about happiness in *Eros and Civilization*, but the Marcuse of *The Aesthetic Dimension*—the Marcuse who wrote that "[t]he inexorable entanglement of joy and sorrow, celebration and despair, Eros and Thanatos cannot be dissolved into the problems of the class struggle."[3] Even a classless society, he added, "would not signal the end of art, the overcoming of tragedy, the reconciliation of the Dionysian and the Apollonian."[4]

To be sure, to invoke today the figure of Marcuse is as anachronistic, if not more, as invoking that of the class struggle.[5] Dominant modes of contemporary political discourse have as little patience for 'utopia' as they have for the philosophy of history. They find themselves preoccupied with the ceaseless deconstruction of an identitarian habit that, in the name of order and meaning, is said to exclude and dominate what is other than itself, to lose sight of what it must eliminate in order to enjoy the pretense of its harmony. In such a context, Marcuse's passion for fulfillment cannot help but seem fatefully involved with a revolution that is perhaps nothing more than an insidious restoration—nothing more than yet another deployment of the pervasiveness of power.[6]

Furthermore, if to invoke Marcuse is already to betray the workings of an ill-fated wish, then to invoke Freud is to confront the endless controversies, the plethora of readings and rereadings to which all great thinkers inevitably give rise.[7] It is in fact to encounter the origins of a cultural event of literally historic proportions.[8] Whatever else may be said about him, Freud was certainly correct in ranking the impact of his discoveries as equal to those of Galileo and Darwin.[9] To approach Freud's work is thus, as if by definition, to approach vexing uncertainties and intractable difficulties, questions as historical as they are theoretical.

This truth at once overwhelms and catalyzes this book. I find in Freud not only an iconoclastic critique of the totalistic illusions of a self that deems itself transparent to itself, but also an effort, an insistence to devise a mode of communication with what this self conceals from itself. Freud *cultivates*, as it were, the soil of disillusion. He not only unveils but also seeks to understand the extravagant, yet meaningful workings of that "internal foreign territory" he named 'the unconscious'. While refusing the possibility of a transparent univocity, for example, Freud's concept of 'over-determination' stops short of an apotheosis of indeterminacy. His critique of absolute meaning is misconstrued as an absolute denial of meaning. Psychoanalysis neither imposes a truth held by authority, nor concludes thereby that there is no such thing as truth. In fact, psychoanalysis has its inception at the point where faith in authority has waned, lost its hold. It seizes the death of God precisely as an occasion for a new lease on life.

From what he took to be the demise of Christianity, Nietzsche hoped to cultivate the possibility of an encounter with suffering no longer complicated by the gnawing of a guilty conscience. He looked forward to a mode of life that has ceased, as he put it, to place "all suffering under the perspective of *guilt*" (emphasis in original).[10] Like his proposed 'transvaluation of all values', Nietzsche's 'gay science' speaks the language of a tragic wisdom: it seeks an abolition not of pain but of guilt, an encounter with mortality no longer grasped from the perspective of sin. Whether Freud's critical exposure of the dynamics of guilt can live up to such a tall order is a question this book both constantly evokes—and carefully leaves unanswered. My intent is far more modest: I want only to explore once again the terrain that defines Freud as a philosopher of culture. More specifically, I want to undo the widespread image of a resigned, pessimistic Freud, an image to which even those among his most illustrious disciples—asserting the need for this or that redeeming 'reinterpretation'—have succumbed.

I am guided in this effort by an old adage as psychoanalytic as it is existential: that the repudiation of death is but a facilitation of its return—
whether as the gnawing of guilt or as the ravages of war.

Freud's theory of culture is incomprehensible apart from his elaboration of the lifelong implications of the premature birth of the human infant. The human infant's "intra-uterine existence," Freud tells us, "seems
to be short in comparison with that of most animals, and it is sent into the
world in a less finished state."[11] For Freud, this means that human beings
come into the world ill equipped to deal with the exigencies of life, the experiences of otherness or loss, of frustration, they will of necessity traverse. Unable to encounter life, the helpless infant has no recourse but to
take refuge in a universe of fantasy, in illusions seeking to foreclose, as a
rule unsuccessfully, the painfulness of loss. Yet what in the infant appears
as a seemingly innocuous wish to return whence it came, persists in the
adult. Birth gives rise not only to the claims of life but also to a tendency
running counter to the movement of life. "The emergence of life," Freud
writes, "would thus be the cause of the continuance of life and also at the
same time of the striving towards death; and life itself would be a conflict
and compromise between these two trends."[12] Precisely in and through its
prematurity, birth inaugurates the primordial "struggle between Eros and
Death."[13]

In essence, the point at issue is that life, for Freud, is not given naturally
and spontaneously. On the contrary, it is itself the product of work, of a
continuous effort against that about us which runs counter to the movements of life. Freud's claim is that we cultivate life not only materially,
through the labor that seeks to wrest our livelihood from nature, but also
psychically, through the labor that forever struggles against our longing
to return whence we came. Freud specified this life-sustaining labor—the
work of Eros—as a "work of mourning."[14] To refuse it is to refuse life itself. To have discovered and investigated it is among Freud's most significant insights.

The first chapter of this book presents an exegesis of Freud's 1915 text,
"Thoughts for the Times on War and Death." Freud's reflection, as Peter
Gay has it, is "an elegy for a civilization destroying itself."[15] I see it as an
untimely meditation—a wistful warning seeking to enjoin a culture bent
upon destructiveness to learn to relate to death in some way other than
that of war. Freud's is a proposal of a new attitude to death. His text indicts
a culture whose denial of death betrays its inability to deal adequately
with the predicament of loss. In so doing, it intimates the possibility of a
different culture that, in learning to encounter rather than deny death, concretizes the possibility not of happiness, but of a life worth living.

In chapter 2, I attempt to locate Freud's theory of culture in the Western
tradition of political philosophy by way of comparisons with Hobbes and

Hegel. Freud's claim that "whatever fosters the growth of civilization works at the same time against war"[16] has given rise to an unfortunate impression of the Hobbesian roots of his conception. In order to undo this impression, I argue that Freud's deployment of the problem of death in terms of fear and loss is, despite some superficial similarities, markedly distinct from Hobbes's deployment of that same problem exclusively in terms of fear. Central to my argument is the observation that Freud and Hobbes maintained substantively different views of human nature. For Freud, the sphere of culture is not solely negative or restrictive in the sense of providing necessary prohibitions and protections; it is simultaneously positive or developmental in the sense of being the field in and through which human beings develop as cultural beings. The infant's fearful and painful encounter with the reality of the other is simultaneously a humanizing encounter.

At the same time, however, the unveiling of the positive or developmental dimension of Freud's theory of culture necessitates a comparison with Hegel, so as to explore the ways in which the thrust of Freud's movement beyond Hobbes stops short of a Hegelian conception of community. Freud's theory of culture specifies a domain both between and beyond the centrifugal forces evidenced in Hobbes's instrumental collection of pre-constituted atoms, on the one hand, and the centripetal forces evidenced in Hegel's all-encompassing totality that both transcends and thoroughly comprehends the moments in and through which it finds its concreteness, on the other. The second chapter is thus an interpretation of Freud's aphoristic statement that culture is a struggle between Eros and Death. If the unifying powers of Eros intimate a critique of Hobbes, the divisive powers of Death intimate a critique of Hegel.

The third chapter, structurally and thematically the central chapter, is also the most ambitious and most problematic. It attempts to formulate a fundamental continuity between the 'clinical' and 'cultural' dimensions of Freud's work. Clinically, psychoanalysis originates in Freud's confrontation with the shortcomings of hypnosis as a therapeutic tool. The discovery of the eminently psychoanalytic fields of 'transference' and 'resistance' takes place in the context of Freud's investigation of the repeated failures of hypnosis in the treatment of neurosis. It is in and through these discoveries that Freud comes to see the dynamics of cure neither as obedience to hypnotic suggestions, nor as exclusively cathartic relief, but rather as a laborious, interpretative reconstruction of the hidden, yet still operative meanings of the past.

The mode of action Freud named 'psychoanalysis' thus appears on the scene as an effort to transvaluate the power of the past over the present and the future. At the heart of the operative power of the past and of the hypnotist's attempted deployment of that power, Freud discerns the human infant's ill-fated wish to refuse the painfulness of loss. For Freud, the correlate of the infant's helplessness is the at once fearful and pro-tective omnipotence of parental figures. The infant's desire is, as it were, fated to be duped into an enmeshment with authority. The power of the past is the persistent power both of the infant's desire and of the au-thoritative figures who have come to represent its satisfaction. As against this, the work of psychoanalysis is essentially a work of mourn-ing: it seeks to facilitate a protracted detachment from the figures that, for the subject, have come to represent the alleviation of its helplessness and have thus come to inherit the power of its wish to foreclose loss.

Thus whereas hypnotic suggestion seeks to redeploy that power in the service of a normalizing obedience, psychoanalysis aims at its dissolution. Freud defines the goal of psychoanalysis as the resolution of transference because such resolution has as its horizon the subject's detachment from its wish to foreclose loss, from its love of immortality. This detachment is inextricably mournful in that it presupposes the subject's encounter not only with loss but also with its own death. For Freud, the practice of psy-choanalysis is a specific mode of labor in and through which the human subject attempts to rupture illusions that, in foreclosing its intuition of its own death, preclude its own accession into the field of temporality, into the world where things pass away. It seeks a sensibility able to live its past not repetitively but as an ever-renewed longing to reach the elusive con-temporaneity of the present—and to seize thereby the possibility of a no longer repetitive future. For Freud, the mournful emergence of death spells, asymptotically, the death of the power of the past.

This understanding of the work of psychoanalysis reveals the continuity between Freud's abandonment of hypnosis, on the one hand, and the cri-tique of authority that lies at the heart of his theory of culture, on the other. In *Group Psychology and the Analysis of the Ego,* Freud reopens the problem-atics of hypnosis in the context of an examination of the dynamics of soci-ety. Like that of the hypnotist, the power of society is ultimately rooted in the convergence of the human infant's wish to foreclose loss and the per-sistent power of parental figures in the life of the adult. Freud derives the power of the social from the prematurity of the human infant.

The thrust of this analysis is deepened in *Civilization and Its Discontents.* The infant's biologically determined prematurity fates it to a long period of helplessness and dependence, the crucial memorial to which is what Freud called the "superego." The process of acculturation, at once re-sented and desired, amounts to a gradual yet forceful sedimentation of authoritative figures in the growing infant's psyche, a protracted incarna-tion of obedience at the heart of the mature individual. As the advocate of an omnipotent perfection, the superego bonds us to the love of an ideal to which we are helplessly inferior.[17] The intolerable discontents of culture thus dramatize, in the concreteness of everyday life, the predicament of an obedient subject that cannot help but judge itself as unworthy of living from the point of view of an illusory life from which the realities of loss and death have been foreclosed. The clinical onset of psychoanalysis as a critique of that foreclosure informs and prefigures Freud's subsequent critique of a culture whose palliatives complicate the suffering they claim to alleviate.

In *The Future of an Illusion*, Freud both broaches the explicitly political dimension of his theory of culture and proposes the waning of religion in the modern world as an opportunity to deploy a far-reaching pedagogical effort of cultural transformation, an "irreligious education."[18] On the one hand, he exposes the juncture between the denial of death and authority, illusion and domination, that he discerns at the heart of all "present day cultures."[19] On the other, he claims that, when conceived as an opportunity, the death of God might issue not in a nihilistic collapse of cultural life *per se*, but in a renewed encounter with the perennial painfulness of loss and death. *The Future of an Illusion* amounts to a diagnosis of a particular historical situation in terms of which Freud ventures to posit the task of psychoanalysis. This task is the formulation of the principles of an alternative mode of acculturation, of pedagogical practices that, informed by the psychoanalytic unveiling of the psychical specificity of the human infant, would seek to facilitate, rather than preclude, the developmental work of mourning. The fourth chapter of this book explores Freud's remarkable audacity: his hope to have unveiled an opportunity wherein his own abandonment of hypnosis emerges, pedagogically, as a concrete historical possibility for Western culture as a whole.

Civilization and Its Discontents culminates with a question, a "fateful question," Freud tells us, about whether and to what extent we might manage to master the disturbance of our communal life by "the human instinct of aggression and self-destruction."[20] Freud's understanding of the deeply cultural task this question leaves us with is inextricably connected to his grasp of the relation between generations as central to the production and reproduction of cultural forms. For Freud, cultural forms sustain themselves not magically, as it were, but in and through concrete pedagogical practices—"upbringing" in the widest sense—that give particular content to the recalcitrant yet historically shifting relations between generations. The question Freud raises as he concludes *Civilization and Its Discontents* is about the degree to which we might self-consciously intervene in this dimension of the historical process.

The central problem Freud identifies in that regard is that adults cannot properly educate children because, as their 'infantile amnesia' evidences, they no longer understand their own childhood. The unprecedented contribution of psychoanalysis to the life of culture is to have minimized our estrangement from childhood. On a distinctively cultural plane, the essence of psychoanalysis is to have raised a most difficult question, in Freud's phrase, about the "upbringing of the next generation."[21] For Freud, the heart of this upbringing is an effort to carefully guide the prematurely born—and therefore helpless and dependent human infant—through the experiences of loss it is destined to encounter.

In chapter 5, I examine this exceedingly problematic aspect of Freud's theory of culture. By daring to imagine the application of the practice he founded to the terrain of cultural life, Freud self-consciously wrestled, in his own terms, with problems as familiar and intractable as those pertinent to the complex entanglements of politics and pedagogy, power and knowledge, 'city' and 'soul'. Freud's theory of culture thus culminates not in pessimistic resignation but in a richly textured pedagogical reflection. His lifelong attentiveness to the ravages of Death is rooted in an insistent effort to assess, assist, and intimate the precarious chances of Eros. Freud's is a peculiar generosity, distinguished, as Richard Wollheim puts it, by a "refusal to believe that it is in any way the mark of a good or generous mind to give way to hope."[22]

Wollheim is not altogether mistaken in his frankly polemical observation that "[t]o try to find in Freud's writings an articulated or coherent social theory or ethic, an enterprise to which some of the most speculative minds of our day have committed themselves, is a vain task. For Freud had no such theory and no such ethic: as he himself was able to recognize."[23] Freud's hostility to the passion for salvation, a passion never removed from sustained thought about political matters, is unparalleled. His work traverses a paradoxical terrain in which human beings mutilate both themselves and each other in the process of their very growth and development—an uncertain and precarious terrain in which danger and opportunity, mystification and liberation, pain and pleasure constantly intersect and intertwine in the midst of a never-ending struggle.

Yet by the same token, if it is correct to say, with Wollheim, that "[n]o greater disservice can be done to Freud than by those who, in the interest of this or that piety, recruit him to the kind of bland or mindless optimism that he so utterly and so heroically despised,"[24] it is equally correct to say that no greater disservice can be done to Freud than by those who, in the interest of this or that so-called realism, recruit him to the kind of lifeless pessimism against which his very life and thought were a perennial protest. Freud's thought points toward not apathetic withdrawal but, as Wollheim puts it, "justifiable grounds for action."[25] Precisely as ultimately pedagogical concerns about the cultivation of character, Freud's tempered "hopes for the future"[26] have a prima facie claim to be regarded as genuinely political in the deepest sense. They are claims about the presuppositions of a politics no longer as intruded upon by the twin passions for salvation and withdrawal.

The fundamental question to be posed is not whether Freud was a quintessentially political thinker in the purest sense. It is rather whether political philosophy can learn from Freud's uncompromising lessons. The disconcerting challenge he posed in this regard is entailed in his unique understanding of and insistence upon the underestimated and extraordinary weight of childhood experience. My central objective is to facilitate the meaningful emergence of that challenge. We might say that it is a challenge that, perhaps all too hopefully and all too humanly, provokes thoughts about a politics whose tragic sense of life permits it to lengthen creatively, rather than shorten artificially, what Freud called our "circuitous paths to death."[27]

NOTES

1. Herbert Marcuse, *Eros and Civilization: A Philosophical Inquiry into Freud* (Boston: Beacon, 1955); Norman O. Brown, *Life Against Death: The Psychoanalytic Meaning of History* (Middletown, Conn.: Wesleyan University Press, 1959); and Phillip Rieff, *Freud: The Mind of the Moralist* (New York: Viking, 1959).

2. Sigmund Freud, *Civilization and Its Discontents*, in vol. 21 of *The Standard Edition of the Complete Psychological Works of Sigmund Freud*, ed. and trans. James Strachey et al. (London: Hogarth, 1953–1974), 133, 145, and passim.

3. Herbert Marcuse, *The Aesthetic Dimension: Toward a Critique of Marxist Aesthetics*, trans. Herbert Marcuse and Erica Sherover (Boston: Beacon, 1978), 16.

4. Marcuse, *The Aesthetic Dimension*, 29.

5. Thus, for example, Anthony Elliot has recently remarked that "[i]n a reflexive and pluralistic world, a world which has recently witnessed the global crash of Communism, the project of Freudo-Marxism has clearly become a dead tradition of thought." See Anthony Elliot, introduction to *Freud 2000*, ed. Anthony Elliot (New York: Routledge, 1999), 10.

6. See Michel Foucault, *An Introduction*, vol. I of *The History of Sexuality*, trans. Robert Hurley (New York: Vintage, 1980). For a response from Marcuse's point of view, see Gad Horowitz, "The Foucaultian Impasse: No Sex, No Self, No Revolution," *Political Theory* 15 (February 1987): 61–80. See also Eugene Victor Wolfenstein, *Inside/Outside Nietzsche: Psychoanalytic Explorations* (Ithaca, N.Y.: Cornell University Press, 2000).

7. See, for example, Anthony Elliot, *Social Theory and Psychoanalysis in Transition: Self and Society from Freud to Kristeva* (Oxford, UK: Blackwell, 1992).

8. See John Forrester, *Dispatches from the Freud Wars: Psychoanalysis and Its Passions* (Cambridge, Mass.: Harvard University Press, 1997); Barry Richards, *Images of Freud: Cultural Responses to Psychoanalysis* (London: J. M. Dent, 1989); and Sherry Turkle, *Psychoanalytic Politics: Freud's French Revolution* (New York: Basic Books, 1978).

9. See Sigmund Freud, "A Difficulty in the Path of Psycho-Analysis," in vol. 17 of *The Standard Edition*, ed. and trans. James Strachey et al., 135–44; and also Sigmund Freud, "The Resistances to Psycho-Analysis," in vol. 19 of *The Standard Edition*, ed. and trans. James Strachey et al., 211–24.

10. Friedrich Nietzsche, *On the Genealogy of Morals,* trans. Walter Kaufmann and R. J. Hollingdale (New York: Vintage, 1969), 162.

11. Sigmund Freud, *Inhibitions, Symptoms and Anxiety,* in vol. 20 of *The Standard Edition,* ed. and trans. James Strachey et al., 154.

12. Sigmund Freud, *The Ego and the Id,* in vol. 19 of *The Standard Edition,* ed. and trans. James Strachey et al., 40–41.

13. Freud, *Civilization and Its Discontents,* 122.

14. See Sigmund Freud, "Mourning and Melancholia," in vol. 14 of *The Standard Edition,* ed. and trans. James Strachey et al., 237–58.

15. Peter Gay, *Freud: A Life for Our Times* (New York: Anchor Books, 1989), 355.

16. Sigmund Freud, "Why War?" in vol. 22 of *The Standard Edition,* ed. and trans. James Strachey et al., 215.

17. Cf. Leo Bersani, "Erotic Assumptions: Narcissism and Sublimation in Freud," in *The Culture of Redemption* (Cambridge, Mass.: Harvard University Press, 1990), 40.

18. Sigmund Freud, *The Future of an Illusion,* in vol. 21 of *The Standard Edition,* ed. and trans. James Strachey et al., 48.

19. Freud, *Future of an Illusion,* 12.

20. Freud, *Civilization and Its Discontents,* 145.

21. Sigmund Freud, *New Introductory Lectures on Psycho-Analysis,* in vol. 22 of *The Standard Edition,* ed. and trans. James Strachey et al., 146.

22. Richard Wollheim, *Sigmund Freud* (Cambridge, UK: Cambridge University Press, 1971), 255.

23. Wollheim, *Sigmund Freud,* 253.

24. Wollheim, *Sigmund Freud,* 273.

25. Wollheim, *Sigmund Freud,* 272.

26. Freud, *New Introductory Lectures,* 146.

27. Sigmund Freud, *Beyond the Pleasure Principle,* in vol. 18 of *The Standard Edition,* ed. and trans. James Strachey et al., 39.

1

Eros, Loss, and Death

[T]he fatal truth that has laid it down that flight is precisely an instrument that delivers one over to what one is fleeing from.

—Sigmund Freud, "Delusions and Dreams in Jensen's *Gradiva*"

FREUD'S PARTING GLANCE AT EROS

The proverbial pessimism of Freud's theory of culture is so familiar that it scarcely bears repetition. "The liberty of the individual," Freud writes in *Civilization and Its Discontents* (1930), "is no gift of civilization."[1] The dynamics of culture are on the whole those of a systematic imprisonment of the individual. The construction of the "superego," of the moral capacities of a human being, is, in essence, both accomplished and sustained in and through fear and punishment. The sphere of law, even if deeply internalized, is a sphere of compulsion. As much as it is for Hobbes, freedom, for Freud, is in "the silence of the Law."[2] Yet in Freud's case, not "commodious living" but a "permanent internal unhappiness," a profound "sense of guilt," is both the price and the result of culture.[3] To be human is to be unhappy. It is as if the Hobbesian war of every one against every one were translocated and reenacted at the heart of the Freudian psyche: culture weakens and disarms the individual by setting up an agency within him to watch over him, "like a garrison in a conquered city."[4]

Given the familiar features of Freud's pessimism, the optimistic tone of *The Future of an Illusion* (1927) cannot help but surprise us. Written only three years earlier than *Civilization and Its Discontents, The Future of an Illusion* articulates a view of culture premised on a distinction between what is and what can be, a distinction always dear to those who permit themselves to look into the future in search of as yet unrealized possibilities. Indeed, the 1927 text raises questions about education, pedagogical questions conceived in the widest sense, in order seriously to consider the grand project of an alternative mode of acculturation—a project that would, in Freud's own words, point toward "a state of things in which life will become tolerable for everyone and civilization no longer oppressive to anyone."[5]

There are, of course, well-known historical reasons, involving the rise of Nazism and Fascism, that may account for Freud's shift in outlook between 1927 and 1930. Moreover, there are theoretical questions about the gradual development of Freud's understanding of culture, in particular about the progressive incorporation of his hypothesis of the "death drive" into that understanding, that may also help in explaining the shift in outlook.[6] But these same reasons and questions, whether historical or theoretical, would make it even more difficult to understand why, three years *after* the publication of *Civilization and Its Discontents,* in a work as major as the *New Introductory Lectures on Psycho-Analysis* (1933), a work that unambiguously restates the hypothesis of the death drive, Freud chooses, unperturbed, to forcefully evoke *The Future of an Illusion:* he raises once again issues about the education of the young, declares that these issues are nothing less than central to the psychoanalytic enterprise as a whole, and in fact adds that their resolution would presuppose, as he puts it, "a quite other constitution of society."[7] One cannot help but wonder whether, before setting out to explain the discontinuity between the 1927 text and the 1930 text, we would do well to become suspicious about the very perplexity that their juxtaposition appears to generate.

The opposition between optimism and pessimism that gives rise to that perplexity is, after all, certainly not one to which Freud himself subscribed. "It is not a question," he writes in "Analysis Terminable and Interminable" (1937), "of an antithesis between an optimistic and a pessimistic theory of life. Only by the concurrent or mutually opposing action of the two primal instincts—Eros and the death-instinct—, never by one or the other alone, can we explain the rich multiplicity of the phenomena of life."[8] Thus the puzzling relation between the "optimistic" Freud of 1927 and the "pessimistic" Freud of 1930 presents us, not with a shift in outlook, but with a particularly striking indication of a larger structure underlying Freud's thinking as a whole.

My purpose in this chapter is twofold. On the one hand, I want to show that Freud's theory of culture is irretrievably misunderstood if interpreted exclusively in terms of an irreducible antagonism between individual and society.[9] On the other, I seek to establish that Freud's so-called pessimism is, on the contrary, the very standpoint from which he criticizes a culture unable to deal adequately with the predicaments of loss and death. Freud's theory of culture is less a call for resignation than an intertwining of a profound encounter with the necessity of unhappiness and an uncompromising indictment of the culture he describes. It is that unity of loss and critique, mortality and vision, that I wish to bring into relief.

My argument proceeds in three stages. In the first, I underline the often neglected centrality of the loss of loved ones in Freud's theory of culture. In the second, I elaborate this centrality with the intent of articulating its importance in Freud's understanding of intersubjectivity, of relations between people. In the third, I argue that in Freud's work, the category of mourning grounds the possibility of a culture informed by an existential mood closer to a tragic celebration of the living than to a resigned melancholia in the face of loss, death, and destructiveness. Thus the concept of the loved one's death announces the critical content of Freud's theory.

In short, my point is that Freud's encounter with loss and death gives rise to a vision of an alternative configuration of individual-society relations. My examination of that vision in this chapter will permit us, in chapter 2, to differentiate Freud's theory of culture from Hobbes's construal of the ineradicable antagonism between individual and society, as well as from Hegel's insistence upon the possibility of a fully sutured reconciliation. Freud's unique vision offers instead the image of a struggle in which the sustained endurance of loss and death is a continuously renewed cultivation of living in the company of others.

Paradoxically, it is surprisingly easy to *under*estimate the destructiveness that, according to Freud, haunts the highest of human aspirations and achievements. The unhappiness of culture is far more ominous than that of an unfortunate fate to be carried with the dignified elegance of heroic stoicism. The problem Freud has in mind is of a definitively *deathly* quality. Freud interprets the alliance of morality and destructiveness, the proverbial cruelty of the superego, as an alliance of culture and death. His unveiling of the constitutive unhappiness of culture is at the same time a warning: the sense of guilt, he tells us, "will perhaps reach heights that the individual finds hard to tolerate."[10] For Freud, this self-defeating structure of culture intimates the truth that the apparently vital claims of Eros, of the cultural struggle against destructiveness, are in fact those of a long detour to death. Freud posits a veritable *death drive*, a hidden cunning of death, as it were, at the core of culture.[11] His ever-recurrent imagery of war suggests that the remarkable depth of his encounter with destructiveness is paralleled only by that of his line of questioning: Freud's theory of culture is an *inquiry* into the viability of the human species.

Yet such an inquiry, however disturbing, is not the same as a statement of doom. In fact, it is precisely from the point of view of such an inquiry that we can begin to make sense of the peculiar circumstance that the classic statement of Freud's theory of culture, *Civilization and Its Discontents*, concludes on a note that subtly yet significantly modulates the familiar gloom traditionally associated with his position:

> The fateful *question* for the human species seems to me to be whether and to what extent their cultural development will succeed in mastering the disturbance of their communal life by the human instinct of aggression and self-destruction. It may be that in this respect the present time deserves a special interest. Men have gained control over the forces of nature to such an extent that with their help they would have no difficulty in exterminating one another to the last man. They know this, and hence comes a large part of their current unrest, their unhappiness and their mood of anxiety. And now it is to be expected that the other of the two "Heavenly Powers," eternal Eros, will make an effort to assert himself in the struggle with his equally immortal adversary. But who can foresee with what success and with what result?[12] (emphasis added)

Evidently with this passage in mind, Norman O. Brown writes that "psychoanalysis may, like Freud, hope for a rebirth of Eros, but rationally it can only predict the self-destruction of the human race."[13] Similarly, though carefully noting that "in the end, Freud left the decisive question open," Peter Gay comments that "Freud concluded *Civilization and Its Discontents* with a flicker of optimism, though his cheering for the life drive in its duel with death seems far more a matter of duty than conviction."[14] But there is no need to undervalue the genuinely theoretical worth of Freud's parting glance at Eros as he concludes *Civilization and Its Discontents*, a gesture that, indeed, Freud had already made some years earlier, in the concluding sentence of his metapsychological masterpiece, *The Ego and the Id* (1923):

> It would be possible to picture the id as under the domination of the mute but powerful death instincts, which desire to be at peace and (prompted by the pleasure principle) to put Eros, the mischief-maker, to rest; but perhaps that might be to undervalue the part played by Eros.[15]

Freud's repeated evocations of Eros are in fact intrinsic to a theory that aspires to map a paradoxical terrain in which wish and prohibition, pain and pleasure, life and death are ceaselessly interwoven. To absolutize either pole of this interminable struggle is to cancel our view of the tensions and conflicts interminably constitutive of the phenomena Freud sought to unveil.[16] To render Freud's theory as an ultimately pessimistic statement is to miss this most crucial of points: Freud is unable to conclude *Civilization and Its Discontents* without stealing a glance in the direction of Eros because he is, as it were, theoretically debarred from doing so. His theory of culture opens the destiny of the human species as a "fateful question" to be taken up, a *task* to be engaged upon, rather than a definitive fate to be dealt with. However softly, Freud chooses to remind us of the faint contours of an alternative horizon.

Freud's earliest formulation of the problem of culture, "'Civilized' Sexual Morality and Modern Nervous Illness" (1908), concludes with a statement whose content remains untheorized in the body of the text. "Let us add," Freud writes by way of conclusion,

> that a restriction of sexual activity in a community is quite generally accompanied by an increase of anxiety about life and of fear of death which interferes with the individual's capacity for enjoyment and does away with his readiness to face death for any purpose.[17]

Already in 1908, this closing addition prefigures the connection between sexuality and death that, in 1930, in *Civilization and Its Discontents*, Freud is to place at the center of his analysis of culture. With the possible exception of *Totem and Taboo* (1912–1913), however, it is not until 1915, in "Thoughts for the Times on War and Death," that Freud first explicitly and unambiguously incorporates the related themes of loss, death, and destructiveness into his analysis of culture.[18] In that text, written some six months after the outbreak of the Great War, Freud displays a lucidity on the one hand fully cognizant of the loss endured, and on the other both unable and unwilling to give up its attachment to life. Not by chance, the 1915 text concludes with Freud's richest aphoristic formulation of his position:

> To tolerate life remains, after all, the first duty of all living beings. Illusion becomes valueless if it makes this harder for us.[19]

My reexamination of Freud's position is an exegesis of this passage. What interests me about it is that it does not tally very well with Freud's familiarly pessimistic derivation of the inextricability of morality and destructiveness. The "first duty" of which he speaks in this passage connects the sphere of ethics not with death but with life.[20] It insists upon a standpoint from which Freud criticizes a culture that, enamoured with war, has lost access not to happiness, but to the possibility of a life worth living.

DEATH OF A LOVED ONE

The very title of Freud's "Thoughts for the Times on War and Death" already posits a distinction between war and death, destructiveness and mortality. Hence the interpretation of the status of destructiveness in Freud's theory of culture ought not obscure the equally prominent status of mortality. In "Thoughts for the Times," Freud links destructiveness to mortality, war to death, by way of an analysis of the experience of loss—in particular, the loss of loved ones. The category of loss is thus absolutely central to his reflection.

The analysis of the centrality of loss in "Thoughts for the Times" is in fact already an analysis of the centrality of loss in Freud's theory of culture. More specifically, as we shall see in the course of this chapter, it is already an analysis of the way in which Freud's concept of loss intertwines the emergence of ethical imperatives and the development of existential attitudes toward life and death.

Freud presents "Thoughts for the Times" as an analysis of what he calls the "confusion of wartime." He proposes to "pick out two among the factors" responsible for this shared sense of being "at a loss." Alongside "the disillusionment which this war has evoked," Freud finds "the altered attitude to death which this—like every other war—forces upon us."[21] Thus Freud seizes the Great War as a juxtaposition of an overwhelming disappointment regarding the ethical stature of human beings, on the one hand, and a particularly forceful encounter with the fact of mortality, on the other. His selection of these two "factors" indicates that the task he sets before himself when he specifies the "confusion of wartime" as his theoretical object is that of grasping disillusionment and death from a single point of view. The burden of his reflection is to construct a perspective that, in linking murder to mortality, war to death, is simultaneously ethical and existential. Freud's "Thoughts" are *for the times* in that they seek to understand the historically situated "confusion" that they target from the viewpoint of that perspective, of the relation between war and death.[22] As if wistfully untimely, his reflection as a whole informs the culture it addresses that it urgently needs to learn to approach death in some way other than that of war.

To begin with, Freud posits disillusionment as a way of dealing with the shocking truth contained in the war. He sees the glimmerings of a mode of self-cognition. Nonetheless, Freud does not accept but rather *questions* disillusionment. He seeks to derive a strange "consolation" from that which disillusionment reveals:

> our mortification and our painful disillusionment on account of the uncivilized behaviour of our fellow-citizens of the world during this war were unjustified. They were based on an illusion to which we had given way. In reality our fellow-citizens have not sunk so low as we feared, because they had never risen so high as we believed.[23]

Disillusionment speaks of truth, to be sure, yet only from the viewpoint of illusion. Freud can discern its cognitive limits because he speaks from a horizon framed beyond the disjunction of illusion and disillusion, the naive hopefulness of optimism and the hopelessness of despondency. To illuminate the contours of this horizon is to grasp the authentic features of Freud's own standpoint.[24]

The appearance of the problem of death in Freud's reflection is best approached in terms of these limits of disillusionment. To be sure, disillusionment is immediately linked to murder in that it correctly cognizes a murderous propensity at the heart of the human being. But murder is not mortality. Accordingly, if the scope of Freud's reflection in "Thoughts for the Times on War and Death" is to reach beyond war toward death, then it must link the problem of murder to that of mortality, war to death. The clue to this linkage is contained in the observation that in spite of the war, disillusionment cannot afford to posit the human being as unambiguously murderous. To do so is to lose the conditions for the possibility of culture. An unambiguously murderous creature would hardly experience the "confusion of wartime." To expose our participation in the ravages of war need not entail that we forget our grief. For Freud, to question disillusionment is to ask the disillusioned to account for the grief that their disillusionment reveals. In fact, it is precisely the question of the roots of this grief that leads Freud to the problem of death, in particular to the death of loved ones. For it is from the viewpoint of the grief attendant on the loss of loved ones that, in the midst of war, Freud wishes to bring into relief that about human beings which, in spite of their propensity to murder, might nonetheless resist the ravages of war.

"The second factor to which I attribute our present sense of estrangement in this once lovely and congenial world," Freud writes, "is the disturbance that has taken place in the attitude which we have hitherto adopted towards death." "That attitude," he tells us, "was far from straightforward." On the one hand, we are ready to proclaim death as "natural, undeniable and unavoidable." On the other, we display an "unmistakable tendency to put death on one side, to eliminate it from life." We claim to know death yet are in reality "accustomed to behave as if it were otherwise."[25]

What Freud calls our "cultural and conventional attitude towards death" is in fact an attitude of denial. When a death happens, he notes, "we are always deeply affected, and it is as though we were badly shaken in our expectations. Our habit is to lay stress on the fortuitous causation of death—accident, disease, infection, advanced age; in this way we betray an effort to reduce death from a necessity to a chance event."[26]

Yet war erases the conditions for the possibility of these cultural efforts of denial. "It is evident," Freud tells us, "that war is bound to sweep away this conventional treatment of death. Death will no longer be denied; we are forced to believe in it. People really die; and no longer one by one, but many, often tens of thousands, in a single day."[27]

Given this crumbling away of our "conventional treatment" of death, Freud offers not to console but to search for yet another attitude to death. His search, however, is as ambiguous as his earlier "consolation."

The "new" attitude to death he proposes to investigate is rather a truly old one, already within us. It is that about us which the subversion of the "conventional" attitude lays bare. Freud informs us that this attitude of our unconscious toward the problem of death is "almost exactly the same as that of primaeval man."[28] It is as if he were able to tell us about ourselves only through the expedient of a primeval human being.

The primeval human being's attitude to death, he tells us, was "far from consistent"; it was "most contradictory." In a manner reminiscent of but not identical to that of the human being in culture, the primeval human being both acknowledged and refused to acknowledge death:

> On the one hand, he took death seriously, recognized it as the termination of life and made use of it in that sense; on the other hand, he also denied death and reduced it to nothing. This contradiction arose from the fact that he took up radically different attitudes towards the death of other people, of strangers, of enemies, and towards his own. He had no objection to someone else's death; it meant the annihilation of someone he hated, and primitive man had no scruples against bringing it about. He was no doubt a very passionate creature and more cruel and more malignant than other animals. He liked to kill, and killed as a matter of course. The instinct which is said to restrain other animals from killing and devouring their own species need not be attributed to him.[29]

The ease with which we superficially acknowledge death is not truly an acceptance of death. It is merely the ease with which we can accept not our *own* but rather *another's* death—the ease with which we can kill him. Freud is concerned with raising the question of how it is that, given the unscrupulous murderousness of the primeval human being, the scrupulous unease of culture could have been produced in the first place. His intent is to understand the possibility of culture in the midst of the barbaric cruelty evidenced in and through the Great War.

The "contradiction" Freud posits at the heart of the primeval human being's attitude to death is central to Freud's understanding, but the path he follows is circuitous and requires close attention to his text. On the one hand, Freud tells us that the primeval human being simultaneously "recognized" and "denied" death. Yet on the other, Freud himself complicates matters a great deal when he immediately adds that while the "recognition" pertains to the death of others, the "denial" pertains to one's own death. Freud's surprising addition resolves the contradictoriness it wishes to assert. It speaks not of a single, contradictory attitude that "recognizes" and "denies" death at the same time and in the same respect; it speaks, rather, of two "radically different" attitudes to death which may, as such, exist side by side without thereby contradicting one another. I may quite consistently affirm your death while denying mine. In other words, it is only in the context of some as yet unstated unity in mortality of self and other that Freud can write that my negation of my own death contradicts my affirmation of yours.

A similar difficulty concerning the relation between I and not-I becomes visible at the heart of Freud's concept of the "cultural and conventional" denial of death. When Freud first introduces that concept, he tells us that regardless of our superficial protestations of acknowledgment,

> It is indeed impossible to imagine our own death; and whenever we attempt to do so we can perceive that we are in fact still present as spectators. Hence the psycho-analytic school could venture on the assertion that at bottom no one believes in his own death, or, to put the same thing another way, that in the unconscious everyone of us is convinced of his own immortality.[30]

Yet this unconscious belief in our own immortality is not so much a *denial* as a *preclusion* of the very possibility of our own death. The unconscious is immortal not in the sense that it denies its own death. It is immortal, rather, in the sense that it does not know its own death. The unconscious is the locus of a disbelief in the possibility of our own death, a disbelief that we, even at the level of culture, nonetheless share with the primeval human being.

Unlike the primeval human being, however, the cultured human being has difficulty acknowledging even *another's* death. Freud writes:

> When it comes to someone else's death, the civilized man will carefully avoid speaking of such a possibility in the hearing of the person under sentence. *Children alone disregard this restriction;* they unashamedly threaten one another with the possibility of dying, and even go so far as to do the same thing to someone whom they love, as, for instance: "Dear Mummy, when you're dead I'll do this or that." The civilized adult can hardly even entertain the thought of another person's death without seeming to himself hard-hearted or wicked; unless, of course, as a doctor or lawyer or something of the kind, he has to deal with death professionally. Least of all will he allow himself to think of the other person's death if some gain to himself in freedom, property or position is bound up with it.[31] (emphasis added)

To be sure, this civilized "sensitiveness,"[32] as Freud calls it, toward the death of another echoes our indifferent disbelief regarding our own death. Both display a tendency "to put death on one side," "to hush it up,"[33] and Freud does explicitly refer to both as denials of death. Yet whereas we *share* the disbelief with the primeval human being, our sensitiveness is precisely that which *distinguishes* us from his unabashed lack of scruples regarding the death of another. This is why Freud repeatedly emphasizes that the sensitiveness of which he speaks is a "restriction" pertaining to "civilized man"; children, he observes, "disregard" it. According to Freud, then, the "cultural and conventional attitude towards death" is not an inability to perceive but a nonacknowledgment of something at some level already known; thus, it is a denial.

The fact that Freud unequivocally insists that the "cultural and conventional" denial of death is a denial not only of another's but also of one's *own* death is surprising. For according to Freud, I can scarcely deny my own death, since I cannot even think it. To put it otherwise, I can render my belief in my own immortality as a denial of my mortality only to the degree that I can know myself from the viewpoint of another who, unlike me, can know my death. The degree to which I can grasp myself as the stranger whose death I can know is the degree to which I can grasp my own death. I can die only to the extent that I become the stranger—or that the stranger becomes I. Only then is it possible to speak of the cultural and conventional denial of death as a denial of my own death. Once again, like the mysterious "contradiction" he wishes to discern at the heart of the primeval human being, Freud's entire conception of the cultural and conventional denial of death presupposes a suspension of the distinction between I and not-I.

Freud theorizes this suspension in terms of the death of loved ones. He tells us that

> The complement to this cultural and conventional attitude towards death is provided by our complete collapse when death has struck down someone whom we love—a parent or a partner in marriage, a brother or sister, a child or a close friend. Our hopes, our desires and our pleasures lie in the grave with him, we will not be consoled, we will not fill the lost one's place. We behave as if we were a kind of Asra, who die when those they love die.[34]

The death of a loved one pierces the psyche's belief in its own immortality. The loss of loved ones implants death within the psyche. Since, so to speak, we die when those we love die, the death of loved ones provides the ground for an understanding of our psyche's persistent belief in its own immortality as a stubborn, recalcitrant refusal of something the psyche has already learned. It is by way of the death of loved ones, then, that Freud manages to move the psyche's relation to its own death from the sphere of preclusion to that of denial.

Similarly, it is only in the context of the death of loved ones that the "contradiction" Freud posits at the heart of the primeval human being can be meaningfully grasped as indeed a contradiction. My belief in my own immortality contradicts my indifference, acceptance, or even enjoyment of another's death only if that other is simultaneously myself. Freud writes:

But there was for him [primeval man] one case in which the two opposite attitudes to death collided and came into conflict with each other; and this case became highly important and productive of far-reaching consequences. It occurred when primaeval man saw someone who belonged to him die—his wife, his child, his friend—whom he undoubtedly loved as we love ours, for love cannot be much younger than the lust to kill. Then, in his pain, he was forced to learn that one can die, too, oneself, and his whole being revolted against the admission; for each of these loved ones was, after all, a part of his own beloved self. But, on the other hand, deaths such as these pleased him as well, since in each of the loved ones there was also something of the stranger. The law of ambivalence of feeling, which to this day governs our emotional relations with those whom we love most, certainly had a very much wider validity in primaeval times. Thus these beloved dead had also been enemies and strangers who had aroused in him some degree of hostile feeling.[35]

Freud unveils not so much the truism of murder, as much as the far more difficult truth of the *murder of the loved one*. By insisting to unveil this truth, Freud makes clear the roots of our need for concealment. It is only if the other whom he murders is a *loved* other that the primeval human being can object to his own murderousness. Similarly, it is because of our love that the lust to kill evoked by the war can appear, scrupulously, only as disillusionment. We enjoy the deaths not only of strangers but also of those we love.

As soon as Freud accounts both for our need for concealment and for our grief in terms of the death of the loved one, he simultaneously raises the problem of mortality. Not the death of the other per se, but that of the loved one, places before us the possibility of our own death. The loved one is that other whose death is also ours. I can confront my mortality only to the extent that I can survive my own death: I learn of my death only in and through my pain over the loved one's. The death of the loved one is the occasion for the becoming explicit of a contradiction between the relation to death I hold through myself and the relation to death I hold through another. The loved one is both self and other, immortal and mortal. In his figure converge both love and hate and life and death. This is why, as Freud repeatedly insists, the "confusion of wartime" must belong not to "those who themselves risk their lives in battle," but to the noncombatants—to "those who have stayed at home and have only to wait for the loss of one of their dear ones by wounds, disease or infection."[36]

Thus, it is by virtue of the concept of the death of loved ones that Freud's "Thoughts for the Times on War and Death" are as much about mortality as they are about murder, as much about death as they are about war. We shall presently see that it is also in terms of that concept that Freud understands the appearance of culture.

LOSS AND INTERSUBJECTIVITY

Freud's retrieval of the grief of death from the dynamics of disillusion-ment, then, finds a primordial "ambivalence" at the root of the "confusion of wartime." The war confuses us because it places our fundamental am-bivalence before us. This ambivalence itself is what our cultural illusions attempt to obscure, what our cultural attitude to death attempts to dissi-pate. It is with this in mind that, at a crucial juncture of *Civilization and Its Discontents*, Freud writes:

> And now, I think, the meaning of the evolution of civilization is no longer ob-scure to us. It must present the struggle between Eros and Death, between the instinct of life and the instinct of destruction, as it works itself out in the hu-man species. This struggle is what all life essentially consists of, and the evo-lution of civilization may therefore be simply described as the struggle for life of the human species. And it is this battle of the giants that our nurse-maids try to appease with their lullaby about Heaven.[37]

Freud's point is not that this ambivalent convergence of life and death is suppressed because it contradicts the objective needs of the community, the survival of civilization. Freud's point, rather, is that the ambivalence is in and of itself unbearable. The death of a loved one is that by way of which the great "battle of the giants" emerges concretely in the life of the mind. Accordingly, it is also that which propels the cultural "lullaby" aimed at forgetfulness. This centrality of the category of the death of loved ones in Freud's theory of culture requires elaboration.

To begin with, it is important to note that the fundamental contradic-tion to be analyzed is located in the psyche itself, not between the psyche and civilization. The problem of civilization is not that it imposes itself ex-ternally on a unitary psyche that needs to be repressed if it is to survive. The problem, rather, is that the psyche is itself divided. At issue is not a conflict between self and world, but a conflicted psyche dramatized as the world of culture. That this conflict comes to be only in and through the death of the loved one lends culture its dual character. That which fuels culture is precisely that which culture refuses. Culture presupposes knowledge of the death it wishes to deny. Culture is constituted as a fore-closure of its own ground.

In a complex passage worth quoting at length, Freud graphically sum-marizes the paradoxical dynamics of culture:

> Philosophers have declared that the intellectual enigma presented to primae-val man by the picture of death forced him to reflection, and thus became the starting-point of all speculation. I believe that here the philosophers are think-ing too philosophically, and giving too little consideration to the motives that

were primarily operative. I should like therefore to limit and correct their assertion. In my view, primaeval man must have triumphed beside the body of his slain enemy, without being led to rack his brains about the enigma of life and death. What released the spirit of inquiry in man was not the intellectual enigma,[38] and not every death, but the conflict of feeling at the death of loved yet alien and hated persons. Of this conflict of feeling psychology was the first offspring. Man could no longer keep death at a distance, for he had tasted it in his pain about the dead; but he was nevertheless unwilling to acknowledge it, for he could not conceive of himself as dead. So he devised a compromise: he conceded the fact of his own death as well, but denied it the significance of annihilation—a significance which he had no motive for denying where the death of his enemy was concerned. It was beside the dead body of someone he loved that he invented spirits, and his sense of guilt at the satisfaction mingled with his sorrow turned these new-born spirits into evil demons that had to be dreaded.[39]

Culture—which, for Freud, is but another name for "psychology"—is compromise formation. It is constituted as an effort to forget a conflict, a sense of profound fragmentation, which, by way of the loved one's dead body, has become irretrievably lodged at the very heart of the psyche. The psyche immerses itself in illusion in order to avoid the pain of its division. It seeks to (mis)take itself as nothing but its own illusory demand for unity. Its knowledge is rather an attempt not to know what is true. Its intelligence is born as an ill-fated, forever haunted attempt to undo the "conflict of feeling" produced by the death of a loved one. Freud's theory of culture tells the story of this psyche, of its virtually constitutive failure to come to know itself as mortal.

This failure is at the root of Freud's concept of the unconscious. Freud tells us that our unconscious "knows nothing that is negative, and no negation; in it contradictories coincide." It is for that reason, Freud specifies, that "it does not know its own death, for to that we can give only a negative content."[40] The problem, then, is not that the unconscious is the locus of some primitive attachment to life: it is not as if some longing for immortality prevents the emergence of mortality as a problem. On the contrary, the unconscious is ignorant of its own death by definition, due to its very mode of operation, and it is this ignorance that renders it unsuitable, as it were, both for life and for culture.

The centrality of the death of a loved one in Freud's theory of culture is most visible at this point. The death of a loved one somehow manages to render the inaccessible accessible, to intimate the unthinkable: one's own death. The death of a loved one is the category in and through which Freud theorizes the insertion of the "No" into the psyche, the dynamics by way of which the psyche comes to intuit its own finitude. In and through the death of a loved one, the psyche is presented with an opportunity to correct its ignorance of its own death. In the death of loved ones, Freud seeks the seeds of the "No," of the corrective that is to enable a psyche that "knows nothing that is negative" to gain access to the conflicted terrain of its mortal life as it unfolds within the boundaries of culture.[41]

According to Freud, the death of a loved one transforms the coexistence of opposing trends in the unconscious into a contradiction generating pain and anxiety, making a demand for work, insisting to be appeased. It is in this way that the painful struggle of life and death—that, for Freud, is the *truth of life*—appears before the human psyche. Yet the way in which this appearance takes place is no small difficulty. It is certainly not from the viewpoint of the unconscious itself that Freud tells us that "in it contradictories coincide." To speak of contradiction is already to presuppose the "No" whose appearance is precisely what we are trying to understand. It is already to speak of the way in which the demand for unity that is deemed to arise in and through the death of a loved one grasps the coexistence in the unconscious of convergent attitudes to death. In other words, this coexistence is not *as such* contradictory. The unconscious is constituted as non-sense only in and through the demand for sense. The matter at issue is not at all that I become conscious of a preexisting contradiction, but rather that in the very act of becoming conscious I constitute that contradiction as such. Thus, this becoming conscious cannot be satisfactorily explained as a result of a contradiction to which consciousness alone can give rise.

Curiously enough, the poles of the contradiction in question both presuppose the absence of the "No." The death-murder of the stranger is as much an aspect of the nonexistence of contradiction in the unconscious as is the impossibility of one's own death. The conviction of one's own immortality is a conviction of oneself as totality, as everything that is. From its point of view, the other is that which, strictly speaking, *is* not. The other *is* the not-real, that which can and must be murdered.[42] Thus the absence of the "No" in the unconscious signifies the relation between I and not-I as the site of an antagonism, as an occasion for war. But at the same time, in the midst of this antagonism, the death of a loved one suspends the distinction between I and not-I. In so doing, it actually brings to life, as it were in spite of me yet precisely through my love, that strange and truly remarkable mode of being that finds its being in not-being. Thus it faces me with my own death with the same stroke with which, as it were posthumously, it brings the loved stranger to life. Its painful "No" resignifies the relation between I and not-I not as war but as loss, *not as the site of an antagonism but as an occasion for unification.* Thus the primordial ambivalence that the death of a loved one brings to the fore is an antagonism not between

I and not-I, but between that which unifies and that which separates. This is the struggle of Eros and Death.[43]

The fact that the psyche's demand for unity cannot be derived from the unconscious as such is at the heart of Freud's conception of culture. The loved one's death introduces something new; it introduces Eros. To be sure, this does not take place ex nihilo.[44] Freud's point is rather that Eros is something not internal to the *isolated* mortal substance;[45] it is something that happens between people, that is evoked in the sphere of intersubjectivity. It comes to be when I am separated from that which I take to be my own body, when the other becomes separate, itself. Accordingly, Eros is the emblem of loss. So little is it opposed to loss that it both originates and sustains itself only in and through loss. The psyche's properly erotic demand for unity is not something outside loss—it is both constituted by and constitutive of loss. Loss is at the crossroads of life and death. Eros finds its realization, then, not in the return to some illusory happy unity—which is the ruse of Death—but in the mutually mournful revelation of our irreducible solitudes, of each other's death.[46]

The psyche's failure to know itself as mortal is a failure not to come to life but to remain in it. The struggle of life and death is a struggle about how loss (and its attendant conflict of ambivalence) is to be dealt with, about how death is to be signified. By way of its illusions, the psyche manages to avoid not the struggle but the truthful appearance of itself to itself *as* that struggle. It seeks to appease rather than work, forget rather than cognize.

Freud's sense of the loss incurred thereby is truly profound. The problematic that the appearance of the "No" brings into being is as ethical as it is existential. It is existential in that death is at its heart, and it is ethical in that the heart of this death is forever the death-murder of the loved one. At issue in this ethico-existential unity is the crucial circumstance that Freud locates mortality at the level of relations between people, in a radically intersubjective arena.[47] For Freud, the death of the loved one is about not only the appearance of death, but also about the emergence of an entire cultural universe among whose most essential components is a sphere of intersubjective relations, of relations between people. Paradoxically, then, the "conventional" denial of death upon which culture rests coincides with a denial of the reality of the other. These are the subterranean roots of the juncture between progress and barbarism that, like an evil demon, haunts the achievements of culture. The cultural denial of death must of necessity culminate in war because the only way to uphold my immortality in the face of the other is to kill him. Only by way of murder can I continue to regard myself as the totality. Yet the triumphs of my lordship are not only those of destruction but also those of self-destruction. A culture unable and unwilling to endure the ambivalent struggle of life and death that is the truth of life cannot help but end in war. For war is the outcome of its denial of death, and war puts a stop to that denial. War tells the truth of culture: horrified as much as disillusioned, culture discovers in its own midst the uncanny otherness it so helplessly attempted to spit out of itself.

In the denied death of the loved one, Freud discerns the broken features of a lost opportunity. He speaks like a regretful witness deeply sensitive to the gigantic foreclosure of a possible intersubjectivity, an experience of the relation between I and not-I both capable of sustaining the irreducible cleavages of otherness and in fact grounded precisely in an appropriation of those very same cleavages. The death of the loved one is pregnant with a future. It promises a horizon beyond the ravages of an "either-or" that, by way of its stubborn grasp of the relation between I and not-I as the site of cruel antagonisms, turns the world into a madhouse. The death of the loved one allows me to see myself as other, as dead—and the other as myself, as alive. It frightens me not only with the otherness of the other to myself, but also with that of myself to myself. Yet in so doing, it simultaneously prompts me to place a question mark at the door of the ill-fated desire to find oneself either as immortal or as dead, either as all or as nothing. It insists that I come to live both with and as that which dies. The death of the loved one brings both the other and myself to life.[48] Hence, its conceptual specification contains Freud's *distinctive* version of an "'I' that is 'We' and 'We' that is 'I'."[49]

The mere fact that Freud discerns the traces of a profound loss in the denial of the loved one's death does not in and of itself entail that the imagined horizon from which he feels that loss embodies a betrayed possibility, a viable alternative. All the same, the mere fact that Freud refers to the illusions of culture as illusions, as denials, tells us that he speaks from the viewpoint of an intelligence, a mode of cognition capable of recasting or breaking through such denials. Like the war itself, Freud's intelligence presents us with a denial of the cultural denial of death, an undoing of culture's negation of death. Thus, Freud's intelligence follows the lead of war in that it, too, "lays bare the primal man in each of us."[50] But although the war facilitates the articulation of Freud's truth, it by no means coincides with it. Unlike the war, Freud's intelligence seeks a re-cognition of rather than a re-turn to the denied content of culture. Freud does not equate the cultural illusions destroyed by the war with culture as such. Thus, he is not disillusioned by the death of a culture he neither can nor does respect. Rather, he is deeply interested in the possibility of a culture, an ethos, no longer rooted in the precarious and treacherous ground of illusion.

This notion of an intelligence capable of undoing the negation of death within, rather than at the expense of, the confines of culture permits us to observe that, in addition to its ethical and existential dimensions, the concept of the death of the loved one presents a third, philosophical dimension. At the level of the existential, the death of the loved one opposes the fact of mortality to one's inability to think one's own death. At the level of the ethical, it opposes war to dialogue, my wish to murder to the possibility of an intersubjectivity rooted in the assumption of otherness. At the level of the philosophical, the death of the loved one opposes the intelligence that seeks to undo the "conflict of feeling at the death of loved yet alien and hated persons" to the intelligence that insists that such conflict must be *worked through*, dealt with in some other way. At the level of the philosophical, the death of the loved one opposes denial to knowledge, illusion to (re)cognition.

These three dimensions are as inextricable as the opposed poles each of them places before us. They are as inextricable, that is to say, as life and death are from each other. A cognition altogether devoid of illusion is neither possible *nor desirable*. The point at issue here is not the tiresome one that the death of a loved one is about a pain so intolerable that it can by no means be grasped directly, without the softening comforts of illusion. The point, rather, is that the truth Freud seeks to intimate by way of the loved one's death is precisely that of the ceaseless crisscrossing of Eros and Death, the forever ambivalent crossroads of reality and dream.[51] Thus, nowhere is the ruse of Death as insidiously present as in the illusory promise of a "pure" and "mature" knowledge. The illusions of the infantile can be unambiguously transcended as little as the claims of the unconscious can be absolutely mastered. When Freud tells us that culture may be "simply described as the *struggle for life* of the human species" (emphasis added),[52] he is specifying the situation of a living being who can never fully manage to be born, who comes to life from the womb of death, and who begins to die as soon as it is born. At issue here is the crucial observation that, for Freud, it is because we are biologically born prematurely, that we must historically be born posthumously, in the twilight of retroactivity (*Nachträglichkeit*).[53] This is why the intelligence of which Freud speaks must always appear as an undoing of negations, as a critique of illusions. This is not the place to reflect upon Freud's conception of the connection between "the symbol of negation," the "No," and the origins and development of the "function of intellectual judgment."[54] What is important at this point, rather, is that Freud approaches the problem of cognition in terms of the undoing of the negation of the death of the loved one—in a word, in terms of the problem of mourning. Hence, Freud's movement from dis-illusion to cognition takes place in and through a particular kind of labor, the labor of mourning. Only such labor can construct the possibility of an alternative existential mood.

EROS AND TRANSIENCE

This, then, is the statement that the foregoing reflection should allow us to illuminate:

> To tolerate life remains, after all, the first duty of all living beings. Illusion becomes valueless if it makes this harder for us.[55]

Once again, we may begin with the death of the loved one. The fact that the loved one is that other whose death is also mine indicates the profound depth of the ambivalence Freud has in mind. Since I am that other about whose death I feel ambivalent, my ambivalence toward that other is simultaneously ambivalence toward myself. Our ambivalence is ambivalence toward existence as such, toward the very fact of being. As the living substance of culture, we are the very field in which Eros and Death wage their primordial struggle.

Illusions are deathly in that their denial of our ambivalence, their refusal to endure the death of the loved one, removes us both from ourselves and from the struggle constitutive of life itself. In this respect, Freud's choice is clear: his injunction to endure life is an injunction against Death. For Freud, the content of our "first duty" as living beings is deeply erotic. Freud presents Eros itself under the rubric of duty, as the duty to love without illusion, to live in truth. This is why the renunciation of illusion results not in disillusionment but in (re)cognition, in a reclaiming of the only life that is our own, of the forgotten fragments of a life from which we would no longer be as distanced.

Freud's brief paper "On Transience" (1916), another of his meditations on the Great War, may be grasped as an explication of his distinction between disillusion and cognition proper. In "On Transience," Freud invites us to a "summer walk through a smiling countryside in the company of a taciturn friend and of a young but already famous poet." The conversation is to explore the circumstance that "[t]he poet admired the beauty of the scene around us but felt no joy in it." The poet is captured between an ebbing capacity to admire beauty and a lost capacity for joy. He is enthralled by a debilitating experience of transience:

> All that he would otherwise have loved and admired seemed to him to be shorn of its worth by the transience which was its doom.[56]

"I could not see my way to dispute the transience of all things, nor could I insist upon an exception in favour of what is beautiful and perfect," Freud admits. "But," he adds immediately, "I did dispute the pessimistic poet's view that the transience of what is beautiful involves any loss in its worth." Thus, on the one hand, it is true, Freud tells us that "what is painful may none the less be true." Yet, on the other, he reminds us that he is no pessimist, at least not in the sense in which the "pessimistic" young poet is. Freud opposes his own capacity for joy to the young poet's "aching despondency."[57] In so doing, he proposes an alternative attitude to transience.

The way in which Freud considers and then dismisses the poet's attitude reveals the remarkable degree to which Freud regards his own capacity for joy as virtually self-evident. Freud states that he cannot even understand what the poet is talking about. He finds it "incomprehensible," he tells us unabashedly, "that the thought of the transience of beauty should interfere with our joy in it":

> A flower that blossoms only for a single night does not seem to us on that account less lovely. Nor can I understand any better why the beauty and perfection of a work of art or of an intellectual achievement should lose its worth because of its temporal limitation. A time may indeed come when the pictures and statues which we admire to-day will crumble to dust, or a race of men may follow us who no longer understand the works of our poets and thinkers, or a geological epoch may even arrive when all animate life upon the earth ceases; but since the value of all this beauty and perfection is determined only by its significance for our own emotional lives, it has no need to survive us and is therefore independent of absolute duration.[58]

Freud's efforts to enjoin his disillusioned audience toward a love of the transient, however, fall on deaf ears. "I noticed," he tells us, "that I had made no impression either upon the poet or upon my friend." Nonetheless, Freud persists in regarding his own capacity for joy and its implications as "incontestable." From his failure to persuade the poet and his friend, Freud infers not that he himself ought to question his enjoyment, but rather that "some powerful emotional factor was at work which was disturbing their judgment." Freud even adds that "I believed later that I had discovered what it was."[59]

Like the disillusionment of the war, then, the poet's despondency is as much knowledge as it is illusion, a concealing as much as a revealing. It is a revealing to the extent that it cognizes the transience of all things. It is a concealing to the extent that it equates the appearance of truth in and through despondency—with truth itself. In this latter aspect, the cognitive content of the poet's despondency lies not in what it tells us about that which is cognized, but rather, about he who cognizes. Recognition of the painfulness of what is true by no means entails that life itself be condemned by the living. In this way, Freud differentiates the transience of all things from the paralyzing despondency in and through which the truth of transience arises in the poet's mind. The young poet's disillusionment is but a signpost on the way to unveiling his enthralling belief that only that which does not die is worthy of being and of being loved.

Thus, for Freud, the young poet's refusal to enjoy beauty is in fact a "demand for immortality"[60]:

> What spoilt their enjoyment of beauty must have been a revolt in their minds against mourning.[61]

Yet a revolt against mourning is a revolt against death itself—a revolt that, in attempting to keep death at a distance, manages to lose life. The poet refuses to love or enjoy that which must of necessity be mourned. For Freud, only love of the temporal, the transient, is truly erotic.

Toward the conclusion of a crucial paper on psychoanalytic technique, "The Dynamics of Transference" (1912), Freud makes a statement that once again brings to mind this conception of the movement into the truth of life as a movement into the field of temporality:

> The unconscious impulses do not want to be remembered in the way the treatment desires them to be, but endeavour to reproduce themselves in accordance with the timelessness of the unconscious and its capacity for hallucination.[62]

Freud's task is to transform the repetitiveness produced by the timelessness of the unconscious into a memory that allows itself to be forgotten. The mode of remembrance he seeks, then, is precisely that of constructing the possibility of forgetfulness, of introducing unconscious processes into the field of temporality. To become conscious is to become involved in the universe of time. Freud seeks to transform Thanatos into Eros, the repetitive timelessness of death into the open expanse of life. The struggle Freud wages against illusion, against the hallucinatory satisfactions of the unconscious, is a struggle against Thanatos, the death drive. Thanatos is a refusal to love what will die. We may regard it as a kind of loyalty whose stubborn illusions foreclose the death of what is loved, resist the loss of old loves, the birth of new ones. In Freud's universe, Death seduces us with the promise of immortality.

This is why, for Freud, the movement into life must of necessity be mediated in and through consciousness of death. Eros, the life drive, can find its predominance only in and through the recognition of death and finitude. Only such recognition can liberate our longing from attachments to unreal, immortal objects. Only the *work of mourning* involved in such detachment can direct our longing toward real, mortal objects. The young poet's disillusionment is but the symptom whereby the illusion of immortality casts its shadow over the fragments of existence.[63] The poet's love of the immortal "spoils his enjoyment"—it is but a secret love of death. Thus the poet cannot love anything that, like his own mortal body, is truly alive.

For Freud, the only true pleasure is pleasure in time. The truth of life is the transience of what we love. Love is always love of what will die. As distinct from the pessimistic poet's, that is, Freud's attitude is less a call for resignation than an attempt to (re)claim death as an occasion to be born. Freud grasps the wound of death not as an argument against life, but as an opportunity to deploy an eroticism that has made truthfulness a condition of its love. In proposing a new attitude to death, Freud proposes a new attitude to life. And this new existential mood is the deeply erotic content of our "first duty" as living beings.

This alternative existential mood brings in its wake an alternative ethical universe. The refusal to enter temporality is a refusal to enter the field of society, of intersubjectivity. The young poet refuses not only to live but also to live with others, to find the fragments of his own life amidst those of others. "To turn away from reality," Freud writes, "is at the same time to withdraw from the community of man."[64] Thus, Freud's proposed new attitude to death intimates an entire culture, a new ethos. Accordingly, it adumbrates an alternative conception of guilt, of a new superego whose commands require us to fulfill our "first duty" as living beings.[65]

The complexity of Freud's conception of guilt is proverbial. Without by any means pretending to do justice to it, let it here suffice to underline the relation between guilt and death; or, more precisely, to visualize guilt as a mode of relatedness between the living and the dead.[66] Freud tells us that it is beside the dead body of someone we love that we come to invent spirits. He observes that these newborn spirits allow us both to concede and to deny death simultaneously—in other words, to deny death the "significance of annihilation." He then adds that these spirits turn into "evil demons" that are to be dreaded.[67] "[T]he first-born spirits," he tells us in *Totem and Taboo*, "were *evil* spirits" (emphasis in original).[68] It is as if

> *all* of the dead were vampires, all of them had a grudge against the living and sought to injure them and rob them of their lives. It was from corpses that the concept of evil spirits first arose.[69] (emphasis in original)

Death turns our loved ones into malignant demons. The loved yet also hated dead become possessors of the hostility we had directed against them. In and through their haunting enmity, our own murderousness now confronts us as something alien, as if from the outside. "The survivor," Freud tells us, "thus denies that he has ever harboured any hostile feelings against the dead loved one; the soul of the dead harbours them instead and seeks to put them into action during the whole period of mourning."[70] For Freud, these are the origins of the gnawing throes of conscience, the "pure culture" of the death drive that typifies the hostile superego,[71] the discontent of civilization. Guilt is the token of unfinished business with the dead—the sign that mourning work is still to be done.[72]

This refusal to mourn, of course, is a refusal to (re)cognize the death of the loved one. In "Thoughts for the Times on War and Death," as he introduces the concept of the cultural and conventional denial of death, Freud makes a cryptic remark about our relation to the dead:

> Towards the actual person who has died we adopt a special attitude—something almost like admiration for someone who has accomplished a very difficult task. We suspend criticism of him, overlook his possible misdeeds, declare that *"de mortuis nil nisi bonum,"* and think it justifiable to set out all that is most favourable to his memory in the funeral oration and upon the tombstone. Consideration for the dead, who, after all, no longer need it, is more important to us than the truth, and certainly, for most of us, than consideration for the living.[73] (emphasis in original)

It is at this juncture that we can capture Freud's critique of illusion, of the denial of death, as an injunction envisioning a different culture. The critique of illusion takes place in the name of a care for truth—and for the living. It is uttered, that is, from the viewpoint of an ethos informed by our "first duty" as living beings. For Freud, guilt—the predominance of Thanatos, the death drive—is guilt over the opportunity not seized, the life not lived. It is guilt over not having fulfilled our "first duty." Freud's ethos does not speak like a punitive voice from the distant past that mortifies us with what we have done and with what we refuse to lose. Freud's voice, rather, enjoins us to endure the loss of a life truly lived. In the name of Eros, Freud wishes not to eliminate but to transvaluate our relation to death and to the dead. As distinct from the ravages of war, the capacity to mourn the dead is coeval with a tragic celebration of the living. It moves us in the direction of "consideration for the living." This is why Freud's critique of illusion is the critique of a culture fascinated by war, a death-culture, a pure culture of the death drive. Freud's observation is that we would rather go to war than talk of death.[74] His profound concern is that our times might no longer wish to endure life.

Freud's parting glance at Eros as he concludes *Civilization and Its Discontents* is enough to alert us to the fact that the intent of his legendary portrayal of the discontents of culture is not merely to demonstrate the necessity of suffering. Rather, his portrayal is premised on the insight that the fruitless attempt to avoid necessary suffering cannot help but culminate in the production of unnecessary suffering. Illusions complicate the very suffering they wish to eliminate. For Freud, the harsh truth of pain is superior to the illusion of happiness. The truth his so-called pessimism offers is the truth of mourning, not of melancholia. His "fateful question" specifies a task to be engaged upon rather than a definitive fate to be accepted despondently. Accordingly, his own standpoint must be carefully and subtly distinguished from the discontents of the culture he portrays. Freud mounts a nuanced critique of the melancholic discontents of culture. At stake in that critique is Freud's attempt to awaken a culture whose illusions pervert the truth of pain into an argument against the possibility of a life worth living. Freud's is not a theory about the regrettable yet necessary imprisonment of the individual in the cultural. It is a critical theory about how human beings fall short of who they can be by refusing to be the mortal beings that they are.

NOTES

1. Sigmund Freud, *Civilization and Its Discontents*, in vol. 21 of *The Standard Edition of the Complete Psychological Works of Sigmund Freud*, ed. and trans. James Strachey et al. (London: Hogarth, 1953–1974), 95.

2. Thomas Hobbes, *Leviathan*, ed. C. B. Macpherson (Middlesex, UK: Penguin, 1968), 271.

3. Freud, *Civilization and Its Discontents*, 128.

4. Freud, *Civilization and Its Discontents*, 124. I compare Freud and Hobbes in chapter 2, in "Hobbes's Fear of Violent Death."

5. Sigmund Freud, *The Future of an Illusion*, in vol. 21 of *The Standard Edition*, ed. and trans. James Strachey et al., 50.

6. See John Deigh, "Freud's Later Theory of Civilization: Changes and Implications," in *The Cambridge Companion to Freud*, ed. Jerome Neu (Cambridge, UK: Cambridge University Press, 1992), 287–308. Freud's first explicit articulation of the death drive took place in 1920, in Sigmund Freud, *Beyond the Pleasure Principle*, in vol. 18 of *The Standard Edition*, ed. and trans. James Strachey et al., 1–64.

7. Sigmund Freud, *New Introductory Lectures on Psycho-Analysis*, in vol. 22 of *The Standard Edition*, ed. and trans. James Strachey et al., 146, 149.

8. Sigmund Freud, "Analysis Terminable and Interminable," in vol. 23 of *The Standard Edition*, ed. and trans. James Strachey et al., 243. Jacques Lacan may have this passage in mind when he states that "[t]he death instinct isn't an admission of impotence, it isn't a coming to a halt before an irreducible, an ineffable last thing, it is a concept." See Jacques Lacan, *The Seminar of Jacques Lacan: Book II, The Ego in Freud's Theory and in the Technique of Psychoanalysis 1954–1955*, ed. Jacques-Allain Miller and trans. Sylvana Tomaselli (London: Norton, 1988), 70.

9. Freud says as much explicitly: "But this struggle between the individual and society is *not* a derivative of the contradiction—probably an irreconcilable one—between the primal instincts of Eros and death. It is a dispute within the economics of the libido, comparable to the contest concerning the distribution of libido between ego and objects; *and it does admit of an eventual accommodation in the individual, as, it may be hoped, it will also do in the future of civilization, however much that civilization may oppress the life of the individual to-day*" (emphases added). Freud, *Civilization and Its Discontents*, 141.

10. Freud, *Civilization and Its Discontents*, 133. See also 145.

11. The Hegelian "cunning of Reason," one might say, here appears as a "cunning of unreason." Recall that Freud's books were among those publicly burned by the Nazis in Berlin on May 10, 1933. But note also that scarcely three months before he left Vienna, on June 4, 1938, in the wake of Hitler's invasion of Austria, Freud still writes not simply that progress *is* barbarism, but rather that "[w]e are

living in a specially remarkable period," in which "progress *has allied* itself with barbarism." Sigmund Freud, *Moses and Monotheism: Three Essays,* in vol. 23 of *The Standard Edition,* ed. and trans. James Strachey et al., 54 (emphasis added). On this period of Freud's life, see Peter Gay, *Freud: A Life for Our Times* (New York: Anchor, 1989) 588–629.

12. Freud, *Civilization and Its Discontents,* 145. The editors of *The Standard Edition* note that Freud added the final sentence of this passage "in 1931—when the menace of Hitler was already beginning to be apparent."

13. Norman O. Brown, *Life Against Death: The Psychoanalytic Meaning of History* (Middletown, Conn.: Wesleyan University Press, 1959), 98–99.

14. Gay, *A Life for Our Times,* 551 and 553.

15. Sigmund Freud, *The Ego and the Id,* in vol. 19 of *The Standard Edition,* ed. and trans. James Strachey et al. 59.

16. Thus, in *New Introductory Lectures,* Freud writes: "From the concurrent and opposing action of these two [i.e., Eros and Death] proceed the phenomena of life which are brought to an end by death. . . . We are not asserting that death is the only aim of life; we are not overlooking the fact that there is life as well as death. We recognize two basic instincts and give each of them its own aim." Freud, *New Introductory Lectures,* 107. See also Freud's final and unfinished *An Outline of Psycho-Analysis,* in vol. 23 of *The Standard Edition,* ed. and trans. James Strachey et al., 149; and the passage cited in note 8 above.

17. Sigmund Freud, "'Civilized' Sexual Morality and Modern Nervous Illness," in vol. 9 of *The Standard Edition,* ed. and trans. James Strachey et al., 203.

18. Sigmund Freud, "Thoughts for the Times on War and Death," in vol. 14 of *The Standard Edition,* ed. and trans. James Strachey et al., 299. The complexity of the development of Freud's thought between 1908 and 1930 can hardly be overestimated. Two crucial moments in that manifold development are here worth recalling briefly. First, Freud's paper "On Narcissism: An Introduction," completed in March 1914, a year before the publication of "Thoughts for the Times," is widely and rightly regarded as deserving the most prominent of places in any account of the development of Freud's thought in that period. The status of the pioneering "libido theory" articulated in 1905 in the *Three Essays on the Theory of Sexuality* seems to hang by a thread in the 1914 paper. Indeed, the sense of an uncertain and uneasy suspension of Freud's drive theory is not transcended, if ever at all, until 1920, when *Beyond the Pleasure Principle* sets forth the new dualism of life and death that is to succeed the old dualism of sexuality and self-preservation, and that, in 1930, will make its dramatic appearance in Freud's mature theory of culture. See Ernest Jones, *The Life and Work of Sigmund Freud,* 3 vols. (London: Hogarth, 1955), vol. 2, 339–42; Marthe Robert, *The Psychoanalytic Revolution: Sigmund Freud's Life and Achievement,* trans. Kenneth Morgan (London: Allen & Unwin, 1966), 309–12; and Gay, *A Life for Our Times,* 340–42. Yet as early as 1915, in the midst of war, Freud's concern with death in "Thoughts for the Times" already announces the new dualism. "Thoughts for the Times" is a kind of companion piece to "On Narcissism": whereas the latter destroys the old world, the former begins to visualize the new one. Second, "Mourning and Melancholia" (1917), the first draft of which was written in February 1915, at about the same time as "Thoughts for the Times," offers Freud's first systematic elaboration of the concept of 'mourning', and hence of the

role of loss in the formation of the human personality. Grasped as a whole, "On Narcissism" and "Mourning and Melancholia" in fact contain the seeds of the hypothesis of the superego that, through *The Ego and the Id,* will then become the centerpiece of *Civilization and Its Discontents.* Composed in the midst of that fruitful period, Freud's early account of culture in "Thoughts for the Times" thus promises, in retrospect, to shed light on central aspects of *Civilization and Its Discontents.* Freud exaggerates only slightly when, in *Civilization and Its Discontents,* he explicitly insists that his consideration of the sphere of Death does not amount to an "alteration of the psycho-analytic theory of the instincts." Rather, "it is merely a matter of bringing into sharper focus a turn of thought arrived at long ago and of following out its consequences." Freud, *Civilization and Its Discontents,* 117. On Freud's drive theory, see André Green, "Instinct in the Late Works of Freud," in *On Freud's "Analysis Terminable and Interminable,"* ed. Joseph Sandler (New Haven, Conn.: Yale University Press, 1991), 124–141.

19. Freud, "Thoughts for the Times," 299. E. Colburn Mayne translates this passage as follows: "To endure life remains, when all is said, the first duty of all living beings. Illusion can have no value if it makes this more difficult for us." See Sigmund Freud, "Thoughts for the Times on War and Death," trans. E. Colburn Mayne, in vol. 4 of Sigmund Freud, *Collected Papers,* trans. Joan Riviere et al. (New York: Basic, 1959), 317.

20. See Barry Richards, *Images of Freud: Cultural Responses to Psychoanalysis* (London: J. M. Dent, 1989), 33–52. See also Joanne Brown and Barry Richards, "The Humanist Freud," in *Freud 2000,* ed. Anthony Elliot (New York: Routledge, 1999), 235–61.

21. Freud, "Thoughts for the Times," 275.

22. The historical dimension of Freud's reflection is evidenced in that he speaks of the disillusionment that *this,* not *every other war,* has evoked. At the height of Western civilization, "[n]ot only is it [i.e., this war] more bloody and more destructive than any war of other days, because of the enormously increased perfection of weapons of attack and defense; it is at least as cruel, as embittered, as implacable as any that has preceded it." Freud, "Thoughts for the Times," 278. For a brief, precise, and informative appreciation of how the Great War "destroyed a world," see Gay, *A Life for Our Times,* 342–49.

23. Freud, "Thoughts for the Times," 285.

24. Peter Gay follows Ernest Jones in taking Freud's "consolation" at face value, as an essay to "help his readers survive the war years." Jones, *The Life and Work,* 412–16. See Gay, *A Life for Our Times,* 356. To be sure, plenty in Freud's text supports such a reading. But it would be most unfortunate if we were to confuse the life that is to be endured with a symptom—like the war itself—already indicative of a refusal to endure life. See Jacqueline Rose, "Why War?" in *Why War?—Psychoanalysis, Politics, and the Return to Melanie Klein* (Oxford, UK: Blackwell, 1993), 15–40; and Richards, *Images of Freud,* 34.

25. Freud, "Thoughts for the Times," 289.
26. Freud, "Thoughts for the Times," 290.
27. Freud, "Thoughts for the Times," 291.
28. Freud, "Thoughts for the Times," 296.
29. Freud, "Thoughts for the Times," 292.

30. Freud, "Thoughts for the Times," 289.

31. Freud, "Thoughts for the Times," 289–90.

32. Freud, "Thoughts for the Times," 290.

33. Freud, "Thoughts for the Times," 289.

34. Freud, "Thoughts for the Times," 290.

35. Freud, "Thoughts for the Times," 293.

36. Freud, "Thoughts for the Times," 291. Jones informs us that two weeks into the war, in early August 1914, Freud's "eldest son Martin volunteered for the Army and became a gunner." Jones, *Life and Work,* 194. "It would have been *intolerable* for me," Martin wrote to his father from the front, "to remain behind alone when all others are marching off" (reported by Gay, *A Life for Our Times,* 352, emphasis added). In "Thoughts for the Times," Freud explicitly identifies the "noncombatant classes of the population" as composed of "women who take no part in war-work" and "children." Freud, "Thoughts for the Times," 278. "When the furious struggle of the present war has been decided," he writes elsewhere in that essay, "each one of the victorious fighters will return home joyfully to his wife and children. . . ." Freud, "Thoughts for the Times," 295. In yet another passage, he tells us that he himself is a member of the noncombatant population. Freud, "Thoughts for the Times," 292. Consider in this regard the dream about his own son's death that, in a section entitled "Wish-Fulfilment," Freud adds in 1919 to chapter VII of *The Interpretation of Dreams.* Sigmund Freud, *The Interpretation of Dreams,* in vol. 5 of *The Standard Edition,* ed. and trans. James Strachey et al., 558–60. "[W]e had once more been without news of our son at the front for over a week," Freud tells us. "It is easy to see," he adds, "that the content of the dream expressed a conviction that he had been wounded or killed." Freud, *The Interpretation of Dreams,* 559. See also Sarah Kofman's remarks in *The Enigma of Woman: Woman in Freud's Writings,* trans. Catherine Porter (Ithaca, N.Y.: Cornell University Press, 1985), 22–23; Jacques Lacan's discussion of the dream about a "dead son" that opens chapter VII of *The Interpretation of Dreams* in *The Four Fundamental Concepts of Psychoanalysis,* ed. Jacques-Alain Miller, trans. Alan Sheridan (New York: Norton, 1981), 29–41; and Jane Gallop's commentary in *Reading Lacan* (Ithaca, N.Y.: Cornell University Press, 1985), 157–85.

37. Freud, *Civilization and Its Discontents,* 122.

38. The reference is to Schopenhauer. See Freud's explicit reference in Sigmund Freud, *Totem and Taboo,* in vol. 13 of *The Standard Edition,* ed. and trans. James Strachey et al., 87. Yet Freud's claim may also remind us of Plato. See book VII of Plato, *Republic,* trans. Paul Shorey in *Plato: The Collected Dialogues,* ed. Edith Hamilton and Huntington Cairns (Princeton, N.J.: Princeton University Press, 1963), 753, 755, and 757, where Socrates is concerned with a "contradictory perception" (523c) that "would compel the soul to be at a loss and to inquire, by arousing thought in itself" (524e), thereby drawing "the soul away from the world of becoming to the world of being" (521d).

39. Freud, "Thoughts for the Times," 293–94.

40. Freud, "Thoughts for the Times," 296.

41. Speaking of Freud's early formulations of the psyche's accession into the sphere of culture, Gay notes that Freud was implicitly "paving the way for a psychoanalytic social psychology." Gay, *A Life for Our Times,* 337–38. The experiences

of frustration, loss, and conflict that are to catalyze the development of the organism born of a human womb into a cultural being are inseparable from "*the great social No*" giving rise to them (emphasis added).

42. See Sigmund Freud, "Instincts and Their Vicissitudes," in vol. 14 of *The Standard Edition*, ed. and trans. James Strachey et al., 136 and 139.

43. Freud writes: "After long hesitancies and vacillations we have decided to assume the existence of only two basic instincts, *Eros* and *the destructive instinct*. (The contrast between the instincts of self-preservation and the preservation of the species, as well as the contrast between ego-love and object-love, falls within Eros.) The aim of the first of these basic instincts is to establish ever greater unities and to preserve them thus—in short, to bind together; the aim of the second is, on the contrary, to undo connections and so to destroy things" (emphases in original). Freud, *An Outline of Psycho-Analysis*, 148.

44. Consider the enigmatic last sentence of *The Ego and the Id*, cited above in note 15: "It would be possible to picture the id as under the domination of the mute but powerful death instincts, which desire to be at peace and (prompted by the pleasure principle) to put Eros, the mischief-maker, to rest; but perhaps that might be to undervalue the part played by Eros." Freud, *The Ego and the Id*, 59. Consider also the following passage from *An Outline of Psycho-Analysis*: "There can be no question of restricting one or the other of the basic instincts to one of the provinces of the mind. They must necessarily be met with everywhere." Freud, *An Outline of Psycho-Analysis*, 149. Similarly, in "Thoughts for the Times," while insisting upon the absence of the "No" in the unconscious, Freud nonetheless tells us that "ambivalence" is itself a dimension of the "primal man in each of us" that the war "lays bare": "To sum up: our unconscious is just as inaccessible to the idea of our own death, just as murderously inclined towards strangers, just as divided (that is, ambivalent) towards those we love, as was primeval man." Freud, "Thoughts for the Times," 299.

45. Paul Ricoeur writes: "Freud does not look for the drive for life in some will to live inscribed in each living substance: in the living substance *by itself* he finds only death" (emphasis in original). Paul Ricoeur, *Freud and Philosophy: An Essay on Interpretation*, trans. Denis Savage (New Haven, Conn.: Yale University Press, 1970), 291.

46. Cf. Jessica Benjamin, *The Bonds of Love: Psychoanalysis, Feminism and the Problem of Domination* (New York: Pantheon, 1988), especially 82–84. See also C. Fred Alford, "Freud and Violence," in *Freud 2000*, ed. Anthony Elliot (New York: Routledge, 1999), 61–87.

47. See Edward S. Casey and J. Melvin Woody, "Hegel, Heidegger, Lacan: The Dialectic of Desire," in *Interpreting Lacan*, ed. Joseph H. Smith and William Kerrigan (New Haven, Conn.: Yale University Press, 1983), 101–2.

48. If the psyche is to find its way into the universe of culture, of intersubjectivity, then it must learn of its own death as it learns about the claims of independent others. The category of loss is central to Freud's theory of culture because it is in terms of that category that he understands the psyche's cultural task of learning about its own death. Loss is that which educates, that which catalyzes a movement from a mode of mental functioning that knows nothing that is negative, to a mode of mental functioning capable of cognizing and respecting otherness. Loss,

in short, catalyzes the movement from pleasure principle to reality principle. Thus, in "Negation," Freud writes that "a precondition for the setting up of reality-testing is that objects shall have been *lost* which once brought real satisfaction" (emphasis added). Sigmund Freud, "Negation," in vol. 19 of *The Standard Edition*, ed. and trans. James Strachey et al., 238. See also Sigmund Freud, "Formulations on the Two Principles of Mental Functioning," in vol. 12 of *The Standard Edition*, 213–26.

49. See G. W. F. Hegel, *Phenomenology of Spirit*, trans. A. V. Miller (Oxford, UK: Oxford University Press, 1977), 110. I compare Freud and Hegel in chapter 2, in "Those Who Have Stayed at Home."

50. Freud, "Thoughts for the Times," 299.

51. Cf. Jean Laplanche, *Life and Death in Psychoanalysis*, trans. Jeffrey Mehlman (Baltimore: Johns Hopkins University Press, 1976), 125–26.

52. Freud, *Civilization and Its Discontents*, 122.

53. I deal with this concept in chapter 3, in "From Hypnosis to Psychoanalysis." Some excellent discussions are Madeleine Baranger, Willy Baranger, and Jorge Mario Mom, "The Infantile Psychic Trauma from Us to Freud: Pure Trauma, Retroactivity and Reconstruction," *International Journal of Psychoanalysis* 69 (1988): 113–28; Jean Laplanche, *Life and Death*, chapter 2; Jean Laplanche, "Psychoanalysis, Time and Translation" and "Notes on Afterwardsness," in *Jean Laplanche: Seduction, Translation, Drives*, trans. Martin Stanton, ed. John Fletcher and Martin Stanton (London: Institute of Contemporary Arts, 1992), 161–77 and 217–23. In *The Language of Psycho-Analysis*, Jean Laplanche and Jean-Bertrand Pontalis define Freud's Nachträglichkeit—translated as "deferred action" in *The Standard Edition*—as follows: "Term frequently used by Freud in connection with his view of psychical temporality and causality: experiences, impressions and memory-traces may be revised at a later date to fit in with fresh experiences or with the attainment of a new stage of development. They may in that event be endowed not only with a new meaning but also with psychical effectiveness." Jean Laplanche and Jean-Bertrand Pontalis, *The Language of Psycho-Analysis*, trans. Donald Nicholson-Smith (New York: Hogarth, 1973), 111. Laplanche and Pontalis also note, inter alia, that (a) "It is not lived experience in general that undergoes deferred revision but, specifically, whatever it has been impossible in the first instance to incorporate fully into a meaningful context. The traumatic event is the epitome of such unassimilated experience" (112); that (b) "Deferred revision is occasioned by events and situations, or by organic maturation, which allow the subject to gain access to a new level of meaning and to rework his earlier experiences" (112); and that (c) "deferred action . . . might at first sight be construed as a delayed discharge, but we should notice that for Freud a real working over is involved—a 'work of recollection' which is not the mere discharge of accumulated tension but a complex set of psychological operations . . ." (114).

54. Freud, "Negation," 236. "The study of judgment," Freud writes, "affords us, perhaps for the first time, an insight into the origin of an intellectual function from the interplay of the primary instinctual impulses." Freud, "Negation," 238–39. Some discussions are Jean Hyppolite, "A Spoken Commentary on Freud's *Verneinung*," in *The Seminar of Jacques Lacan: Book I, Freud's Papers on Technique, 1953–1954*, trans. John Forrester, ed. Jacques-Alain Miller (New York: Norton,

1988), 289–97; J.-B. Pontalis, "On Death-work," in *Frontiers in Psychoanalysis: Between the Dream and Psychic Pain*, trans. Catherine Cullen and Phillip Cullen (London: Hogarth, 1981), 184–93; André Green, "Negation and Contradiction," in *On Private Madness* (London: Hogarth, 1986), 254–76; and Richard Boothby, *Death and Desire: Psychoanalytic Theory in Lacan's Return to Freud* (New York: Routledge, 1991), see especially 188–91. I return to Freud's "Negation" in chapter 3, in "The Critique of the Hypnotist's Authority."

55. Freud, "Thoughts for the Times," 299.

56. Sigmund Freud, "On Transience," in vol. 14 of *The Standard Edition*, ed. and trans. James Strachey et al., 305.

57. Freud, "On Transience," 305.

58. Freud, "On Transience," 305–6.

59. Freud, "On Transience," 306.

60. Freud, "On Transience," 305.

61. Freud, "On Transience," 306.

62. Sigmund Freud, "The Dynamics of Transference," in vol. 12 of *The Standard Edition*, ed. and trans. James Strachey et al., 108.

63. In *Introductory Lectures on Psycho-Analysis*, Freud remarks that neurotic symptoms "give the patient himself the impression of being all-powerful guests from an alien world, *immortal beings intruding into the turmoil of mortal life*" (emphasis added). Freud, *Introductory Lectures on Psycho-Analysis*, in vol. 16 of *The Standard Edition*, ed. and trans. James Strachey et al., 278. In yet another formulation, Freud writes that "[a] neurotic is incapable of enjoyment . . . because his libido is not directed on to any real object." Freud, *Introductory Lectures*, 453. Recall that while Freud sees the developmental installation of the reality principle as involving a protracted effort to endure loss and frustration, he grasps that installation not only negatively as a recognition of the limits of satisfaction but also positively as essential to growth and to the maximization of the chances of satisfaction. See Freud, "Formulations on the Two Principles," 213–26.

64. Freud, *Totem and Taboo*, 74.

65. Cf. Richard Boothby, *Death and Desire*, 167–76; Herbert Marcuse, *Eros and Civilization: A Philosophical Inquiry into Freud* (Boston: Beacon, 1955), 228–31; and Roy Schafer, "The Loving and Beloved Superego in Freud's Structural Theory," *Psychoanalytic Study of the Child* XV (1960): 163–88.

66. Cf. Ricoeur, *Freud and Philosophy*, 298.

67. Freud, "Thoughts for the Times," 294.

68. Freud, *Totem and Taboo*, 92.

69. Freud, *Totem and Taboo*, 59, citing Rudolf Kleinpaul, *Die Lebendigen und die Toten in Volksglauben, Religion und Sage* (Leipzig: G. J. Göschen, 1898).

70. Freud, *Totem and Taboo*, 61.

71. Freud, *The Ego and the Id*, 53.

72. Freud writes, "Mourning has a quite specific psychical task to perform: its function is to detach the survivors' memories and hopes from the dead. When this has been achieved, the pain grows less and with it the remorse and self-reproaches and consequently the fear of the demon as well. And the same spirits who to begin with were feared as demons may now expect to meet with friendlier treatment, they are revered as ancestors and appeals are made to them for help."

Freud, *Totem and Taboo*, 65–66. In *Civilization and Its Discontents,* Death renders our business with the dead into something far more difficult than a transitional period to be spontaneously transcended. It frames the task of mourning as an "interminable" struggle of life and death, a perpetual posing and reposing of the "fateful question" that defines us. In that it precludes the question from arising, victory in this struggle is always the victory of Death. Eros is nowhere but in the posing of the question in all of its modalities. Ponder, for example, the role of "wit" in Freud's thought. See Freud, *Jokes and Their Relation to the Unconscious,* in vol. 8 of *The Standard Edition,* ed. and trans. James Strachey et al.; and Sigmund Freud, "Humour," in vol. 21 of *The Standard Edition,* 159–66.

73. Freud, "Thoughts for the Times," 290.

74. In his letter to Einstein, Freud writes that "there is no question of getting rid entirely of human aggressive impulses; it is enough to try to divert them to such an extent that they need not find expression in war." Sigmund Freud, "Why War?" in vol. 22 of *The Standard Edition,* ed. and trans. James Strachey et al., 212. Consider Leo Bersani's remark, about "an *historical* violence which . . . may be the catastrophic symptom of our refusal to recognize the violence in which our sexuality is grounded" (emphasis in original). Leo Bersani, *The Freudian Body: Psychoanalysis and Art* (New York: Columbia University Press, 1986), 114. See also Boothby, *Death and Desire,* 184.

2

Between Hobbes and Hegel

It is not a question of an antithesis between an optimistic and a pessimistic theory of life. Only by the concurrent or mutually opposing action of the two primal instincts—Eros and the death-instinct—, never by one or the other alone, can we explain the rich multiplicity of the phenomena of life.

—Sigmund Freud, "Analysis Terminable and Interminable"

NEITHER HOBBES NOR HEGEL

The foregoing reflection claims that the *question* Freud leaves us with at the end of *Civilization and Its Discontents* is in fact the most fundamental *conclusion* of his theory of culture. I have argued that it is only in the light of a retrieval of the critical content of that theory that the task Freud places before us can be adequately understood. Freud's "fateful question" is about the relation between war and death; it raises the possibility that, in learning to relate to death in some way other than that of war, our culture might manage to deploy an alternative attitude to life—and thus to maximize the accessibility of joy within the bounds of our mortal condition.

According to Freud, the central purpose of *Civilization and Its Discontents* is "to represent the sense of guilt as the most important problem in the development of civilization and to show that the price we pay for our advance in civilization is a loss of happiness through the heightening of the sense of guilt."[1] The exposure of this self-defeating structure at the

41

heart of culture animates Freud's profound concern regarding the fate of our times—and, in fact, of our species. In this regard, Freud's theory of culture adumbrates a conception of guilt intimating a new superego whose commands require us to fulfill our "first duty" as living beings.

In this chapter, I want to begin to broach the political import of Freud's theory in terms of a juxtaposition of Freud and Hobbes. On the one hand, my intent is to develop further the observation that Freud's theory of culture is irretrievably misunderstood if interpreted *exclusively* in the wake of Hobbes's well-known opposition of individual and society, passion and order, war and peace. I wish to place Freud in the Western tradition of political philosophy by interpreting Freud's "Thoughts for the Times on War and Death" rather as thoughts *for Hobbes* on war and death. Such a juxtaposition of Freud and Hobbes reveals the degree to which, for Freud, the sphere of culture is not simply negative or restrictive in the sense of providing necessary prohibitions and protections. On the contrary, it is also positive or developmental in the sense of being the very field in and through which human individuals can and do develop as cultural beings. My reflection in this chapter thus proceeds to a discussion of the relation between Freud and *Hegel* as regards the theorization of relations between people, of intersubjectivity. This discussion will serve to illustrate that the thrust of Freud's movement beyond Hobbes stops short of a Hegelian conception of comprehensive community. As a whole, this chapter introduces a reflection—to be articulated in the chapter that follows it—about the juncture between death and authority, illusion and domination, that, as we shall see, Freud posits at the heart of the culture he criticizes.

It is difficult to overestimate the weight and complexity of fear in Hobbes's political philosophy. More than any other emotion, fear captures most adequately Hobbes's rendering of the natural condition of humankind. For Hobbes, fear is absolutely central to human nature. To be human is to fear. Accordingly, the dynamics of fear are fundamental to Hobbes's conception of both the foundation and the sustenance of political society. This is why, for Hobbes, the transition from the state of nature to the social state, from war to peace, has to do not with an elimination of fear, but with a creative deployment of that essentially human emotion.[2]

Since the fear of which Hobbes speaks involves a fear of violent death, the category of death is as central to Hobbes's thought as that of fear. But what, precisely, *is* the role of death in Hobbes's thought? Why must fear, to put it otherwise, necessarily be, in the final analysis, the fear of violent death? What is it about Hobbes's thought that accounts for his deployment of the category of death in terms of that of fear? My claim in this regard is that to understand Hobbes's rendering of death in terms of fear is to understand why he conceptualized political society as something that stands, like an awesome sword, outside and above the individuals who compose it.

As regards the juxtaposition of Hobbes and Freud, my interest in the role of death in Hobbes's thought is to ascertain that to render death, with Freud, in some way different from Hobbes's fearful way, is to have access to a different understanding of society. The essential point I wish to argue is that Freud's concept of the death of a loved one allows him to move beyond Hobbes's instrumentalization of the sphere of relations between people, toward a theorization of the constitutive role of social relations in the construction of the human subject as such. To juxtapose Hobbes and Freud in terms of the problem of death is to deepen our appreciation of both thinkers—and also to grasp Freud's theory of culture not as some kind of psychological elaboration of but rather as a critique of Hobbes's political theory. The upshot of my discussion is that Freud's theory of culture captures a dimension of social life beyond the reach of Hobbes's position. This dimension is the dimension of Eros.

As we noted in chapter 1, the conceptual specification of Freud's concept of the loved one's death contains his *distinctive* version of an "'I' that is 'We' and 'We' that is 'I'."[3] Accordingly, the present chapter differentiates Freud's from Hegel's conception of relations between people. This differentiation shall enable us to locate Freud's conceptualization of social relations both between and beyond Hobbes's instrumental collection of competitive and preconstituted atoms, on the one hand, and Hegel's all-encompassing totality that both transcends and comprehends the moments in and through which it finds its concreteness, on the other. If the unifying powers of Eros intimate a critique of Hobbes, the divisive powers of Death intimate one of Hegel. In that vein, I return, by way of conclusion to this chapter, to the problem of Freud's purported pessimism.

HOBBES'S FEAR OF VIOLENT DEATH

According to Hobbes, human nature is such that war necessarily ensues as soon as human beings come into contact with each other in the absence of a common authority to overawe each and all. The state of nature—the prepolitical state—is a state of war. For Hobbes, the absence of government is eo ipso the presence of war. We owe everything to government because without government we have nothing but war.

Yet this state of nature which is a horrible state of war is not a historical reality but a hypothesis designed with a particular purpose: to frighten us into submission to an absolutely sovereign government that has no obligations whatsoever toward its subjects. The unbearable horrors of the state of war are such that Hobbes is able to suggest that any government is better than no government. Some governments are better than others, but this does not alter the fact that there is very little that the most corrupt and most despotic of governments can do that would be worse than the absence of government. The terrors of the war of every one against every one that takes place in Hobbes's state of nature are such that we cannot help but consider ourselves fortunate to have government. Hobbes's state of nature is a device intended to help us appreciate the indispensability of political authority.

The purpose that Hobbes's hypothesis is intended to fulfill, however, already leads us to a central problem that Hobbes's political philosophy must face. On the one hand, Hobbes's description of the state of nature must be horrifying enough so as to be able to frighten us into submission. On the other hand, and at the same time, the more horrifying Hobbes's description gets, the more difficult it becomes for Hobbes to think his way out of the state of nature and into civil society. Indeed, how can the thoroughly self-involved and self-regarding, power-seeking Hobbesian individual be thought of as a reliable participant in the contract that, according to Hobbes, underlies the very fabric of society? Can the individuals Hobbes describes by way of his state of nature be understood as individuals capable of living in a society and obeying the requirements of social existence? Thus, Hobbes's imaginative strategy runs the risk of running contrary to its own purpose: his concept of human nature appears to come dangerously close to making it impossible to understand how it is that human society is at all possible.

I am interested not so much in a solution to this problem as much as in what we may learn about Hobbes from the very fact that this problem arises. From the many lessons that may be drawn from it, I wish to pick out two. The first is clear enough. Hobbes's concept of human nature seeks not to prove the impossibility of human society, but rather to dramatize its vulnerable, precarious, deeply problematic character. The second lesson to be learned is already contained in the first. We may put it like this: Hobbes's concept of human nature is ambiguous because Hobbes thinks that there is an ambiguity at the very heart of human nature. The ambiguity belongs not to Hobbes's concept but to the reality it is attempting to capture. Hobbes is telling us that human beings, by nature, are neither completely social nor completely antisocial. I can be neither completely in nor completely out of society. I need others to satisfy my desires, to be sure; but the very presence of these others is a profound problem for me. Society is necessary—*and* it is a problem. Thus, there is a contradiction not only between myself and society, between "I" and "You," but also one between myself and myself, between my need of you, on the one hand, and my experience of you as an obstacle to be overcome, on the other. We need each other in order to make the possibility of a mutually desired "commodious living" a reality, yet at the same time, and at the very heart of this "commodious living," each of us relates instrumentally to the other as the mere object of his passions. The paradox is that we need others to satisfy ourselves, but once we are together we compete savagely and brutally: we are at war.

This ambiguity of the neither completely social nor completely anti-social nature of human beings is quite clearly stated by Hobbes at the end of chapter XIII of *Leviathan*, the chapter on the state of nature. He tells us that in the war of every one against every one, "there be no Propriety, no Dominion, no *Mine* and *Thine* distinct; but only that to be every mans that he can get; and for so long, as he can keep it" (emphasis in original).[4] And then he immediately adds: "And thus much for the ill condition, which man by meer Nature is actually placed in; *though with a possibility to come out of it,* consisting partly in the Passions, partly in his Reason" (emphasis added).[5] The "ill condition" of "meer Nature," then, contains both the fact of war and the possibility of peace. It is this promise of society already given at the level of "meer" nature that politics, as that which moves us beyond "meer" nature, is to actualize through the instrumentalities of both passions and reason.

Hobbes goes on:

> The Passions that encline men to Peace, are Feare of Death; Desire of such things as are necessary to commodious living; and a Hope by their Industry to obtain them. And Reason suggesteth convenient Articles of Peace, upon which men may be drawn to agreement. These Articles, are they, which otherwise are called Lawes of Nature: whereof I shall speak more particularly, in the two following Chapters.[6]

The chapter on the state of nature, then, concludes with an evocation of the possibility of a way out. The passions provide the end of peace and the energy required to achieve it; reason provides the means and the know-how, the conveniences or contraptions required to get there. In this combination of passion and reason, Nature already contains the potentiality for the "generation"—to use Hobbes's word[7]—of the artificial. In this way, Hobbes unfolds the artificial from the natural.

To think a movement from "x" to "y" requires that one find in "x" something that already points toward "y." Thus Hobbes must show us how, in the very midst of the chaos of the hypothetical state of war, he manages to glimpse the promise of the order of society. It is as if Hobbes were telling us that if we did not need each other, if there were not in human nature some kind of passion conducive to society and peace, then there would not be war either. In fact, we might even say that there is war precisely because we need each other. If we did not need each other, then we would be indifferent to one another, and each would live his own life separately. The fact that, in "meer" nature, we inevitably wind up in war means that we do indeed need something from each other. Total independence or total solitude produce not war but indifference. Strangely enough, war is a mode of relatedness. It is true that, unlike the bees and ants Hobbes compares us to,[8] we do not naturally fall into some kind of harmony. Our togetherness is not given by nature. But this does not mean that by nature we are separate. Hobbes tells us that by nature we are at war. He tells us that we are opposed, not separate. Hence, in the very midst of our antisocial proclivity, Hobbes begins to glimpse the promise of some sort of connectedness.

We might grasp this better if we allow ourselves to observe how truly remarkable and truly interesting Hobbes's concept of solitude is. In chapter XIII, in a well-known passage, Hobbes tells us that in the natural condition of humankind there is "continuall feare, and danger of violent death; And the life of man, solitary, poore, nasty, brutish, and short."[9] The solitude of this solitary condition, however, cannot by any means be one of complete isolation, since it is constantly and, according to Hobbes, necessarily invaded by the agitations of fear in and through which an other is indeed always already present. If I fear, I am not truly alone. You accompany me precisely to the degree to which I fear you. Hobbes refuses, consistently, the isolated separateness of a truly profound solitude. By nature we are connected, and the thread that links us is the thread that links those who cannot help but fear one another.

With this in mind, we are in a position to understand the task Hobbes assigns to politics. Politics is a matter of putting this natural and paradoxical connectedness to better use. It is as if nature had given us an incomplete or deficient connectedness, a chance to live together, to live in society, that, without the intervention of politics, ends up in war. It is as if war were an incomplete and unsuccessful attempt to come together. The task of politics is to use, for the purpose of maintaining peace, the very same needs and passions that, in the absence of politics, produce war.

Of course, if the deficient connectedness that nature leaves us with is that of fear, then it is fear that Hobbes will use to hold society together. To remedy the deficiencies of nature, Hobbes wants to use the very same fear that lies at the root of those deficiencies, at the root of the anxious and uncertain condition of the state of war. For Hobbes, politics is of necessity about power because politics is of necessity about the manipulation of fear. Politics achieves a kind of shifting of places, a translocation of fear from the dispersed and disaggregated fear that every one has of every one in the state of nature, to the concentrated and aggregated fear that each and all have of the Leviathan in the social state. Each now fears not so much the power of every other, as much as the absolute power of the Leviathan.

This, then, is the question I wish to bring to Hobbes: why must power be the power to kill? *Would not the capacity to inflict harm of any kind or degree be enough to ensure law and order?* Why must the fear evoked and concentrated by the power of the Leviathan be, in the final analysis, the fear of violent death?

The transition from dispersed to centralized fear and power is effected by means of the "Covenant of every man with every man." This covenant is informed by reason. At the end of chapter XIII, Hobbes in fact tells us that reason suggests "Articles of Peace" known as the "Lawes of Nature." He then spends the next two chapters of the *Leviathan*, chapters XIV and XV, outlining this contribution of reason to the establishment of the social order. Toward the end of chapter XV, he meets an objection that, not by chance, he himself raises. Hobbes is aware that chapters XIV and XV might be regarded as very complex and difficult to understand. Of course, he does not wish to give the impression that one must be a sophisticated student of political philosophy in order to be able to participate in the contract that lies at the root of the social order. Accordingly, he says that he does not want his deduction of the laws of nature to seem too subtle to be understood by all. As if anticipating subterfuge or quarrelsomeness, he tells us that, in order to "leave all men unexcusable," he has summarized the laws of nature into one easy statement, "intelligible," he adds, "even to the meanest capacity." The statement is: *"Do not that to another, which thou wouldest not have done to thy selfe"* (emphasis in original).[10] This is reason reduced to a single maxim, a maxim at the heart of social coexistence and peace.

In the same passage, Hobbes goes on to say that in order to learn the laws of nature we have to do nothing more than put ourselves in the place of others, and others in our place. He writes:

> he has no more to do in learning the Lawes of Nature, but, when weighing the actions of other men with his own, they seem too heavy, to put them into the other part of the ballance, and his own into their place, that his own passions, and self-love, may adde nothing to the weight; and then there is none of these Lawes of Nature that will not appear unto him very reasonable.[11]

Once again Hobbes appeals to a shifting of places, a kind of translocation. The point of this placing oneself in the place of another while simultaneously placing that other in one's own place is to prevent one's own passions and self-love from blinding one to the *equality* between oneself and others. The movement into the social order requires that we acknowledge an equality that our self-love, even in the face of the urging and urgent terrors of the state of war, refuses to see.

Of course, given the nature of Hobbes's individual, we can hardly expect his reason alone to accomplish this task of acknowledging equality.

It is Hobbes himself who warns us that the self-love of a human being is enough to lead him, in the name of his own aggrandizement, to attempt to dispute or suppress the simplest truths of geometry.[12] And if it is passion that prevents us from acknowledging or even seeing equality, then it must be passion, too, that somehow disposes us to acknowledge it. Hobbes's answer in this regard is deceptively simple: our self-love is to be beaten into submission by way of fear. Fear of the consequences of disregarding the equality at the heart of the covenant shall force us to acknowledge equality—or at least to behave as if we acknowledged it. Hobbes is very clear:

> For the Lawes of Nature (as *Justice, Equity, Modesty, Mercy,* and (in summe) *doing to others, as wee would be done to,*) of themselves, without the terrour of some Power, to cause them to be observed, are *contrary to our naturall Passions,* that carry us to Partiality, Pride, Revenge, and the like. And Covenants, without the Sword, are but Words, and of no strength to secure a man at all.[13] (last emphasis added)

Why this sword must be a sword that kills and why the fear it embodies must be the fear of violent death can be understood as soon as we recall that Hobbes defines equality as nothing other than the equal capacity of human beings to kill each other. As Hobbes puts it, "the weakest has strength enough to kill the strongest."[14] The fear that is to beat the partiality of our self-love into submission must be the fear of violent death because the possibility of such a death is at the very root of equality. In Hobbes, fear and death are necessarily connected by way of equality. It is because of the way in which he defines our equality of power and vulnerability that fear is in the end the fear of violent death.

We might wish to rest content with this egalitarian response to my question regarding the intertwining of fear and death in Hobbes's thought. Yet we can rest content with that response only so long as we refrain from asking why it is that Hobbes chooses to define our equality in terms of our equal capacity to kill each other. Why, indeed, would Hobbes insist upon murder as a starting point? Why would he seek the foundations of our community in the violence of murder?

The answer is as simple to state as it is difficult to grasp. We can state it both positively and negatively. Positively put, the answer is that pride plays a deeply significant role in Hobbes's thought. Hobbes defines pride as the breach or violation of the precept that "*every man acknowledge other for his Equall by Nature*" (emphasis in original).[15] This, then, is what pride really amounts to: since our equality resides in our equal capacity to kill one another, it is clear that pride, as a refusal of such equality, is indeed a refusal to acknowledge the possibility that I can be killed. The horrifying imagery of the war of every one against every one is not in and of itself enough to counteract this persistent foolishness. It is almost as if the proud Hobbesian individual finds it impossible to believe in his own death. His egoism is such that he somehow manages to fancy himself invulnerable. So, Hobbes must literally drive into the individual, by way of the awesome and organized fear of the Leviathan, the idea of his own limits, of his own mortality. Without such an idea of limits, the Hobbesian individual can hardly acknowledge the existence of another, let alone his rightful equality. Hence, it is because of the depth of the Hobbesian individual's pride that Hobbes must, so to speak, seek equality in the womb of murder.

Negatively put, the answer is that in Hobbes, the sphere of love is rather that of *self*-love. The egalitarian capacity to place oneself in the place of another does not come naturally or spontaneously to Hobbes's individual. It is only the fleeting result of a geometric deduction, a precise calculation performed by a delicate and precarious reason that requires the violence of fear to be at all effective. This fear must be the fear of death because only such fear can teach the thoroughly self-involved Hobbesian individual about others and their claims. It is as if the sword of the Leviathan serves as a reminder of the presence of others—of the fact that, in spite of one's self-love, one can indeed be killed. Since love of others does not come spontaneously to the Hobbesian individual, he must be constantly warned that if he insists on behaving as if they did not exist, he will be promptly eliminated, murdered. Thus, Hobbes's individual is violently reminded of his humanity by that *"Mortall God"* (emphasis in original),[16] the Leviathan, who bears the name of he who came into the world to crush human pride.[17]

This presence of pride and this absence of love are but aspects of the same coin. The Hobbesian individual experiences other individuals either as means or as obstacles to his own satisfaction. That which is other is forever posed either instrumentally or antagonistically, irretrievably as that which is outside and alien to the self. The Hobbesian individual's incessant motion—his "perpetuall and restlesse desire of Power after power, that ceaseth onely in Death"[18]—is motion directed to the preservation of his self-definition as that which excludes and repudiates everything other than itself. According to Hobbes, the "cause" of the individual's perpetual motion is

> not always that a man hopes for a more intensive delight, than he has already attained to; or that he cannot be content with a moderate power: but because he cannot assure the power and means to live well, which he hath present, without the acquisition of more.[19]

To be able to live—and to do so "well"—is to have command over the future. The unforeseen and the unforeseeable cannot help but appear to me, as if by definition, not only as that which is radically *other* than me, but also as that which is thereby *opposed*, like an ominous threat, to the motion that constitutes the continued possibility of my life. Thus, the motion of Hobbes's individual is the motion of life itself, of a mode of self-preservation recurrently haunted by an urgent need to assert that it is and must be, in order to live, the master in its own house.

In the context of this ceaseless striving for mastery, fear is adequately grasped as the converse of power; it is, so to speak, that in and through which my ultimate powerlessness to avert future disaster becomes manifest. Paradoxically, then, it is precisely the thoroughly foreseeable certainty of my inevitable death that functions as an image of my powerlessness, of my irremediable inability to command the future. Accordingly, the irreducible otherness that death places before the Hobbesian individual is, *by definition,* to be feared in the sense of its instantiating and representing the shocking physical pain of the violent arrest of motion—in a word, of violent death.

The point here is by no means to deny the possibility of a natural, peaceful death in the social state. The point, rather, is to discern that even such a protected death, however preferable to the diffidence of the state of war, cannot be said to escape the definitional trappings in terms of which Hobbes casts the fact of mortality. At issue is the Hobbesian individual's *attitude* to the otherness of death. In this regard, the crucial point to be brought into relief is that, at least with respect to his theorization of the generation of society, *Hobbes casts mortality in the guise of murder, death in the guise of war.* It is worth repeating that for Hobbes, the accession to the social order concerns not an elimination but a translocation of the fear of violent death from the fear that every one has of every one in the state of war to the fear that all have of the Leviathan in the social state. Thus, the result of the Hobbesian individual's attitude to death is that the sphere of relations between people is rendered as the arena of the necessary limitation of a preconstituted individual whose relations to others are inherently instrumental, and whose only alternative to subjection is the violence of the state of war. Not surprisingly, then, freedom, for Hobbes, is in "the silence of the Law,"[20] a law wielded by that absolutely sovereign power who, in representing the image of my death, also preserves that of my safety, and whose awesome sword, in the final analysis, is the fundamental means of guaranteeing the possibility of peace.

Of course, it would be regrettable to neglect the fact that Hobbes explicitly states that the power of the Leviathan cannot be maintained by "terrour of legal punishment" alone.[21] In his study of Hobbes, Norman Jacobson warns that although the "fear of retaliation, what men call punishment . . . has provided the chief text for most commentaries [of Hobbes's work] . . . there is another feature of his thought that has scarcely received attention."[22] According to Jacobson, this other feature is "political education."[23] In fact, Hobbes tells us that in the absence of a widespread apprehension of the grounds of the Leviathan's absolute sovereign authority, the people would take punishment "but for an act of Hostility; which when they think they have strength enough, they will endeavour by acts of Hostility, to avoyd."[24] Hobbes thus concerns himself with the "Instruction of the people."[25] Not only fear but also "Instruction"—not only the Sword but also *words*—are to be employed in Hobbes's struggle against the disease of prideful sedition. "Besides wishing to politicize the wolf," Jacobson notes, "Hobbes entertains dreams of *civilizing* him."[26]

Yet having demonstrated that the solution to the predicament Hobbes grasps by way of the hypothesis of the state of war is a "twofold" solution, on the one hand "legal" and on the other "pedagogical,"[27] Jacobson does not fail to remind us that

> If Hobbes's theories of sovereignty and obligation seem stern, it is crucial to recognize that in his view men and states are always poised between pride and fear. . . . Pride leads backward into a state of war. Fear leads forward into a civil society. Given this tension, *the role of law and of political education is identical. It is to tip the balance to civil society by evoking the fear of violent death. . . .*[28] (emphasis added)

If it is an error to forget Hobbes's effort to *teach* the grounds of the Leviathan's authority by way of words, it is equally erroneous to forget Hobbes's fearful words that "Covenants, without the Sword, are but words, and of no strength to secure a man at all."[29] Whether evoked "legally" by the Leviathan himself, or "pedagogically" by Hobbes in *Leviathan*, the fear of violent death—that most "rational" of passions[30]—is what finally sustains the possibility of peace.

For Hobbes, then, the "Articles of Peace" or "Lawes of Nature" suggested by reason as instrumentalities facilitating the movement into society, require the human subject, when weighing the actions of another, to place itself in the position of that other, and that other in its own place, so as to preclude thereby the partiality emanating from the subject's pride or self-love. Yet even as he ascertains passions that do indeed "encline men to Peace," Hobbes tells us that this shifting of places conducive to an appreciation of the "reasonableness" of the laws of nature is "contrary to our naturall Passions." Fear—and in particular the fear of violent death—is the "Passion to be reckoned upon"[31] because the sustained behavioral acknowledgment of equality, constitutive of the possibility of peace, is to be sought in each individual's vulnerability to murder by any other. For Hobbes, the sphere of one's own death fulfills an indispensable political function to the degree to which it is inextricable from that of equality. As a specifically political category, that is to say, death arises in a radically intersubjective arena, at the level of my relation to feared others who might kill me, and whose capacity to do so instantiates our equality. Only the humbling awareness of the possibility of one's own death (i.e., murder) can serve as a corrective to the war-conducive exaggerations of pride or self-love. Fundamentally, this is why the ordering power of the Leviathan must of necessity be the awesome monopolization of each individual's fearful capacity to kill any other. Thus the image of the sword concretizes Hobbes's deployment of the political meaning of death in terms of murder.

To what extent, however, might the sphere of *murder* be distinguished from that of *mortality?* Might the mysteries of death not contain still another meaning that, though as fundamental in the constitution of society, is not reducible to the possibility of murder? Might death, to put it otherwise, not arise in a context other than war? It is with this question in mind that I want now to proceed to broach the import of Freud's theory of culture as regards the evaluation of Hobbes's position.

As we noted in chapter 1, Freud deploys the role of death in the constitution of society not only in terms of murder but also, and simultaneously, in terms of an encounter with mortality. As its very title indicates, Freud's "Thoughts for the Times on War and Death" is premised on a *distinction* between war and death. Freud's reflection is in fact an effort to differentiate the sphere of murder from that of mortality as regards the generation of social relations. It is this differentiation that makes visible what we might term a *conflation* of war and death at the heart of Hobbes's political thought.

To be sure, it is true that Hobbes, as much as Freud, posits death intersubjectively, at the level of relations between people. But, in a manner markedly distinct from that of Hobbes, Freud deploys the socially constitutive role of the sphere of one's own death not in terms of one's relation to a *feared* other who might kill one, but rather in terms of one's relation to a *loved* other whose death teaches one about one's own. Unlike Hobbes's, Freud's subject learns of death not so much by way of fear as much as by way of its pain over the loved one's death. Thus, if in Hobbes the movement of the individual into the social order is mediated in and through the dynamics of fear, in Freud the construction of the human subject as a social and cultural being is mediated in and through the dynamics of what he called the "work of mourning."[32] That which Hobbes must accomplish by way of an expedient calculation supported by the fear of violent death, Freud seeks in an alternative *attitude* to death. Freud's differentiation of the sphere of death from that of war—of mortality from murder—grounds his intimation of a different view of intersubjectivity. Accordingly, the "fateful question" at which Freud's theory of culture comes to fruition is that of the extent to which the unifying powers of Eros might assert themselves so as to (re)signify the relation between I and not-I not as war but as loss, not as the site of an antagonism but as an occasion for a mutually constitutive (re)unification.

The central category of the loved one's death thus permits Freud to move beyond Hobbes's image of a fearful sword as the concretizing image of the ordering power of the social. In and through that category, Freud's theory of culture presents the field of relations between people not only as externally compulsive but also as inherently constitutive of the human subject as such. In the sense of its being the emblem of a loss rendering the other as constitutive of self, the unifying power of *Eros* is a concept thoroughly foreign to Hobbes's work. Paradoxically, when Hobbes consistently refuses the profound separateness of solitude, he refuses the solitariness known only to those who can access community, the loss accessible only to those who know of love. The Hobbesian subject's insistence to remain the master in its own house prevents it from enduring, in and as life, the loss of a life truly lived. It is as if the ceaseless agitations of war prevent Hobbes from hearing the deafening yet pregnant silence of the law of death, of mortality. His conception of the human subject is by definition unable to discern the difference between the violent arrest of motion and the peaceful stillness of death. One might say that Hobbes could have found the elusive community he longed for had he managed to seek, in death, not only fear but also loss and solitude, mortality as well as murder.

Even where Freud appears most fully Hobbesian, he in fact differs substantively from Hobbes. In a memorable passage in *Civilization and Its Discontents,* Freud tells us that people are far too "ready to disavow"

> that men are not gentle creatures who want to be loved, and who at the most can defend themselves if they are attacked; they are, on the contrary, creatures among whose instinctual endowments is to be reckoned a powerful share of aggressiveness. As a result, their neighbour is for them not only a potential helper or sexual object, but also someone who tempts them to satisfy their aggressiveness on him, to exploit his capacity for work without compensation, to use him sexually without his consent, to seize his possessions, to humiliate him, to cause him pain, to torture and to kill him. *Homo homini lupus.*[33] (emphasis in original)

This is a far cry from Hobbes's thoroughly consistent claim that he does not "conceive it possible" that "any man should take pleasure in other mens great harm, without other end of his own."[34] Regardless of whether Freud would have regarded Hobbes's claim as a "disavowal," the important point here at issue is that, having grasped our *anti*-social propensities far more deeply than Hobbes, Freud unveiled, in seeking to understand the possibility of culture, our *social* propensities in a starker light. "If anyone were inclined to put forward the paradoxical proposition that the normal man is not only far more immoral," Freud writes, "but also far more moral than he knows, psychoanalysis, on whose findings the first half of the assertion rests, would have no objection to raise against the second half."[35] "This proposition," he adds, "is only apparently a paradox":

> it simply states that human nature has a far greater extent, both for good and for evil, than it thinks it has—i.e. than its ego is aware of through conscious perception.[36]

Thus, Freud's theory of culture posits not a fear of death that catalyzes the rational pursuit of self-interest, but the forgotten claims of Eros as the unifying force to be deployed in the fateful struggle against the centrifugal forces of Death. For Freud, it is not rational self-interest in and of itself, but rather "libidinal ties" that hold society together.[37] *Freud maintained a view of human nature substantively different from that of Hobbes.*

THOSE WHO HAVE STAYED AT HOME

In 1924, while relating the origins of psychoanalysis, Freud writes:

> Psycho-analysis grew up in a narrowly-restricted field. At the outset, it had only a single aim—that of understanding something of the nature of what were known as the "functional" nervous diseases, with a view to overcoming the impotence which had so far characterized their medical treatment. The neurologists of that period had been brought up to have a high respect for chemico-physical and pathologico-anatomical facts; and they were latterly under the influence of the findings of Hitzig and Fritsch, of Ferrier, Goltz and others, who seemed to have established an intimate and possibly exclusive connection between certain functions and particular parts of the brain. They did not know what to make of the *psychical factor* and could not understand it. They left it to the philosophers, the mystics and—the quacks; and they considered it unscientific to have anything to do with it.[38] (emphasis added)

We need not disregard Hobbes's eminently psychological analyses of the dynamics of pride and glory in order to discern the importance of this passage in the context of a juxtaposition of Freud and Hobbes. For Freud, psychoanalysis originates in a retrieval of a dimension of human life distinct from that of the physical, a retrieval so crucial that Freud views it as fundamental in the delineation of the domain of the discipline he founded. In fact, it is precisely this retrieval of what Freud calls the "psychical factor" that both permits and compels, beyond Hobbes, the conceptualization of social relations as internal to the human subject as such. The pain Freud associates with the field of intersubjectivity is the *psychic* pain of mortality, the pain of loss.[39] Freud understands the emergence of the cultural from the natural in terms not of the contractarian aggregation of preconstituted atoms in motion, but rather of the death of loved ones—

in terms, that is, of the *specifically psychic* pain of mourning. In so doing, he posits otherness as irretrievably constitutive of self. The point here at issue is that, unlike Hobbes, *Freud can think about the constitutive role of intersubjectivity because his subject is not physiologistically conceived—at least not exclusively and by no means mechanistically—as mere matter in motion.*[40] The otherness of death is not something that Freud's subject encounters as an external obstacle precluding its motion, but rather something that it cannot help but meet living immanently, as it were, within itself. This is why Freud speaks not of "commodious living" but of the necessary, constitutive *unhappiness* of the human psyche.[41]

In Hegelian terms, we might say, as Hegel does of the lord in his description of the dialectic of lordship and bondage, that Hobbes's subject cannot ultimately *learn* to do to *itself* what it "does to the other."[42] It cannot, that is, negate itself so as to *recognize* that other as someone that, indeed, negates *it* in turn.[43] Thus, the fearful sword of the Leviathan is and must be there so as to ensure the order and cohesiveness that, for the "commodious" benefit of the subject itself, is to issue from that subject's— as Hobbes has it—weighing "the actions of other men with his own," putting "them into the other part of the ballance, and his own into their place."[44] In other words, the Leviathan guarantees for Hobbes what for Hegel can develop only in and through the serious, painful, patient "labour of the negative"[45] at the heart of the subject's historically and intersubjectively mediated learning experience. This is the point I am driving at: the profound differences between *Freud* and Hegel need not deter us from observing that *what appears in Hegel as the labor of the negative, appears in Freud as the labor of mourning.*[46]

In this vein, the upshot of the foregoing juxtaposition of Freud and Hobbes is that the retrieval of the "psychical factor" introduces into Freud's universe the concept of *psychic pain,* of a mode of dying, so to speak, thoroughly unthinkable from the viewpoint of Hobbes's individual as matter in motion. If at the level of the *physical* death is the complete obliteration of life, at the level of the *psychical* death is rather, as Hegel has it, a mode of negation "which supersedes in such a way as to preserve and maintain what is superseded, and consequently survives its own supersession."[47] As much as in Hegel, in Freud the concept of a *mental life* carries a profound paradox at its core: the "life" of the "mental" both comes to be and sustains itself only in and through death.

Yet if in Hegel the dialectic of recognition enables consciousness to emerge out of its submergence in the immediacy of life so as to initiate a progressive movement culminating in the *daylight* wherein Spirit finally interiorizes Nature as its own other, in Freud the loved one's death irremediably lodges the interminable struggle of life and death, Eros and Death, in the life of the mind. Whereas Hegel writes that "it is only through staking one's life that freedom is won,"[48] Freud tells us that the "confusion" from which culture originates belongs *not* to "*those who themselves risk their lives in battle*," but to "those who have stayed at home and have only to wait for the loss of one of their dear ones by wounds, disease or infection" (emphasis added).[49] It is to a brief elaboration of this difference between Freud and Hegel that I now turn.

To begin with, it is important to note that Freud's notion of psychic pain as the womb of intersubjectivity does not entail the quite different proposition that the site of relations between people is merely "mental." The birth of the human in and through death is not to be grasped as a spiritualistic transcendence of the body. Intersubjectivity is not exclusively a meeting of minds. On the contrary, Freud is relentless in his insistence that the "human need for love, taken in its widest sense"[50] is a bodily "drive." Freud's earliest formulation of the theory of sexuality, in 1905, asserts that the concept of drive lies "on the *frontier* between the mental and the physical" (emphasis added).[51] This "frontier" already intimates the genuinely mytho-poetic longing Freud chooses to obey when, in 1920, he finally lodges the cosmic "battle of the giants," Eros and Death, at the heart of his science. In fact, as late as 1933, Freud continues to write that the theory of the drives is "so to say our mythology." Drives, he tells us, are "mythical entities, magnificent in their indefiniteness."[52] Yet however elusive, this intricate and indefinite complexity of Freud's conception of the drives need not obscure the observation that Eros is by no means an exclusively mental phenomenon: the body, too, seeks the other.

To be sure, it is true that Hegel, as much as Freud, posits the denial of the body and its mortality as itself the preclusion of the emergence of intersubjectivity. Hegel explicitly tells us that the subject must learn that "life is the *natural* setting of consciousness," that "life is as essential to it as pure self-consciousness" (emphasis in original).[53] For Freud, however, the body is not merely the speechless "natural setting" of the life of the mental. Rather, it is closely associated with a particular mode of mental functioning—the *primary process*—that Freud claims to have discovered, that is essential to the psychoanalytic enterprise as a whole, and that renders the body as a site of *meanings* amenable to the deciphering work of psychoanalytic hermeneutics. For Freud, as Maurice Merleau-Ponty notes, the body is itself part and parcel of the field of communication between people, of intersubjectivity.[54]

At the same time, this openness to culture on the part of the Freudian body/subject is not to be construed as an openness regarding the possibility that the body/subject be either contained by or absorbed into culture.[55] Such a (mis)construing would amount to a repetition of the illusion of human goodness, an illusion Freud finds rooted in an overestimation of what he terms our "susceptibility to culture."[56] That Freud can think social relations as constitutive of or internal to the subject does not mean that he thinks social relations as exhaustive of that subject's identity. For Freud, culture is a painful, mournful developmental movement never to be completed, not even at the level of an ultimately all-encompassing philosophical comprehension. On the one hand, it is true that the Freudian body/subject's erotic susceptibility to culture permits Freud to move beyond an exclusively compulsive and/or instrumental conception of social relations. But on the other, Freud simultaneously conceives the intersubjectively mediated cultural labor of developmental transformation as radically "interminable"—in fact, as ultimately impossible. Freud's forever "ambivalent" body/subject refuses as much as it seeks the other.[57]

Paradoxically, then, the struggle constitutive of Freud's subject means that this subject can never finally find itself at home in the intersubjective "we-ness" in and through which it is constituted. When Freud states that culture may be "simply described as the *struggle for life* of the human species" (emphasis added),[58] he is specifying the situation of a living being who cannot, with Hegel, fully and finally step "out into the spiritual daylight of the present."[59] The matter is not one of imputing to Hegel the thoroughly inappropriate image of a facile positivity. It was Hegel who taught us about the "devastation" of "utter dismemberment," the "dreadful" hardship of "tarrying with the negative."[60] The matter, rather, is that of discerning that Freud's movement beyond Hobbes falls short of invoking the ultimately consoling community of a Hegel who sought to absorb the irreducible otherness of the other—the cleavages of death—into the comforting home of a Reason that can become transparent to itself. If Freud's Eros is to be grasped adequately as a critique of Hobbes, then Freud's Death must be broached simultaneously as a critique of Hegel.

The elusive and precarious dimension of the culture Freud conceptualizes—which is but Freud's way of heeding the insistent and ineradicable possibility of war—is best captured in and through the observation that for Freud, "regression" is always and frequently possible. Though developmental, Freud's conceptualization is not framed in terms of the linear temporality of the progressive and necessary unfolding of the Hegelian Spirit in its relentless *Aufhebung* (meaning "sublation") of Nature. (Hegel's dialectical spiral of History has a linear axis threading its core.) For Freud, time cannot be finally eradicated. Thus, precisely because Freud's temporality is not Hegel's, it would be a mistake to grasp the incompleteness of culture in Freud as if it were that of a Hegel who cannot quite manage to be himself, as the incompleteness of a linearity that never reaches its goal. We must rather grasp the Freudian suspension between life and death not merely negatively as the Hegelian life it cannot be, but rather positively as a universe in its own right.

The unhappiness of Freud's psyche is that of a nature that cannot quite become culture, of a culture which, even at the level of philosophy, forever hovers over a nature that is somehow alien to it. The question at issue concerns the meaning of this 'alienation'.[61] In their discussion of the unhappiness of the Freudian psyche, Casey and Woody conclude— apparently with Freud and Lacan—that "the subjection of man to culture foredooms him to what Hegel called 'the unhappy consciousness,' the 'consciousness of self as a dual-natured, merely contradictory being.'" Casey and Woody take Lacan to be reinforcing "Freud's grim conclusion that the contradiction is insuperable, that history can promise no final reconciliation, no splendid synthesis, not even an arena for the attainment of authenticity: cuttings and splittings, human lives in tatters, are all that remain in this darkened vision."[62] Yet it is Lacan himself who, in the *Écrits*, exclaims:

> Who cannot see the distance that separates the unhappy consciousness—of which, however strongly it is engraven in Hegel, it can be said that it is still no more than the suspension of a corpus of knowledge—from the "discontents of civilization" in Freud, even if it is only a mere phrase, uttered as if disavowed, that marks for us what, on reading it, cannot be articulated otherwise than the "skew" relation that separates the subject from sexuality?[63]

Freud's conception of the constitutive cleavage at the heart of the human psyche does not take us back, as it were, to Hegel's unhappy consciousness. Lacan's statement is in fact an effort to capture the discontents of civilization in Freudian rather than Hegelian terms. To be sure, the contradiction Casey and Woody so skillfully bring into relief is not in any way at all less than "insuperable." But that need not preclude us from holding fast the insight that the meaning of this insuperability is adequately seized only in a context able to differentiate between the unhappiness of Hegel's unhappy consciousness and the unhappiness of Freud's psyche. Lacan is surely correct to insist that we "designate the *gap* that separates those two relations of the subject to knowledge, the Freudian and the Hegelian" (emphasis added).[64]

What Casey and Woody wish to retain as the unhappy consciousness is "the emphasis on differentiation at the expense of totalization."[65] "What is most primordial and most valued," they tell us, "is not systematic totality but dispersal or discontinuity itself—in a word, *difference* rather than *identity*" (emphases in original).[66] Yet the dispersal and the difference that are to be valued are more than *mere* dispersal, more than *mere* difference. That which is to be reclaimed amidst the ruins of the collapse of the totalistic illusions of the ego is not the mere opposite of those illusions, not the mere opposite of Hegel's totality. Disillusionment, one might say, issues out of Freud's critique of illusion as little as does nihilism out of Nietzsche's critique of Christianity.[67] Freud proceeds in the context of an effort aiming at transvaluation. This is why, between "human lives in tatters" and "splendid finalities," he stakes the erotic claims of his "darkened vision," the enjoinments of a critical tragic vision seeking respect for our "first duty" as "living beings." These enjoinments are not empty voluntarist imperatives: they are concretely grounded in the labor seeking to liberate desire from the seductions of the immortal, to work through the imprisonment to which the unhappy consciousness, in a manner reminiscent of Freud's young poet in "On Transience," is still subject. Freud's darkened vision is of a perennial *twilight* that is neither dusk nor dawn: it is a life whose wakefulness is such that it can find itself only when it stumbles, as if by chance, upon one of its dreams.

FREUD'S COMMON UNHAPPINESS

By way of conclusion to *Studies on Hysteria* (1895), in a classic and deservedly famous formulation, Freud replies to the objection that he cannot fulfill what he permits himself to *promise*:

> When I have promised my patients help or improvement by means of a cathartic treatment I have often been faced by this objection: "Why, you tell me yourself that my illness is probably connected with my circumstances and the events of my life. You cannot alter these in any way. How do you propose to help me, then?" And I have been able to make this reply: "No doubt fate would find it easier than I do to relieve you of your illness. But you will be able to convince yourself that much will be gained if we succeed in transforming your hysterical misery into common unhappiness. With a *mental life* that has been restored to health you will be better armed against that unhappiness."[68] (emphasis added)

Freud's analysand confronts Freud with the weight of the unalterable. For his part, Freud presents to us this unendurable and unalterable weight in the shape of a particular position that his analysand assumes in regard to the field of temporality. He tells us that the analysand's complaint is that Freud "cannot alter" the future because he can alter neither the overwhelming sway of present "circumstances" nor the lingering and stubborn dominance of past "events." Without further ado, Freud requests in response that the analysand give up his attachment to "fate." In so doing, he intimates that what is to be transformed is precisely the particular attitude that the analysand assumes in regard to the field of temporality.

"No doubt," Freud begins his communication, "the gracious omnipotence of fate could help you, but we cannot count on fate here; we must proceed with what we have to work with. It is not fate but I, Sigmund

Freud, who will help you." With these words, Freud seeks to avail himself of the mysterious powers of fate. He seeks to attach his analysand's
hope to his own person. But at the same time, Freud induces yet another
movement of detachment. "It is I, Freud, who will help you—but I am not
omnipotent, I am not as powerful as fate itself." With this admission,
Freud refuses within himself what he, in 1925, comes to call "something
positively seductive in working with hypnotism," the "sense of having
overcome one's helplessness," the flattery of enjoying a "reputation of being a miracle-worker."[69] Thus Freud goes on to inform his analysand that
it is in fact "*we*," not I, who might "succeed in transforming your hysterical misery into common unhappiness." The movement from "fate" *to*
Freud takes place in the context of a simultaneous movement *away* from
Freud. Accordingly, the second sentence of Freud's communication introduces the analysand himself as actor—neither fate, nor Freud alone, are
the agents here at issue. Rather, the analysand himself comes to take a
place next to Freud's in regard to the ill fate in which he is at first thoroughly immersed. Freud no longer appears in the third sentence of his
communication. The subject is now himself "armed"—as Freud has it—
no longer the recipient either of fate's or of Freud's favors.

The editors of *The Standard Edition* remind us that in the German edi-
tions of Freud's text previous to 1925, the preceding passage from *Studies
on Hysteria* spoke not of a "mental life" but of a *nervous system* that has
been restored to health.[70] This shift in what Freud chooses to tell his
analysands is of course not a matter of indifference. It signals, even if
retroactively, Freud's definitive retrieval of the "psychical factor." It is precisely this retrieval that, as we shall see in the following chapter, permits
Freud to seek the future in the past, to alter the unalterable, to alter the future by way of a retroactive transformation of the past. This, I think, is the
import of Freud's profound request that the attachment to "fate" be given
up: the owl of Minerva can spread its wings *before* actuality is there cut
and dried, not because it wishes to give instruction as to what the world
ought to be, but because, since the life of the psychical is but an interminable struggling to be, actuality can never, in fact, be there cut and
dried.[71] The conceptual specification of this most remarkable of Freudian
acts is to be found at the very origin of psychoanalysis, in Freud's abandonment of hypnosis. Freud illuminates the delicate theoretical constella-
tion comprising the concepts of 'death of a loved one', 'mourning', 'sexuality', and 'temporality' in terms of the dynamics of transference. Only by
way of this circuitous path through the specificity of the psychoanalytic
situation shall we find ourselves in a position to seize the deeply political
meaning of Freud's urgent and insistent duty to pose the destiny of the
human species as a "fateful question" to be taken up rather than a definitive fate to be dealt with.

NOTES

1. Sigmund Freud, *Civilization and Its Discontents*, in vol. 21 of *The Standard Edition of the Complete Psychological Works of Sigmund Freud*, ed. and trans. James Strachey et al. (London: Hogarth, 1953–1974), 134.

2. On the centrality of fear in Hobbes's political philosophy, see Leo Strauss, *The Political Philosophy of Hobbes* (Chicago: University of Chicago Press, 1952), especially chapter II, 6–29. But see also Macpherson's important comments on Strauss's reading in C. B. Macpherson, *The Political Theory of Possessive Individualism: From Hobbes to Locke* (Oxford, UK: Oxford University Press, 1962), 42–46. Michael Oakeshott's "The Moral Life in the Writings of Thomas Hobbes" is an intriguing attempt to articulate Hobbes's conception of the binding power of social relations in terms not of fear but of a particular deployment of pride. Michael Oakeshott, "The Moral Life in the Writings of Thomas Hobbes," in *Rationalism in Politics and Other Essays* (London: Methuen, 1962), 248–300.

3. See chapter 1, "Loss and Intersubjectivity."

4. Thomas Hobbes, *Leviathan*, ed. C. B. Macpherson (Middlesex, UK: Penguin, 1968), 188.

5. Hobbes, *Leviathan*, 188.

6. Hobbes, *Leviathan*, 188.

7. Hobbes, *Leviathan*, 227.

8. Hobbes, *Leviathan*, 225–26.

9. Hobbes, *Leviathan*, 186.

10. Hobbes, *Leviathan*, 214.

11. Hobbes, *Leviathan*, 214–15.

12. Hobbes, *Leviathan*, 166.

13. Hobbes, *Leviathan*, 223.

14. Hobbes, *Leviathan*, 183.

15. Hobbes, *Leviathan*, 211.

16. Hobbes, *Leviathan*, 227.

17. Hobbes, *Leviathan*, 362.

18. Hobbes, *Leviathan*, 161.

19. Hobbes, *Leviathan*, 161.

20. Hobbes, *Leviathan*, 271.

21. Hobbes, *Leviathan*, 377.

22. Norman Jacobson, "Behold *Leviathan*! The Systematic Solace of Thomas Hobbes," in *Pride and Solace: The Function and Limits of Political Theory* (New York: Methuen, 1978), 57.

23. Jacobson, "Behold *Leviathan*!" 66.

24. Hobbes, *Leviathan*, 377.

25. Hobbes, *Leviathan*, 384.

26. Jacobson, "Behold *Leviathan*!" 87.

27. Jacobson, "Behold *Leviathan*!" 62–63.

28. Jacobson, "Behold *Leviathan*!" 66. Jacobson distinguishes Hobbes from Freud on 82 and 87. But consider in particular the following passage: "The state of war between nature and reason is reflected in a war between two lexicons representing the adversaries. There exists a perennial antagonism between

fancies, imaginings, and passions expressed in metaphor, poetry, and other imprecise and extravagant modes of speech, and their adversary, discourse, a name given by Hobbes to the language of scientific reason. Rational scientific discourse must seek always to still the terrible and insistent voices of the inner self. We must study ourselves in order to disarm ourselves; must investigate ourselves, *not as with Freud so we may choose by learning how to listen;* the self in Hobbes's system is overcome by learning how *not* to listen" (first emphasis added). Jacobson, "Behold *Leviathan!*" 89–90. At stake in this truly insightful opposition of what we might call Hobbes's cure of silence to Freud's eminently *"talking* cure" is Freud's fundamental discovery of a *language* of the passions: his invention of a hermeneutic of the imprecise and extravagant, yet profoundly *meaningful* poetry of dreams. What for Hobbes is a failure in precision, for Freud is rather a failure in *translation.* See chapter 4, "Eros and Logos." Joel Schwartz's "Freud and Freedom of Speech" attempts to construct a psychoanalytic defense of freedom of speech. Joel Schwartz, "Freud and Freedom of Speech," *American Political Science Review* 80 (December 1986): 1227–48. For discussions of the question of translation in psychoanalysis, see Jean Laplanche, "Psychoanalysis, Time and Translation," trans. Martin Stanton, in *Jean Laplanche: Seduction, Translation, Drives,* ed. John Fletcher and Martin Stanton (London: Institute of Contemporary Arts, 1992), 161–77; and Andrew Benjamin, "Structuring as a Translation," in *Jean Laplanche: Seduction, Translation, Drives,* ed. John Fletcher and Martin Stanton (London: Institute of Contemporary Arts, 1992), 137–57.

29. Hobbes, *Leviathan,* 223.

30. See Strauss, *Political Philosophy of Hobbes,* 22.

31. Hobbes, *Leviathan,* 200.

32. See chapter 1, especially "Eros and Transience." See also Sigmund Freud, "Mourning and Melancholia," in vol. 14 of *The Standard Edition,* ed. and trans. James Strachey et al., 237–58; and Sigmund Freud, *The Ego and the Id,* in vol. 19 of *The Standard Edition,* 1–66, especially chapters III and V.

33. Freud, *Civilization and Its Discontents,* 111.

34. Hobbes, *Leviathan,* 126.

35. Freud, *The Ego and the Id,* 52.

36. Freud, *The Ego and the Id,* 52, n. 1.

37. Sigmund Freud, *Group Psychology and the Analysis of the Ego,* in vol. 18 of *The Standard Edition,* ed. and trans. James Strachey et al., 96. "[A] group," Freud writes, "is clearly held together by a power of some kind: and to what power could this feat be better ascribed than to Eros, which holds together everything in the world?" Freud, *Group Psychology,* 92. See chapter 3, "The Critique of Culture."

38. Sigmund Freud, "A Short Account of Psycho-Analysis," in vol. 19 of *The Standard Edition,* ed. and trans. James Strachey et al., 191.

39. J.-B. Pontalis tells the story of Freud's retrieval of "psychic space." J.-B. Pontalis, "Between Freud and Charcot: From One Scene to the Other," in *Frontiers in Psychoanalysis: Between the Dream and Psychic Pain,* trans. Catherine Cullen and Philip Cullen (London: Hogarth, 1981), 17–22. "On Psychic Pain" is the title of the last chapter of Pontalis's book.

40. On Hobbes's materialism, see Macpherson, *Possessive Individualism*, 10 and 78–81. See also C. B. Macpherson, "Hobbes's Bourgeois Man," in *Democratic Theory: Essays in Retrieval* (Oxford, UK: Clarendon, 1973), 238–50.

41. Jean Hyppolite writes, "Otherness has become the Superego." Jean Hyppolite, "Hegel's Phenomenology and Psychoanalysis," in *New Studies in Hegel's Philosophy*, ed. Warren E. Steinkraus (New York: Holt, Rinehart and Winston, 1971), 63. For a study of the Hegel-Freud relation, see Darrel E. Christensen, "Hegel's Phenomenological Analysis and Freud's Psychoanalysis," *International Philosophical Quarterly* 8 (1968): 356–78.

42. G. W. F. Hegel, *Phenomenology of Spirit*, trans. A. V. Miller (Oxford, UK: Oxford University Press, 1981), 116. On the dialectic of Lordship and Bondage, see George Armstrong Kelly's classic, "Notes on Hegel's 'Lordship and Bondage,'" *Review of Metaphysics* 19 (June 1966): 780–802; Alexandre Kojève's *Introduction to the Reading of Hegel: Lectures on the* Phenomenology of Spirit, trans. James H. Nichols Jr., ed. Allan Bloom (Ithaca, N.Y.: Cornell University Press, 1969), 3–30; and Jean Hyppolite, *Genesis and Structure of Hegel's* Phenomenology of Spirit, trans. Samuel Cherniak and John Heckman (Evanston, Ill.: Northwestern University Press, 1974), 156–77. See also Howard Adelman, "Of Human Bondage: Labour, Bondage and Freedom in the *Phenomenology*," in *Hegel's Social and Political Thought*, ed. Donald P. Verene (Atlantic Highlands, N.J.: Humanities Press, 1980), 119–35; Henry S. Harris, "The Concept of Recognition in Hegel's Jena Manuscripts," in *Hegel Studien/Beiheft 20*, ed. Klaus Dusing and Dieter Henrich (Bonn: Bouvier, 1980), 229–48. For a reading of Hegel's thought as a whole, see Charles Taylor, *Hegel* (Cambridge, UK: Cambridge University Press, 1979).

43. Cf. Asher Horowitz and Gad Horowitz's comparison of Hobbes and Hegel. Asher Horowitz and Gad Horowitz, *"Everywhere They Are in Chains": Political Theory from Rousseau to Marx* (Scarborough, Ont.: Nelson Canada, 1988), 201–4. On the Hobbes-Hegel relation, see Ludwig Siep, "The Struggle for Recognition: Hegel's Dispute with Hobbes in the Jena Writings," in *Hegel's Dialectic of Desire and Recognition: Texts and Commentary*, ed. John O'Neil (Albany: State University of New York Press, 1996), 273–88.

44. Hobbes, *Leviathan*, 214–15.

45. Hegel, *Phenomenology*, 10.

46. For comparisons of Hegel and Freud with particular emphases on the problem of negation, see Michael S. Roth, *Psycho-Analysis as History: Negation and Freedom in Freud* (Ithaca, N.Y.: Cornell University Press, 1987), 120–33; and Richard Boothby, *Death and Desire: Psychoanalytic Theory in Lacan's Return to Freud* (New York: Routledge, 1991), 188–91. See also Edward S. Casey and J. Melvin Woody, "Hegel, Heidegger, Lacan: The Dialectic of Desire," in *Interpreting Lacan*, ed. Joseph H. Smith and William Kerrigan (New Haven, Conn.: Yale University Press, 1983), 75–112; Wilfred Ver Eecke, "Hegel as Lacan's Source for Necessity in Psychoanalytic Theory," in *Interpreting Lacan*, ed. Joseph H. Smith and William Kerrigan (New Haven, Conn.: Yale University Press, 1983), 113–38; and John P. Muller, "Negation in 'The Purloined Letter': Hegel, Poe, Lacan," in *The Purloined Poe: Lacan, Derrida, and Psychoanalytic Reading*, ed. John P. Muller and William J. Richardson (Baltimore: Johns Hopkins University Press, 1988), 343–68.

47. Hegel, *Phenomenology*, 114–15.

48. Hegel, *Phenomenology*, 114.

49. Sigmund Freud, "Thoughts for the Times on War and Death," in vol. 14 of *The Standard Edition*, ed. and trans. James Strachey et al., 291.

50. Freud, "Thoughts for the Times," 282.

51. Sigmund Freud, *Three Essays on the Theory of Sexuality*, in vol. 7 of *The Standard Edition*, ed. and trans. James Strachey et al., 168.

52. Sigmund Freud, *New Introductory Lectures on Psycho-Analysis*, in vol. 22 of *The Standard Edition*, ed. and trans. James Strachey et al., 95.

53. Hegel, *Phenomenology*, 114–15.

54. "Whatever their philosophical formulations may be," Merleau-Ponty writes, "there is no denying that Freud had an increasingly clear view of the body's mental function and the mind's incarnation." As cited by Boothby, *Death and Desire*, 223. See Merleau-Ponty's truly insightful comments on Freud in Maurice Merleau-Ponty, "Man and Adversity," in *Signs*, trans. Richard C. McCleary (Evanston, Ill.: Northwestern University Press, 1964), 226–32. Similarly, Jerome Neu writes that "sexuality is as much a matter of thought or the mind as of the body. To think one can get away from sexuality via the denial of the body is to mistake the half for the whole." Jerome Neu, "Freud and Perversion," in *The Cambridge Companion to Freud*, ed. Jerome Neu (Cambridge, UK: Cambridge University Press, 1991), 199. See also Philip Rieff, "Science and Moral Psychology" in *Freud: The Mind of the Moralist* (New York: Viking, 1959), 3–27; Jean Laplanche and J.-B. Pontalis, "Fantasy and the Origins of Sexuality," *International Journal of Psychoanalysis* 49 (1968): 1–18; and Steven Marcus, "The Origins of Psychoanalysis Revisited," in *Freud and the Culture of Psychoanalysis* (New York: Norton, 1984), 6–21.

55. Casey and Woody write in their discussion of Lacan, "Desire belongs *neither* to the natural *nor* to the symbolic order. It is situated at the intersection of the natural and the signifying, but neither the natural nor the signifying is left uninfected by the encounter" (emphases in original). Casey and Woody, "Hegel, Heidegger, Lacan," 106. According to Laplanche and Pontalis, Freud's concept of "infantile sexuality is difficult to comprehend: it cannot be accounted for either by an approach that reduces it to a physiological function or by an interpretation 'from above' that claims that what Freud calls infantile sexuality is the love relationship in its varied embodiments. In fact it is always in the form of *desire* that Freud identifies infantile sexuality in psycho-analysis: as opposed to love, desire is directly dependent on a specific somatic foundation; in contrast to need, it subordinates satisfaction to conditions in the phantasy world which strictly determine object-choice and the orientation of activity." Jean Laplanche and Jean Bertrand Pontalis, *The Language of Psycho-Analysis*, trans. Donald Nicholson-Smith (New York: Hogarth, 1973), 421–22.

56. See Freud, "Thoughts for the Times," 283.

57. "[C]apable," Merleau-Ponty says, "of feeling the lack of and need for others, but incapable of finding his resting place in others." Merleau-Ponty, "Man and Adversity," 231.

58. Freud, *Civilization and Its Discontents*, 122.

59. Hegel, *Phenomenology*, 111.

60. Hegel, *Phenomenology*, 19.

61. See, for example, Boothby's discussion in *Death and Desire*, 41–45.

62. Casey and Woody, "Hegel, Heidegger, Lacan," 111.

63. Jacques Lacan, *Écrits: A Selection*, trans. Alan Sheridan (New York: Norton, 1977), 297.

64. Lacan, *Écrits*, 301.

65. Casey and Woody, "Hegel, Heidegger, Lacan," 99.

66. Casey and Woody, "Hegel, Heidegger, Lacan," 98.

67. For an instructive juxtaposition of Hegel and Nietzsche, see Murray Greene, "Hegel's 'Unhappy Consciousness' and Nietzsche's 'Slave Morality,'" in *Hegel and the Philosophy of Religion: The Wofford Symposium*, ed. Darrel E. Christensen (The Hague: Martinus Nijhoff, 1970), 125–41. See also Joseph C. Flay's "Comment" on Greene's paper and Greene's "Reply," in *Hegel and the Philosophy of Religion: The Wofford Symposium*, ed. Darrel E. Christensen (The Hague: Martinus Nijhoff, 1970), 142–46 and 153–54; and Joseph C. Flay, *Hegel's Quest for Certainty* (Albany: State University of New York Press, 1984), especially 110–12 and 249–67. Freud acknowledges that "Nietzsche, another philosopher whose guesses and intuitions often agree in the most astonishing way with the laborious findings of psychoanalysis, was for a long time avoided by me on that very account; I was less concerned with the question of priority than with keeping my mind unembarrassed." Sigmund Freud, *An Autobiographical Study*, in vol. 20 of *The Standard Edition*, ed. and trans. James Strachey et al., 60. See also Sigmund Freud, *On the History of the Psycho-Analytic Movement*, in vol. 14 of *The Standard Edition*, 15–16. Irvin D. Yalom, *When Nietzsche Wept: A Novel of Obsession* (New York: Basic, 1992) is a study, in the form of a novel, of the relation between Nietzsche's thought and psychoanalysis. On Freud, psychoanalysis, Nietzsche, and critical theory, see Eugene Victor Wolfenstein, *Inside/Outside Nietzsche: Psychoanalytic Explorations* (Ithaca, N.Y.: Cornell University Press, 2000).

68. Sigmund Freud, "The Psychotherapy of Hysteria," in Sigmund Freud and Josef Breuer, *Studies on Hysteria*, in vol. 2 of *The Standard Edition*, ed. and trans. James Strachey et al., 305.

69. Freud, *Autobiographical Study*, 17.

70. See James Strachey, "Editor's Introduction" to Freud and Breuer, *Studies on Hysteria*, in vol. 2 of *The Standard Edition*, ed. and trans. James Strachey et al., xxv, n. 1.

71. The image of the owl of Minerva appears in the preface to Hegel's *Philosophy of Right*, trans. T. M. Know (Oxford, UK: Oxford University Press, 1967), 13.

3

The Abandonment of Hypnosis

Transference is merely uncovered and isolated by analysis. It is a universal phenomenon of the human mind, it decides the success of all medical influence, and in fact dominates the whole of each person's relations to his human environment.

—Sigmund Freud, *An Autobiographical Study*

THERAPY AND CULTURE

In *On the History of the Psycho-Analytic Movement* (1914), immersed in a polemic effort to enunciate the specificity of psychoanalysis, Freud writes:

The theory of repression is the corner-stone on which the whole structure of psycho-analysis rests. It is the most essential part of it; and yet it is nothing but a theoretical formulation of a phenomenon which may be observed as often as one pleases if one undertakes an analysis of a neurotic without resorting to hypnosis. In such cases one comes across a resistance which opposes the work of analysis and in order to frustrate it pleads a failure of memory. The use of hypnosis was bound to hide this resistance; *the history of psycho-analysis proper, therefore, only begins with the new technique that dispenses with hypnosis.* The theoretical consideration of the fact that this resistance coincides with an amnesia leads inevitably to the view of unconscious mental activity which is peculiar to psycho-analysis. . . . *It may thus be said that the theory of psycho-analysis is an attempt to account for two striking and unexpected facts of observation which emerge whenever an attempt is made to trace the symptoms of a neurotic back to their sources in his past life: the facts of transference and of resist-ance.*[1] (emphases added)

In the present chapter, I wish to examine Freud's historic abandonment of hypnosis with the intent of demonstrating that Freud understands psychoanalysis as a mode of self-constitutive labor in and through which the human subject attempts its own accession into the field of temporality. Neurotic symptoms, Freud tells us, "give the patient himself the impression of being all-powerful guests from an alien world, immortal beings intruding into the turmoil of mortal life."[2] Accordingly, psychoanalysis seeks the liberation of "mortal life" from the intrusions of the immortal. The essence of its mode of action, I shall argue, is historicization.[3]

The profound significance of Freud's location of the onset of psychoanalysis at the heart of his abandonment of hypnosis is best broached in terms of this task of historicization. "Hypnotism," he writes, "has not fulfilled its original promise as a therapeutic agent. We psycho-analysts may claim to be its legitimate heirs and we do not forget how much encouragement and theoretical clarification we owe to it."[4] Freud's understanding of the dynamics accounting for the failure of hypnosis contains his theorization of an inextricable connection between the possibility of a psychoanalytic historicization, on the one hand, and the transcendence of attitudes to life and death whose authority would otherwise remain unchallenged, on the other. To examine Freud's critique of hypnosis is to examine a juncture between authority and death: the human subject's precarious intuition of its own death is coeval with a critique of unquestioned authority. Freud's complex bequeathal of the hypnotist's authority to the psychoanalyst is therefore simultaneously a relinquishment. For Freud, psychoanalysis is an effort to transvaluate the authority of the past over the present and the future, of the dead over the living. Fundamentally, as we shall see, this is why he posits the analytico-historical dissolution of symptoms as the resolution of transference. The analysand's intuition of his own death is eo ipso an intuition of the analyst's mortality, a dissolution of transferential authority. The struggle between Eros and Death, between death and its denial, is thus waged on the terrain of psychoanalysis.

Freud's earliest formulation of the problem of culture, "'Civilized' Sexual Morality and Modern Nervous Illness" (1908), already offers a "number of technical papers" on the theory of neurosis as evidence for the injuriousness of civilization.[5] From the very beginning, Freud claims to establish an essential continuity between the 'clinical' and the 'cultural' dimensions of his work. His lifelong refusal to sever these dimensions is enough to arouse the suspicion that the psychoanalytic critique of culture can by no means culminate in the image of an isolated yet rational individual either well adjusted to or freed therapeutically from the pernicious influences of culture. On the contrary, the critical image of psychoanalysis is rather the emblem of an alternative intersubjectivity, of a mode of relatedness—both ethical and existential—more closely attuned to the erotic claims of our "first duty" as living beings. It is an image not so much of the liberation of the individual from culture as of the liberation of culture from illusion.

In this vein, the onus of the present chapter is to outline the conceptual movements whereby Freud's initial *therapeutic* protest against hypnosis transforms itself into Freud's subsequent *cultural* protest against a culture rooted in illusion. This outline will enable us, in the chapter following this one, to grasp the emerging logic of psychoanalysis as the logic of a new culture—of the culture Freud permits himself to intimate when he suggests, in *Civilization and Its Discontents,* that Eros might "assert himself in the struggle with his equally immortal adversary."

The present chapter begins with an analysis of Freud and Breuer's "Preliminary Communication," an 1893 text containing Freud's initial exploration of the dynamics of hysterical phenomena. The following section chronicles Freud's movement beyond the "Preliminary Communication"; his transition, by way of the abandonment of hypnosis, from Breuer's 'cathartic method' into 'psychoanalysis proper.' I then render the mode of therapeutic action Freud named 'psychoanalysis' as in fact a critique of the hypnotist's at once unquestioned and ill-fated authority; and connect that critique to Freud's central concept of the loved one's death, specifically by setting forth the degree to which the dynamics of psychoanalysis resemble a protracted labor of mourning, a renunciation of the illusions sustaining the power of hypnosis. The chapter concludes with a deployment of Freud's *Group Psychology and the Analysis of the Ego* intended to bring into relief the fertile convergence between his critique of hypnosis and his critique of culture.

PRELIMINARY COMMUNICATION

In their "Preliminary Communication," Freud and Breuer set out, on the basis of what they term a "chance observation," to "investigate a great variety of different forms and symptoms of hysteria, with a view to discovering their precipitating cause—the event which provoked the first occurrence, often many years earlier, of the phenomenon in question."[6] The "chance observation" at issue refers to a "highly remarkable phenomenon"; namely, that *"each individual hysterical symptom immediately and permanently disappeared when we had succeeded in bringing clearly to light the*

memory of the event by which it was provoked and in arousing its accompanying
affect, and when the patient had described that event in the greatest possible de-
tails and had put the affect into words" (emphasis in original).[7] "*Hysterics,*"
Freud and Breuer conclude, "*suffer mainly from reminiscences*" (emphasis in
original).[8]

The mode of causation that, according to Freud and Breuer, underlies
the formation of hysterical symptoms is of the utmost importance:

> But the causal relation between the determining psychical trauma and the
> hysterical phenomenon is not of a kind implying that the trauma merely acts
> as an *agent provocateur* in releasing the symptom, which thereafter leads an
> independent existence. We must presume rather that the psychical trauma—
> or more precisely the memory of the trauma—acts like a foreign body which
> long after its entry must continue to be regarded as an agent that is still at
> work. . . .[9] (emphasis in original)

A kind of failed forgetfulness is at the root of hysterical phenomena.
Symptoms embody in the present the lingering power of the past.[10] In
and through symptoms, the past presents itself anachronistically, operates as a contemporary experience. That which *has been* presents itself
rather as that which *is*. Freud and Breuer thus grasp the "foreign" or
enigmatic quality of hysterical symptoms as a temporal relation, as the
recalcitrance of a past that refuses to be itself, to be done with. The
power of the symptomatic is the embodied power of that which refuses
to die.

Accordingly, Freud and Breuer now proceed to theorize the possibility
that "events experienced so long ago should continue to operate so in-
tensely—that their recollection should not be liable to the wearing away
process to which, after all, we see all our memories succumb." The absence of forgetfulness is to be understood by reference to the processes
that, in general, account for "the fading away of a memory or the losing
of its affect." Such forgetfulness, Freud and Breuer tell us, "depends on
various factors," of which the "most important" is

> *whether there has been an energetic reaction to the event that provokes an affect.* By
> 'reaction' we here understand the whole class of voluntary and involuntary
> reflexes—from tears to acts of revenge—in which, as experience shows us,
> the affects are discharged. If this reaction takes place to a sufficient amount a
> large part of the affect disappears as a result. Linguistic usage bears witness
> to this fact of daily observation by such phrases as "to cry oneself out," . . .
> and to "blow off steam". . . . If the reaction is suppressed, the affect remains
> attached to the memory. An injury that has been repaid, even if only in
> words, is recollected quite differently from one that has had to be accepted.
> Language recognizes this distinction, too, in its mental and physical conse-

quences; it very characteristically describes an injury that has been suffered in silence as "a mortification". . . .[11] (emphasis in original)

Pathogenic memories are monuments to injuries "suffered in silence," to psychical traumas deprived of the possibility of a cathartic "abreaction."[12] Memories constituting an exception to the expected wearing-away process must therefore *"correspond to traumas that have not been sufficiently abreacted"* (emphasis in original).[13]

Freud and Breuer surmise that this failure to produce an "adequate" reaction to trauma is due either to "the nature of the trauma," to "the psychical states in which the patient received the experiences in question," or to some combination of both these conditions. As examples of the former condition, Freud and Breuer list (1) the "apparently irreparable loss of a loved person," (2) "social circumstances [which] made a reaction impossible" and (3) situations in which "it was a question of things which the patient wished to forget, and therefore intentionally repressed from his conscious thought and inhibited and suppressed." As regards the latter condition, Freud and Breuer tell us that they find "among the causes of hysterical symptoms ideas which are not in themselves significant, but whose persistence is due to the fact that they originated during the prevalence of severely paralysing affects, such as fright, or during positively abnormal psychical states, such as the semi-hypnotic twilight state of day-dreaming, auto-hypnoses, and so on. In such cases it is the nature of the states which makes a reaction to the event impossible."[14]

Nonetheless, "abreaction" is not the only way in which a memory may be divested of its affect. As an alternative, the memory of a psychical trauma, "even if it has not been abreacted," may enter what Freud and Breuer call "the great complex of associations." In so doing,

> it comes alongside other experiences, which may contradict it, and is subjected to rectification by other ideas. After an accident, for instance, the memory of the danger and the (mitigated) repetition of the fright becomes associated with the memory of what happened afterwards—rescue and the consciousness of present safety. Again, a person's memory of a humiliation is corrected by his putting the facts right, by considering his own worth, etc. In this way a normal person is able to bring about the disappearance of the accompanying affect through the process of association.[15]

Thus, as Laplanche and Pontalis put it, the psychical work involved in this process manages to integrate the memory "into a series of associations which allows the event to be corrected—to be put in its proper place."[16]

The conditions preventing abreaction, however, at the same time preclude the possibility of association. Whether the failure to abreact is produced due to the nature of the trauma itself or due to that of the psychical state in which it is received, both determinants

> have in common the fact that the psychical traumas which have not been dis-
> posed of by reaction cannot be disposed of either by being worked over by
> means of association. In the first group [that due to the nature of the trauma
> itself] the patient is determined to forget the distressing experiences and ac-
> cordingly *excludes* them so far as possible from association; while in the sec-
> ond group [that due to the mental state in which the trauma is received] the
> associative working-over fails to occur because there is *no extensive associative
> connection* between the normal state of consciousness and the pathological
> ones in which the ideas made their appearance.[17] (emphasis added)

Accordingly, Freud and Breuer conclude that *"it may therefore be said that
the ideas which have become pathological have persisted with such freshness and
affective strength because they have been denied the normal wearing-away
processes by means of abreaction and reproduction in states of uninhibited association"* (emphasis in original).[18]

This conception of an excluded content devoid of an extensive connection to the rest of the subject introduces a spatial dimension to the temporal framing of the problematic of hysterical phenomena. As Freud and
Breuer tell us, the "remarkable fact" is that the pathogenic *"experiences are
completely absent from the patients' memory when they are in a normal psychical state, or are only present in a highly summary form"* (emphasis in original).[19] The operative memory, that is to say, is itself forgotten: it is found
not in the patient's normal memory but "in his memory when he is hypnotized." The lingering presence of the past thus coincides with a "splitting" of the personality:

> The longer we have been occupied with these phenomena the more we have
> become convinced that *the splitting of consciousness which is so striking in the
> well-known classical cases under the form of* 'double conscience' *is present to a
> rudimentary degree in every hysteria, and that a tendency to such a dissociation, and
> with it the emergence of abnormal states of consciousness (which we shall bring to-
> gether under the term* 'hypnoid') *is the basic phenomenon of this neurosis.*[20] (em-
> phasis in original)

At issue in this dissociation of the personality is Freud and Breuer's conclusion that "the basis and *sine qua non* of hysteria is the existence of hypnoid states." These states, they tell us, share with hypnosis the fact that
"the ideas which emerge in them are very intense but are cut off from as-
sociative communication with the rest of the content of consciousness"

(emphasis in original).[21] The authority of the past operates in and through this excluded layer of the personality, in a manner analogous to that in which, in the phenomenon of "posthypnotic suggestion," a subject obeys a hypnotist's commands, "though not knowing why."[22] In the wake of this ascertaining of ideas on the one hand withdrawn from consciousness, yet on the other nonetheless powerfully active, Freud and Breuer, as early as 1893, understand hysterical phenomena by way of a comparison to the mysterious universe of dreams: "Whereas . . . our dream-psychoses have no effect upon our waking state," they write, "the products of hypnoid states intrude into waking life in the form of hysterical symptoms."[23]

On that basis, Freud and Breuer formulate the effectiveness of the cathartic method as a psychotherapeutic procedure in the following manner:

> *It brings to an end the operative force of the idea which was not abreacted in the first instance, by allowing its strangulated affect to find a way out through speech; and it subjects it to associative correction by introducing it into normal consciousness (under light hypnosis) or by removing it through the physician's suggestion, as is done in somnambulism accompanied by amnesia.*[24] (emphasis in original)

According to Freud and Breuer, this cathartic method is "a radical one." As distinct from the merely cosmetic efforts of direct suggestion—efforts that attempt no more than a superimposition of the hypnotist's authority over that of the symptom—Freud and Breuer's method operates by way of a cathartic dissolution of the symptom's determinants. "[I]n this respect," they write, "it [the cathartic method] seems to us far superior in its efficacy to removal through direct suggestion, as it is practiced to-day by psycho-therapists."[25]

The subsequent development of Freud's position, however, questions this allegedly "radical" character of the cathartic method. Freud tells us that, as a result of his abandonment of hypnosis, "[a] different view had now to be taken of the task of therapy."[26] The abandonment of hypnosis led Freud not only to a specifically psychoanalytic mode of action but also to an alternative view of the dynamics of hysterical phenomena. As we shall presently see, the shift at the level of therapeutic technique carries with it a profound shift in Freud's conceptualization of the constitution of subjectivity.

FROM HYPNOSIS TO PSYCHOANALYSIS

The seeds of Freud's movement beyond Breuer are already present in their joint "Preliminary Communication." As we have seen, their understanding of the conditions accounting for the impossibility of abreaction concerned either the subject's mental ('hypnoid') state at the moment of the trauma's occurrence or the nature of the trauma itself. In this latter condition, Freud and Breuer included either external circumstances preventing a suitable affective discharge ('retention') or an effort on the part of the subject to forget distressing "things" by way of exclusion from his conscious thought ('defense'). Thus, the pathogenic conditions identified by Freud and Breuer amounted to a threefold classification of hysteria into *hypnoid* hysteria, *retention* hysteria, and *defense* hysteria.[27]

Nevertheless, the "Preliminary Communication" placed the concept of the *hypnoid* state in a predominant position. As we noted, when it comes to the theoretical formulation of the psychical "splitting" at the root of hysterical phenomena, Freud and Breuer state that hypnoid states are the "basic phenomenon of this neurosis," the "*sine qua non* of hysteria."

In this regard, the transition into "psychoanalysis proper" is best grasped as Freud's effort to assert the primacy of the concept of *defense*. "The first difference between Breuer and myself," Freud writes,

> came to light on a question concerning the finer psychical mechanism of hysteria. He gave preference to a theory which was still to some extent *physiological*, as one might say; he tried to explain the mental splitting in hysterical patients by the absence of communication between various mental states ("states of consciousness," as we called them at the time), and he therefore constructed the theory of "hypnoid states," the products of which were supposed to penetrate into 'waking consciousness' like unassimilated foreign bodies. I had taken the matter less scientifically; everywhere I seemed to discern motives and tendencies analogous to those of everyday life, and *I looked upon psychical splitting itself as an effect of a process of repelling which at that time I called 'defense,' and later, 'repression.'*[28] (emphases added)

As Laplanche and Pontalis put it, "it was by bringing the notion of defense to the fore in dealing with hysteria—and, soon afterwards, with the other psychoneuroses—that Freud developed his own conception of mental life in contrast to the views of his contemporaries."[29]

Freud's abandonment of hypnoid states as a theoretical tool is inextricable from his abandonment of hypnosis as a technical one. Though present in the "Preliminary Communication," the concept of defense comes into its own only in and through Freud's change in technique. "Hypnosis," he writes, "had screened from view an interplay of forces which now came in sight and the understanding of which gave a solid foundation to my theory." In the absence of hypnosis, Freud observes the intractable difficulty of the effort of remembrance intended to bring excluded contents within the purview of the subject's consciousness. "[I]t was necessary," he tells us, "to overcome something that fought against one in the patient; it was necessary to make efforts of one's own so as to urge and compel him to remember."[30] *Resistance* is the name Freud gives to the subject's effort to oppose the work of remembrance.

Freud registers the implications of his experience of resistance as early as his theoretical contribution to *Studies on Hysteria*, entitled "The Psychotherapy of Hysteria":

> In what I have hitherto said the idea of resistance has forced its way into the foreground. I have shown how, in the course of our therapeutic work, we have been led to the view that hysteria originates through the repression of an incompatible idea from a motive of defense. . . . Breuer has put forward for . . . cases of hypnoid hysteria a psychical mechanism which is substantially different from that of defense. . . . In his view what happens in hypnoid hysteria is that an idea becomes pathogenic because it has been received during a special psychical state and has from the first remained outside the ego. *No psychical force has therefore been required in order to keep it apart from the ego and no resistance need be aroused if we introduce it into the ego with the help of mental activity during somnambulism.*[31] (emphasis added)

In 1914, while retelling the history of his movement beyond Breuer, Freud writes that "I made a short lived attempt to allow the two mechanisms a separate existence side by side, but as observation showed me always and only one thing, it was not long before my 'defense' theory took up its stand opposite his 'hypnoid' one."[32]

Freud's encounter with resistances leads to the formulation of the cornerstone concept of repression and thereby to an alternative conceptualization both of the mechanism of symptom formation and of the therapeutic task. As we shall presently see, this shift concerns both the spatial and the temporal dimensions of the views developed in the "Preliminary Communication."

As regards the spatial dimension, Freud advances—in the absence of Breuer's hypnoid states—a different "view of hysterical dissociation (the splitting of consciousness)."[33] To begin with, Freud surmises that "the same forces which, in the form of resistance, were now offering opposition to the forgotten material's being made conscious, must formerly have brought about the forgetting and must have pushed the pathogenic experiences in question out of consciousness." Thus the pathogenic exclusion of psychical contents is derived not from the existence of hypnoid states but rather from that of a hypothesized process of active exclusion on the part of the subject. "I gave the name of '*repression*' to this hypothetical process," Freud writes, "and I considered that it was proved by the undeniable existence of resistance" (emphasis in original).[34]

Conflict, according to Freud, is at the root of repression. The cathartic method had made it possible to observe that all pathogenic experiences "involved the emergence of a wishful impulse which was in sharp contrast to the subject's other wishes and which proved incompatible with the ethical and aesthetic standards of his personality."[35] Repression thus appears as a strategic move on the part of a subject who finds himself as the very field in which mutually incompatible "powerful impulsions" carry out a momentous struggle.[36] The incompatible wish is, as it were, exiled from the subject's consciousness: "An acceptance of the incompatible wishful impulse or a prolongation of the conflict would have produced a high degree of unpleasure; this unpleasure was avoided by means of repression, which was thus revealed as one of the devices serving to protect the mental personality."[37]

Flight, however, is "of no avail." The subject, Freud insists, "cannot escape from itself."[38] At the root of symptom formation, Freud finds a failure on the part of the "ostrich-like" strategy of repression.[39] "[T]he repressed wishful impulse," he writes, "continues to exist in the unconscious" (emphasis in original).[40] To trace the path from repression to symptom formation is to decipher the symbolic unconscious processes whereby excluded wishes disguise themselves so as to return—like "all-powerful guests from an alien world, immortal beings intruding into the turmoil of mortal life"[41]—to haunt the conscious personality in the shape of symptoms. This *return of the repressed* as an "unrecognizable *substitute*" is, precisely as both disguised and excluded, "proof against further attacks from the defensive ego; and in place of the short conflict an ailment now appears which is *not brought to an end by the passage of time*" (last emphasis added).[42] The unsuccessfully avoided conflict persists, as it were, behind the back of the fragmented subject.

Freud's dynamic account of "splitting" as a result of an interplay of forces deeply transforms his conceptualization of the task of therapy. Symptoms are grasped as rooted not in the impossibility of abreaction but rather in the avoidance of psychical conflict. The old distinction between the normal wearing-away process and the hysterical exception to that process now appears as one between "normal" and "neurotic" conflict:

> In this connection people usually overlook the one essential point—that the pathogenic conflict in neurotics is not to be confused with a normal struggle between mental impulses both of which are on the same psychological footing. In the former case the dissension is between two powers, one of which has made its way to the stage of what is . . . conscious while the other has been held back at the stage of the unconscious. For that reason, the conflict cannot be brought to an issue; the disputants can no more come to grips than, in the familiar simile, a polar bear and a whale. A *true decision* can only be reached when they both meet on the same ground. To make this possible is, I think, the *sole* task of our therapy.[43] (emphases added)

Whereas the "Preliminary Communication" concerned itself with the facilitation of discharge by way of hypnosis, Freud now seeks the retrieval of the possibility of what he calls an "act of judgment." His aim, he tells us, is "no longer to 'abreact' an affect which had got on to the wrong lines but to uncover repressions and replace them by *acts of judgment* which might result either in the accepting or in the condemning of what had formerly been repudiated." "I showed my recognition of the new situation," he adds, "by no longer calling my method of investigation and treatment *catharsis* but *psycho-analysis*" (first emphasis added).[44]

Freud's account of "splitting" in terms of a dynamic conflict between opposing mental forces results in a momentous expansion of the field of psychology as distinct from that of physiology.[45] The concept of repression undoes a kind of theoretical somatization of specifically psychical processes. It amounts, that is to say, to a reappropriation of the psychical from its concealing embedment in the physiological.[46] By way of such reappropriation, the concept of repression brings the sphere of the symptomatic within the range of psychical action. Symptoms are results neither of organic disorders nor of passively received experiences, but rather modes of communication in and through which the subject is actively implicated. In fact, it is precisely from the viewpoint of the subject's (self-)implication that Freud manages to seize the possibility of its liberation. The psychical character of the symptom means both that it is a historical rather than a physiological predicament and that, as such, it can in principle be dissolved at the level of specifically psychical agency.

The act of judgment Freud has in mind is an act of historicization. This can be observed as soon as Freud's alteration of the temporal relations presented in the "Preliminary Communication" is incorporated into the examination of his abandonment of hypnosis.

Neurotics, Freud never tired of saying, "give us an *impression* of having been 'fixated' to a particular portion of the past, as though they could not manage to free themselves from it and were for that reason alienated from the present and the future" (emphasis added).[47] On the one hand, it is true, "it is as though these patients had not finished with the traumatic situation, as though they were still faced by it as an immediate task."[48] Yet on the other, however much this "impression" might "tempt" us by offering "a simple determinant for the onset of neurosis,"[49] Freud carefully notes instances in which the "fixation appeared to have passed off without doing any damage," and reappeared "only several years later" in the symptoms of the neurosis. Thus, as regards the onset of illness, Freud suggests a "wealth of determinants" greater than that entailed in the notion of an unfinished traumatic situation.[50]

This subsequent reappearance of the fixation as such is at the heart of Freud's own theorization of the formation of symptoms. According to Freud, the path to symptoms begins with frustration in reality. This frustration initiates a search for alternative routes to satisfaction. If reality remains relentless, the demand for satisfaction "recalls earlier and better times"—it withdraws into the universe of fantasy by regressing to memories of satisfaction.[51] As Freud puts it, we know not only that neurotics are "anchored somewhere in their past," but also that this past is a past "in which they were happy."[52]

At the same time, however, this backward movement gives rise to an *internal* conflict. On the one hand, the reawakened memories claim realization, threaten to overflow the limits of the present. On the other, the retrospective revival of once superseded modes and objects of satisfaction confronts the objections of precisely those aspects of the personality that have moved beyond them. Thus, the regressively activated fixations meet the fate of repression. This repression, however, is but the beginning of the "return of the repressed." The denied demand for satisfaction now endeavors to disguise itself so as to circumvent the encountered prohibitions. It returns in the shape of substitutive, compromised efforts at satisfaction. These compromises, as we have seen, are what Freud calls symptoms.[53]

Schematic as it is, the foregoing description of the processes of symptom construction nonetheless suffices to note that the pathogenicity of fixations is constituted retrospectively. A symptom embodies relations not only between opposing psychical demands—wish and prohibition—but also between distinct moments in time: it emblematizes an empty present seeking a fuller past in order to posit—albeit unsuccessfully—a transvaluated future.[54] In this process, *the significance of the past in the production of symptomatology is inseparable from the present that retrospectively revives it.* The symptom is not an effect of the past on the present but rather a relation between past and present. In regard to the past in question, the repressed, as Lacan has it, returns from the future.[55]

This retrospective dimension of Freud's conception effectively expands the subject's field of action in regard to the construction of symptomatology. Freud renders symptoms as carriers of interpretations constitutive of a past whose repeated presence in the present takes place in and through those same interpretations. The mode of (retro)activity Freud has in mind rebukes his "alleged reduction of all human actions and desires to the level of the infantile past." It makes it clear that "Freud had pointed out from the very beginning that the subject revises past events at a later date (*Nachträglich*), and that it is this revision which invests them with significance and even with efficacity or pathogenic force."[56]

Freud alters the temporal relations explicitly presented in the "Preliminary Communication" in the specific sense that the "precipitating cause" of neurosis appears no longer in and through a mode of causation (however complex) of the *past* on the present, but rather in and through a retroactive mode of causation of the *present* on the past. It is precisely the participation of this retroactivity at the level of the constitution of the neurosis that permits, at the level of its dissolution, the mode of action Freud named psychoanalysis. The retroactive reconstitution of the past is what moves psychoanalysis beyond the mere release of an imprisoned past. The reminiscences from which hysterics suffer are always already modes of casting the past. Accordingly, the resolution of their suffering consists not of mere release but also of psychical work seeking a remolding of the past. The analyst's interpretations are always already reinterpretations. For Freud, the dynamics of cure involve neither obedience to hypnotic suggestion nor exclusively cathartic relief, but rather the laborious construction of an alternative mode of self-interpretation.

As Baranger et al. point out, the presence of the past in the present *"is not simply a deferred action* nor a *cause* that remains latent until it has occasion to appear, but a *retroactive causation* of the present on the past." This retroactivity, they continue, sustains

> the possibility of a specific therapeutic action in psychoanalysis: if this retroactivity in the constitution of the trauma did not exist, there would be no possibility of modifying our history, that is, our treatments would have no future. . . . The same retroactivity that acted in the constitution of the traumatic situation can also be used, through interpretation, to undo what it has constituted, to reintegrate the elements of the traumatic situations into new temporal dynamics. If we were to abide by linear categories of causality and temporality, we would be deprived of all therapeutic efficacy.[57] (emphases in original)

Posed as retroactivity, the act of judgment Freud wishes to facilitate is a movement of retrospective resignification.[58] The erotic struggle against the repetitive intrusions of the immortal takes place in and through a dynamic act of recollection aimed at historicization. *"Analysis,"* Baranger et al. write, *"could be defined as historicization (Nachträglichkeit) versus the death instinct"* (emphasis in original).[59] For Freud, the future is not ahead of us but rather in a transvaluated relation to the past.

THE CRITIQUE OF THE HYPNOTIST'S AUTHORITY

Theoretically, then, Freud's charge against hypnosis is that its concealment of resistances precludes a clear theorization of the processes of symptom formation in terms of a dynamic conflict of opposing mental forces. Hypnosis does not permit us "to recognize the *resistance* with which the patient clings to his disease and thus even fights against his own recovery" (emphasis in original).[60] It operates as a narcotic veiling the inherently conflictual character of the human psyche.

It can hardly escape us that Freud's objections against hypnosis can themselves come to fruition only *retroactively*. It is only in the wake of his abandonment of hypnosis that he can, subsequently, adequately theorize its shortcomings, now informed by the encounter with resistances made possible precisely in and through that abandonment. "It was not until later," Freud tells us, "that I was to discover the drawbacks of the procedure":

> At the moment there were only two points to complain of: first, that I could not succeed in hypnotizing every patient, and secondly, that I was unable to put individual patients into as deep a state of hypnosis as I should have wished.[61]

Yet however much one might wish to ponder the fortunate historical irony that may correctly credit Freud's incompetence as a hypnotist with the emergence of psychoanalytic theory, it is of crucial importance to prevent such pondering from blinding us to the profoundly *ethical* content of his abandonment of hypnosis. In the summer of 1889, attracted by Bernheim's successes with suggestion, Freud traveled to Nancy, France, "with the idea," he tells us, "of perfecting my hypnotic technique." It is there that, beyond his fascination with Bernheim's "astonishing experiments," Freud's complaints against hypnosis present themselves not as an admission of his own incompetence, but rather as a decidedly ethical protest.[62]

Recalling a passage from *Group Psychology and the Analysis of the Ego*, Jacques Lacan is careful to note Freud's experience of "genuine revulsion" when witnessing attempts at suggestion.[63] In that passage, Freud speaks of his feeling "a muffled hostility to this tyranny of suggestion." Especially when opposed by patients, the suggestive technique appears to Freud as "an evident injustice and an act of violence." Referring to a patient who in Freud's presence refused to submit to the power of suggestions and was therefore shouted at by the physician in question, Freud declares that "the man certainly had a *right* to counter-suggestions if people were trying to subdue him with suggestions" (emphasis added).[64] Freud's experience of revulsion is in fact inseparable from the technique he developed as an alternative to hypnosis. Respect for resistances, and hence for persons, is to be posed at the heart of psychoanalysis. As we shall presently see, it is precisely this respect that transforms Freud's abandonment of hypnosis into a critique of authority.

Therapeutically, Freud's claim against hypnosis is that its concealment of resistances in effect precludes their removal. Accordingly, Freud tells us that fundamentally, he gave up the suggestive technique because he "despaired of making suggestion powerful and enduring enough to effect permanent cures." "In every severe case," he continues, "I saw the suggestions which had been applied crumble away again; after which the disease or some substitute for it was back once more."[65] The extent to which the astonishing magic of hypnosis leaves resistances untouched is the extent to which its effectiveness is ultimately illusory. For Freud, to ignore or suppress resistances is to reveal oneself unable to grasp the profound depth of the psychical dynamics that determine them. Hypnosis, Freud observes, "agrees most beautifully with the estimate in which neuroses are still held by the majority of doctors":

> The doctor says to the neurotic patient: "There is nothing wrong with you, it's only a question of nerves; so I can blow away your trouble in two or three minutes with just a few words."[66]

Even if at times behaviorally effective, the superimposition of suggestions—or even purportedly "valid" *reasons*—over the subtly textured network of meanings and emotions that sustain resistances is bound to remain merely formal, empty.[67] "Hypnotic treatment," Freud writes, "leaves the patient inert and *unchanged*, and for that reason, too, equally unable to resist any fresh occasion for falling ill" (emphasis added).[68]

As distinct from hypnosis, then, psychoanalysis is to appear on the scene as an effort of transformation. Accordingly, in an early attempt to illustrate the difference between the suggestive and the analytic technique, Freud invokes Leonardo da Vinci's distinction between painting and sculpture, between work that proceeds *"per via di porre"* (meaning "by adding" or "by putting on") and work that proceeds *"per via di levare"* (meaning "by subtracting" or "by taking away").[69] Painting, Freud tells us, "applies a substance—particles of colour—where there was nothing before, on the colourless canvas." Sculpture, by contrast, "takes away from the block of stone all that hides the surface of the statue contained in it." Thus whereas painting presupposes the nothingness of that on which it works, sculpture is rather premised precisely on the respect of the intrinsic shape or content of its material. "The technique of suggestion," Freud writes,

> aims [in a way similar to that of painting] at proceeding *per via di porre*; it is not concerned with the origin, strength and meaning of the morbid symptoms, but instead, it superimposes something—a suggestion—in the expectation that it will be strong enough to restrain the pathogenic idea from coming to expression. *Analytic therapy, on the other hand, does not seek to add or to introduce anything new, but to take away something, to bring out something*; and to this end concerns itself with the genesis of the morbid symptoms and the psychical context of the pathogenic idea which it seeks to remove.[70] (first emphasis in original)

Whereas hypnosis seeks to "cover up and gloss over something," analysis seeks to "expose and get rid of something."[71] Thus, Freud claims to oppose the *surgical* interventions of psychoanalysis to the *cosmetics* of hypnosis. If the hypnotist wishes to "forbid" symptoms, the psychoanalyst wishes to direct his efforts "further back towards the roots,"[72] aiming at a retroactive alteration of the processes that led to the formation of symptoms in the first place. The prohibitions of the hypnotist, that is to say, are to give way to the historico-archaeological explorations of the psychoanalyst.[73]

Thus psychoanalysis emerges as the taking away of resistances. "An analytic treatment," Freud writes, "demands from both doctor and patient the accomplishment of serious work, which is employed in lifting internal resistances." According to Freud, it is "through the overcoming of these resistances," rather than through their dismissal, that "the patient's mental life is permanently changed, is raised to a high level of development and remains protected against fresh possibilities of falling ill." This protracted work of transformation is in fact "the essential function of analytic treatment."[74] To dispense with hypnosis, in other words, is to devise a therapeutic technique that consists in the employment of "the art of interpretation mainly for the purpose of recognizing . . . resistances."[75] This, as Lacan has it, is Freud's claim to have "substituted the analysis of resistances by speech for the subjugation that operates through suggestion or through hypnosis." Psychoanalysis, Lacan adds, not only respects the person but, indeed, "cannot function without respecting it."[76]

Freud's respectful concern that analytic therapy introduce nothing new already implies that what is to be brought out must of itself wish to be brought out, to be revealed. That which is to appear must present itself, in Hegel's phrase, "of its own volition."[77] The impetus for this removal that is at once a disclosure, this taking away that is at once a bringing out, must itself come from he who takes upon himself the labor of analytic therapy. The analysand is to suffer the violence of the removal, once again in Hegel's phrase, at his "own hands."[78] Freud's hostility to the trappings of externally imposed authority goes as far as the statement that psychoanalysis is not "applicable to people who are not driven to seek treatment by their own sufferings, but who submit to it only because they are forced to by the authority of relatives."[79] In this way, his ethically informed protest against the "tyranny of suggestion" simultaneously appears as a technical necessity.

Yet although Freud thus claims that "in renouncing . . . suggestion we are not giving up anything of irreplaceable value,"[80] the complexity of the therapeutic predicament he faces as a result of that renunciation is difficult to overestimate. On the one hand, *Freud's critique of hypnosis is the cri-*

tique of a practice that by not grounding itself in that which it wishes to trans-
form, cannot help but remain either impotent or authoritarian, either unheeded
or heeded only as a result of violence. But on the other, this same critique
places Freud in a truly problematic position from which he must attempt
to catalyze the (self-)transformation of a conflicted, profoundly *ambivalent*
subject who resists, as much as it seeks, its own transformation. The concept of repression renders not only the terrain of symptom formation, but
also that of psychoanalysis itself as a terrain irretrievably traversed by a
momentous conflict of opposing forces. This means that, in spite of his
sturdy opposition to the arbitrary imposition of authority, Freud must of
necessity avail himself of a power other than that of persuasion alone in
order to wage a struggle against that about the subject which resists that
subject's own movement.

Thus, in a statement as disconcerting as it is significant, Freud readily
admits that *"the results of psycho-analysis rest upon suggestion"* (emphasis
added).[81] We might begin to grasp the meaning of this puzzling claim by
observing that the point at which Freud abandons hypnosis is the point at
which he must ask us to hold fast the paradox that the gaping heteronomy
he unveils at the heart of the human subject is nevertheless somehow to
be seized as that which gives rise to a practice that poses respect for the
human person as the ground of its own possibility. An examination of
Freud's exploration of this predicament will now enable us to see that the
independent "act of judgment" he wishes to facilitate is not only an act of
historicization but also, and at the very same time, an uncompromising
critique of unquestioned authority.

In his paper on "Negation" (1925), Freud tells us that "the content of a
repressed image or idea can make its way into consciousness, on condition that it is *negated.*" Freud is referring to situations wherein a subject
presents his thoughts as if they were not his own: "Now you'll think I
mean to say something insulting, but really I've no such intention." "We
realize," Freud continues, "that this is a rejection, by projection, of an idea
that has just come up" (emphasis in original).[82] The subject thus perceives
its own idea as if it were someone else's. As Jean Hyppolite puts it, Freud
encounters negation as a "mode of presenting what one is in the mode of
not being it." "I am going to tell you what I am not," Hyppolite writes,
"pay attention, that is exactly what I am."[83] The following passage of
Freud's is worth quoting at length:

> Negation is a way of taking cognizance of what is repressed; indeed, it is
> already a lifting of the repression, though not, of course, an acceptance of
> what is repressed. We can see how in this the intellectual function is sepa-
> rated from the affective process. With the help of negation only one con-
> sequence of the process of repression is undone—the fact, namely, of the

ideational content of what is repressed not reaching consciousness. The outcome of this is a kind of intellectual acceptance of the repressed, while at the same time what is essential to the repression persists. In the course of analytic work we often produce a further, very important and somewhat strange variant of the situation. We succeed in conquering the negation as well, and in bringing about a full intellectual acceptance of the repressed; *but the repressive process itself is not yet removed by this.*[84] (emphasis added)

Thus, for Freud, the task of removing resistances is by no means a solely intellectual task. Repeatedly, he warns us that beginners in analytic practice are prone to forget that "giving the resistance a name" cannot result in its "immediate cessation."[85] In and of itself, Freud insists, "conscious knowledge" is "powerless" against the resistances.[86] The intent of this insistence on Freud's part is to urge us beyond a perspective that takes an "intellectualist view of the situation" and thereby sets "a high value on the patient's knowledge of what he had forgotten."[87] On the contrary, Freud tells us that there is "no choice but to cease attributing to the fact of knowing, in itself, the importance that had previously been given to it and to place the emphasis on the resistances which had in the past brought about the state of not knowing and which were still ready to defend that state."[88] It is in terms of this puzzling and conflicted situation, combining both conscious knowledge and ignorance in a single subject, that Freud raises the questions of the "meaning of knowledge" and of the "play of forces" set in motion in and through psychoanalysis.[89]

"The patients now know of the repressed experience in their conscious thought," Freud tells us,

> but this thought lacks any connection with the place where the repressed recollection is in some way or other contained. No change is possible until the conscious thought-process has penetrated to that place and has overcome the resistances of repression there. It is just as though a decree were promulgated by the Ministry of Justice to the effect that juvenile delinquencies should be dealt with in a certain lenient manner. As long as this decree has not come to the knowledge of the local magistrates, or in the event of their not intending to obey it but preferring to administer justice by their own lights, no change can occur in the treatment of particular youthful delinquents.[90]

This means not that consciousness is to be discarded, but rather that the analyst's communications to the analysand, though in and of themselves insufficient, nonetheless set up "a process of thought in the course of which the expected influencing of the unconscious recollection eventually takes place."[91] This process in and through which knowledge gains substantive content is that of the analysand's labor. *Working-through* is the name Freud gives to this mental effort required to overcome resistances. Its goal is that of procuring the conditions for the possibility of establishing the absent "connection" between conscious knowledge and "the place where the repressed recollection is in some way or other contained." As Laplanche and Pontalis put it, "working-through permits the subject to pass from rejection or mere intellectual acceptance to a conviction based on lived experience."[92]

However, on the one hand unable to rely exclusively on the persuasive powers of the intellect, and on the other all too conscious that powerful resistances oppose the analysand's own intended movement, Freud must somehow account for the forces compelling the analysand to undertake the connective labor of working-through. The conception of the analysand's difficult and gradual overcoming of his painful and ambiguous not-knowing, in other words, poses before Freud the question of the impetus of the analysand's movement. "The primary motive force in the therapy," Freud writes,

> is the patient's suffering and the wish to be cured that arises from it. . . . By itself, however, this motive force is not sufficient to get rid of the illness.[93] Two things are lacking in it for this: it does not know what paths to follow to reach this end; and it does not possess the necessary quota of energy with which to oppose the resistances. The analytic treatment helps to remedy both these deficiencies. It supplies the amounts of energy that are needed for overcoming the resistances by making mobile the energies which lie ready for the *transference;* and, by giving the patient information at the right time, it shows him the paths along which he should direct those energies.[94] (emphasis added)

According to Freud, the adequate resolution of the once-avoided conflict activating the production of symptomatology requires the overcoming of resistances so as to place the conflicting forces before the analysand's consciousness with the intent of fostering a normal as distinct from a neurotogenic conflict. *The struggle here at issue, then, is not one between wish and prohibition but rather one between the propensity to repression and the possibility of judgment as alternative modes of dealing with psychic conflict.* It is precisely in the context of this struggle against the propensity to repression that Freud enlists the mobilized energies of the *transference.* Unabashedly, he frames this enlistment as the unavoidable ground of the analyst's *authority:*

> If the patient is to fight his way through the normal conflict with the resistances which we have uncovered for him in the analysis, he is in need of a powerful stimulus which will influence the decision in the sense which we desire, leading to recovery. Otherwise it might happen that he would choose

in favour of repeating the earlier outcome and would allow what had been brought up into consciousness to slip back again into repression. *At this point what turns the scale in his struggle is not his intellectual insight—which is neither strong enough nor free enough for such an achievement—but simply and solely his relation to the doctor.* In so far as his transference bears a "plus" sign, *it clothes the doctor with authority and is transformed into belief* in his communications and explanations. In the absence of such a transference, or if it is a negative one, the patient would never even give a hearing to the doctor and his arguments.[95] (emphasis added)

To be sure, this disclosure of the centrality of transference in analytic practice threatens to dissolve the critical distinction between psychoanalysis and suggestion. If Freud insists upon the "greatest possible antithesis between suggestive and analytic technique,"[96] he nonetheless warns us that "it must dawn on us that in our technique we have abandoned hypnosis only to rediscover suggestion in the shape of transference."[97] Yet, for Freud, the specificity of psychoanalysis lies by no means in the absence of suggestion but rather in the use to which its inevitable appearance is put. "*Direct* suggestion," he tells us,

> is suggestion aimed against the manifestation of the symptoms; it is a struggle between your authority and the motives for the illness.[98] (emphasis added)

The transferential authority of the analyst, on the other hand, struggles not against the symptoms themselves, but against those forces in the analysand that seek to disown conflict by way of forgetfulness. In this struggle against forgetfulness, analysis habituates the analysand to reflect rather than repress, to work through rather than eject out of himself. Psychoanalysis seeks to avail itself of suggestibility precisely in order to counteract the possibility of suggestion. Freud's technique is informed by the adage that the unhealing wound can form scars only by use of the weapon that inflicted the wound.[99] Thus Freud can tell us that the "arduous task" of working-through is "a part of the work which effects the greatest changes in the patient and which distinguishes analytic treatment from any kind of treatment by suggestion."[100] His fundamental claim is that analysis takes care of "the patient's final independence by employing suggestion in order to get him to accomplish a piece of psychical work which has as its necessary result a permanent improvement in his psychical situation."[101]

The fact that Freud locates the concept of working-through at the center of his differentiation of psychoanalysis from suggestion places before us the crucial observation that the labor of working-through is constitutive of analytic truth. At issue is not the acceptance on the analysand's part of a truth held by another, whether hypnotist or psychoanalyst. The psychoanalytic active engagement of the subject in and through working-through means that the truth that is to issue from analysis is none other than the truth of the analysand's own labor.

The essential point to be grasped is that, for Freud, the analyst neither is nor claims to be at all "neutral" regarding his uncompromising commitment to the superiority of judgment, as distinct from repression, as a mode of dealing with psychic conflict. However neutral the analyst may manage to be with respect to the particular outcome of the independent decision that the analysand is to make once confronted with his dividedness, the "extraordinary powers"[102] of the transference are, beyond any kind of spurious neutrality, to be utilized as a weapon seeking to establish the conditions for the possibility of judgment. We might say either that the analysand is to be forced to be free—or rather, that the transferential principality of the analyst is to dissolve itself into the republic of the analysand's soul.

THE WORK OF PSYCHOANALYSIS

When Freud observes that the analysand's attachment to the analyst clothes the latter with authority and is transformed into belief, he is in fact describing what he takes to be not a situation specific to the analytic situation but rather a deeply complex feature of the general genesis of belief as such. According to Freud, the credulousness of the transferential attachment is but an arena wherein the analysand's "belief is *repeating* the story of its own development; it is a derivative of love and, to start with, needed no arguments":

> Only later did he [the analysand] allow them enough room to submit them to examination, provided they were brought forward by someone he loved. Without such supports arguments carried no weight, and in most people's lives they never do. Thus in general a man is only accessible from the intellectual side too, in so far as he is capable of a libidinal cathexis of objects; and we have good reason to recognize and to dread in the amount of his narcissism a barrier against the possibility of being influenced by even the best analytic technique.[103] (emphasis added)

On the one hand, the transferential repetition of the history of belief reveals the depth of the analysand's bondage to previous libidinal attachments. On the other, precisely as a repetition, it simultaneously affords an opportunity for a reconsideration. At the level of this reconsideration—and at this level alone—Freud permits himself to grasp the analytic facilitation of judgment *pedagogically*. Psychoanalysis, he writes, is "a kind of *after-education"* (emphasis in original)[104] that, as such, is to take place in the field of retroaction. The substance of this after-education, as we shall presently see, is an effort to liberate the analysand from his bondage to previous libidinal attachments; *it is a labor of mourning.*

As we noted, Freud's account of symptom formation entails a subject's regression, in the face of external frustration, to "earlier and better times." The poverty of the present appears as a pursuit of a fuller past. Yet the ensuing effort to re-present these once superseded modes and objects of satisfaction comes into conflict with those aspects of the personality no longer at ease with the ways of the past. Thus, the anxiety provoked in and through this internal struggle induces the onset of repression. In this vein, Freud eventually comes to posit the process of repression as itself involving not only the objections on the part of the moral, logical, and aesthetic standards of the personality but also, and at the same time, the *attraction* exercised by what was once apparently lost. "[W]e must reflect," Freud writes, "that it would be inconceivable for the libido to regress so regularly to the period of childhood unless there were something to exercise an *attraction* on it" (emphasis added).[105] Hence, strictly speaking, repression is not so much a repulsion at the behest of the ego, as much as an "after-pressure."[106]

This conception of repression as comprising at least two distinct moments in time both broadens Freud's account of resistances and, correlatively, deepens his grasp of the analytic labor of working-through. "There can be no doubt or mistake," Freud writes,

> about the existence of this resistance on the part of the ego. But we have to ask ourselves whether it covers the whole state of affairs in analysis. For we find that even after the ego has decided to relinquish its resistances it still has difficulty in undoing the repressions; and we have called the period of strenuous effort which follows after its praiseworthy decision, the phase of "working-through." The dynamic factor which makes a working-through of this kind necessary and comprehensible is not far to seek. It must be that after the ego-resistance has been removed the power of the compulsion to repeat—the attraction exerted by the unconscious prototypes upon the repressed instinctual process—has still to be overcome. There is nothing to be said against describing this factor as the *resistance of the unconscious.*[107] (emphasis in original)

Accordingly, the work of analysis takes place on two fronts simultaneously. It struggles not only against "the ego's antipathy to certain trends of the libido—an antipathy expressed in a tendency to repression," but also against "the tenacity or adhesiveness of the libido, which dislikes leaving objects that it has once cathected."[108]

The subject's refusal to endure the external frustration as a result of which his longing conjures seemingly abandoned substitutes from the armory of the past, thus appears as a resolute loyalty not only to that which he loves and has loved but also to the continued presence of his own satisfaction. Rather than an encounter with the frustrating absence of its beloved object in and through mourning, the subject seeks refuge in an illusory universe from which the possibility of loss has been banished. Yet at the same time, this contrived presence robs the subject of the very life in the name of which it sought refuge. "A neurotic," Freud tells us, "is incapable of enjoyment . . . because his libido is not directed on to any real object."[109] Enthralled in and through its illusions, the subject attaches itself not only to unreal objects but also, and thereby, to a hallucinatory mode of psychic functioning premised on the foreclosure of both death and postponement, negation and temporality.[110]

What Freud grasps as the resistance of the unconscious is, in this way, revealed as an instance of the recalcitrant absence of the "No" in the unconscious. In refusing the loss of what it loves, the subject simultaneously refuses its own death. Freud thus renders the subject's denial of the loss that confronts it as alienation from the mortal life that is its own.

It is at this level that the deployment of the transference provides not only the affective force required for the analysand's movement but also, as itself a repetition of the history of the analysand's loves in and through the figure of the analyst, the opportunity for a revision, an influencing of the unconscious in the field of retroaction. "In place of the patient's true illness," Freud writes, "there appears the artificially constructed transference illness, in place of the various unreal objects of his libido there appears a single, and once more imaginary, object in the person of the doctor."[111] The transference consists in a re-edition of the subject's old yet still operative loves in the immediacy of the present. On the basis of this immediacy, the detachment of the subject's longing from illusory modes and objects of satisfaction is to take place in and through the analysis of the analysand's relation to the analyst. "In every other kind of suggestive treatment," Freud writes,

the transference is carefully preserved and left untouched; in analysis it is itself subjected to treatment and is dissected in all the shapes in which it appears. At the end of an analytic treatment the transference must itself be cleared away; and if success is then obtained or continues, it rests, not on suggestion, but on the achievement by its means of an overcoming of internal resistances, on the internal change that has been brought about in the patient.[112]

The analysis of the transferential attachment in the immediacy of the present thus coincides with a retroactive dissolution of the operative power of the past. The past is resurrected in order to be killed: "for when all is said and done," Freud tells us, "it is impossible to destroy anyone *in absentia* or *in effigie*" (emphases in original).[113]

The analyst's task consists in an assumption of the imaginary roles the analysand casts for him, yet precisely only in order to refuse them—in order, that is, to catalyze the renunciation of the analysand's claim for illusory satisfaction that unfolds in and through them. As Lacan puts it, "[i]n persuading the other that he has that which may complement us, we assure ourselves of being able to continue to misunderstand precisely what we lack."[114] The analyst's careful refusal to be thus "persuaded" compels the subject to work through rather than take refuge in its resistance to that which it lacks, in its illusory foreclosure of the painful "No" that the loss of loved ones places before it. This working-through of the resistance of the unconscious facilitates the mournful detachment of the analysand's longing from the figure of the analyst. The republic of the analysand's soul is thus founded on an assumption of a no longer denied experience of loss. For Freud, the gradual emergence of death spells the death of unquestioned authority.

At the same time, the analytic labor of mourning seeks to lure the thereby liberated longing to invest itself within the confines of a now rediscovered mortal condition. The analyst's refusal to dwell in the immortal abode that the analysand's resistance wishes to preserve for itself is thus intended, in Pontalis's deeply hopeful phrase, as "enabling the other to bring himself to life."[115] This is why, as Freud repeatedly tells us, "the transference . . . creates an intermediate region between illness and real life through which the transition from the one to the other is made."[116] Freud's deployment of the transference is simultaneously an invitation to live. Against the subject's narcissism, Freud seeks to cultivate an appreciation of mortal life, a care for the living rather than the dead. The analytic struggle is a struggle to fulfill the erotic claims of one's "first duty" as a living being.[117]

THE CRITIQUE OF CULTURE

To disclose the cultural struggle of life and death, Eros and Death, at the heart of Freud's clinical practice is to invoke a fundamental connectedness between his clinical work and his theory of culture. Freud's proposal to overcome therapeutically what he terms "the neurotic attitude to life"[118] evokes his deployment of alternative attitudes to life and death in "Thoughts for the Times on War and Death."[119] In fact, the glimmerings of a fertile convergence between Freud's critique of hypnosis and his critique of culture are already visible in Freud's analysis, presented in "Thoughts for the Times," of the disillusionment provoked by the Great War. Returning briefly to that text will allow us to see this clearly.

In "Thoughts for the Times," the analysis of disillusionment proceeds as an unmasking of the illusions that give rise to it. In essence, these illusions are errors in judgment concerning the moral stature of the human being in culture. Accordingly, Freud briefly formulates a theory of culture in order to portray the reality which these illusions falsify. In "Thoughts for the Times," this theory is itself introduced as a response to a question about the origins of morality in the individual. The way in which "we imagine the process by which an individual rises to a comparatively high plane of morality," Freud writes, must neither presuppose morality as naturally given, nor project the eradication of evil into some purportedly fully ethical and developed future.[120] For Freud, to speak of morality in the midst of war is to demand a theory of culture that is no longer surprised by the emergence of evil. Freud seeks to understand morality as a developmental achievement while at the same time keeping in mind the insistent reality of war.

According to Freud, the illusions that the Great War had come to discredit were rooted in an overestimation of our "susceptibility" to the ethical demands of culture. The widespread disillusionment the war engendered was the result of a wishful misunderstanding in and through which "we are misled into regarding men as 'better' than they actually are." Contrary to the appearances that, understandably, fuel our illusory self-regard, Freud insists that it may happen that a person subjected to the influence of cultural requirements "will choose to *behave* well in the cultural sense of the phrase, although no ennoblement of instinct, no *transformation* of egoistic into altruistic inclinations, has taken place in him." The illusion of human goodness, then, is sustained by an exaggeration of the admittedly favorable implications of our susceptibility to culture, as well as by a failure to distinguish between behavior and motivation, between *"external compulsion"* and internal "transformation." War disillusions us because it makes it difficult to exaggerate our susceptibility to culture, and because it reveals that what we had self-confidently taken as transformation is in reality nothing more than the result of compulsion (first emphasis added).[121]

This distinction between the merely cosmetic claims of external compulsion and the truly cultural work of internal transformation is, of course, at the heart of Freud's distinction between hypnosis and psychoanalysis. In *An Autobiographical Study,* Freud describes his initial enthusiasm regarding the magic of hypnosis:

> [T]here was something positively seductive in working with hypnotism. For the first time there was a sense of having overcome one's helplessness; and it was highly flattering to enjoy the reputation of being a miracle-worker.[122]

Yet this illusory love affair with omnipotence, as we know, was soon to give way to disillusionment. It is worth recalling that, as early as 1904, Freud tells us he gave up the suggestive technique because he "despaired of making suggestion powerful and enduring enough to effect permanent cures." As if helplessly watching the inevitable waning of his own miraculous powers, he time and again "saw the suggestions which had been applied crumble away again; after which the disease or some substitute for it was back once more."[123] He learned that the behavioral changes he had initially assumed as evidence of transformation were nothing more than the result of an ultimately ill-fated compulsion.

This sobering experience of Freud's permits a crucial insight into the attitude he was to take toward the "crumbling away" of culture he was to witness during the Great War. The essential point here to be grasped is that the critique and, ultimately, the rejection of hypnotic suggestion that lie at the origins of psychoanalysis prefigure and inspire Freud's subsequent critique of the precariousness of a culture rooted in illusion. That which Freud posits as "disease" at the level of the individual is precisely what he posits as war at the level of culture. The observation that, for Freud, the achievements of a culture rooted in illusion are as cosmetic as those of a hypnotist amounts to the statement that Freud's critique of culture mirrors his critique of hypnosis. In this vein, Freud's proposal, in "Thoughts for the Times," to construct an alternative attitude to death cannot help but appear as an invitation *to grasp the emerging logic of psychoanalysis as the logic of an alternative constitution of human beings as cultural beings—of a new culture.*

Freud's articulation of the clinical and cultural dimensions of his work is best approached in terms of the central role he accorded to the power of the hypnotic in the constitution of society. This articulation is to be found in Freud's *Group Psychology and the Analysis of the Ego.* It is to that text, then, that I will now turn by way of conclusion to this chapter.

Freud narrates the episode about his "muffled hostility" to the "tyranny of suggestion" in chapter IV of *Group Psychology.* "Later on," he adds, "my resistance took the direction of protesting against the view that suggestion, which explained everything, was itself to be exempt from explanation." Freud's protest targets the "statement that suggestion (or more correctly suggestibility) is actually an irreducible, primitive phenomenon, a fundamental fact in the mental life of man." "Such," he tells us, "was the opinion of Bernheim, of whose astonishing arts I was a witness in the year of 1889."[124] As we have seen, Freud's resistance to the tyranny of suggestion resulted in an investigation of "the question of the nature and origin of one's authority in suggestive treatment."[125] This investigation, in turn, yielded the central concept of transference, and with it, Freud's insistence that one's credulous attachment to the authority of previous loves is, rather than an irreducible or fundamental fact, a predicament *in principle* resolvable in and through a retroactive reconstitution of the past.

Thirty years later, in 1921, engaged in the composition of *Group Psychology*, Freud once again finds himself in the position of a witness who must resort to protest. This time Freud's resistance targets the "authorities on sociology and group psychology," authorities who, in Freud's view, offer nothing more than the "magic word 'suggestion'" as an explanation of the phenomena of group psychology.[126] Accordingly, Freud announces that, now in the sphere of group psychology, he is once more to approach "the riddle of suggestion after having kept away from it for some thirty years."[127]

Chapter IV of *Group Psychology* is entitled "Suggestion and Libido." In it, Freud revisits the onset of psychoanalysis. Once again, psychoanalysis appears in the wake of Freud's abandonment of hypnosis. Once again, psychoanalysis arises as the field in and through which transference and resistance—though in the guise of suggestions and countersuggestions—make a simultaneous appearance. In this retroactive resignification, however, the abandonment of hypnosis issues in a theorization not of the individual but of society. Or rather, as Freud puts it in the opening sentence of *Group Psychology*, it issues in the claim that "the contrast between individual psychology and social or group psychology, which at a first glance may seem to be full of significance, loses a great deal of its sharpness when it is examined more closely."[128] Freud's movement away from the authorities on sociology and group psychology is thus intended to yield a reconceptualization of the constitution of the social, of intersubjectivity. In place of the concept of suggestion, Freud introduces "the concept of *libido* for the purpose of throwing light upon group psychology" (emphasis in original).[129] In so doing, Freud claims sexuality as that which lies at the foundation of the social.

According to Freud, "the essence of a group lies in the libidinal ties existing in it."[130] These ties are of two kinds: those of the members of a group with each other and those of each of these members with their leader. Of these two kinds of ties, however, Freud tells us that "the tie with the leader seems . . . to be a more ruling factor than the other, which holds between the members of the group."[131] The horizontal connections between the members of a group grow on the soil of the shared vertical connection with their leader.[132] As a rule, Freud writes, "the mutual ties between the members of the group disappear . . . at the same time as the tie with their leader."[133] It is on the basis of this claim about the fundamental importance of the moment of leadership in the processes constitutive of groups that Freud then speaks of the hypnotic foundations of group formation. "The hypnotic relation," he tells us,

> is (if the expression is permissible) a group formation with two members. *Hypnosis is not a good object for comparison with a group formation, because it is truer to say that it is identical with it.* Out of the complicated fabric of the group it isolates one element for us—the behaviour of the individual to the leader.[134] (emphasis added)

What interests me here is neither Freud's complex substantiation of the claim that group relations are libidinal relations, nor his further specification of the dynamics of these relations in terms of the ties among members, on the one hand, and between each of these members and their leader, on the other. What interests me, rather, is the crucial observation that Freud's movement from "suggestion" to "libido" is not merely terminological. On the contrary, the shift from the concept of suggestion to that of libido in regard to the theorization of social relations places Freud's understanding of society in a context that, in a manner analogous to that of his therapeutic movement from hypnosis to psychoanalysis, raises the question of the possibility of a dissolution of unquestioned, hypnotic authority. Freud's critique of the "authorities on sociology and group psychology" thus presents itself as a critique of a society constituted as a subtly textured network of suggestions. By way of a conceptual shift as breathtaking as it is momentous, Freud's critical analysis of the "magical" yet ill-fated therapeutic power of the hypnotist aspires to become nothing less than a critical analysis of the roots of *political* authority.[135]

The common root shared by hypnosis and group formation is to be found in what Freud specifies as the primal situation of infantile helplessness. At issue, for Freud, is *the premature birth of the human infant*, the "biological factor" accounting for

> the long period of time during which the young of the human species is in a condition of *helplessness and dependence*. Its intra-uterine existence seems to be short in comparison with that of most animals, and it is sent into the world in a less finished state. . . . [T]he dangers of the external world have a greater importance for it, *so that the value of the object which can alone protect it against them and take the place of its former intra-uterine life is enormously enhanced.* The biological factor, then, establishes the earliest situations of danger and creates the need to be loved which will accompany the child through the rest of its life.[136] (emphasis added)

"There is much more continuity," Freud tells us, "between intra-uterine life and earliest infancy than the impressive caesura of the act of birth would have us believe. What happens is that the child's biological situation as a foetus is replaced for it by a psychical object-relation to its mother."[137] This imaginary unity of infant and caretaker in the infant's precarious psychical universe is in fact a fundamental component of what Freud calls the *pleasure principle*. On the one hand, the prematurity of the human infant is destined to produce a psychical situation wherein the absence of the infant's needed object presents itself, for the infant, as "a *growing tension due to need*, against which it is helpless" (emphasis in original).[138] But, on the other, once the infant learns by experience that an external, perceptible object can put an end to its distress, the content of that which produces its distress is displaced from the condition of need "on to the condition which determined that situation, viz., the loss of object."[139] Thus, since the infant is "not equipped"[140] to help itself meet the exigencies making demands upon it, it can deal with the absence of its object only at the level of hallucination. The wished-for presence, Freud tells us, is "simply presented in a hallucinatory manner, just as it still happens to-day with our dream-thoughts every night."[141] Under the dominance of the pleasure principle, then, the human subject comes to equate the presence of its objects with its own life, as much as their absence with the dreaded, foreclosed (im)possibility of its own death.

The biologically determined continuity between intrauterine life and life itself frames the human subject in an existential situation wherein it is, as it were, constantly refusing to be born. For Freud, the subject repeatedly refuses to learn from the experiences of loss which, as Hegel would put it, should make it "aware that the object has its own independence."[142]

At the same time, Freud himself tells us that "it was only the non-occurrence of the expected satisfaction, the disappointment experienced, that led to the abandonment of this attempt at satisfaction by means of hallucination."[143] "[I]t is evident," Freud writes in his discussion of the origins of intellectual judgment in "Negation," "that a precondition for the setting up of reality-testing is that objects shall have been lost which once brought real satisfaction."[144] Yet, as Freud says of the protracted replacement of the pleasure principle by the reality principle, this *belated* effort to be born "is not in fact accomplished all at once; nor does it take place simultaneously all along the line."[145] The experience of loss plunges the human subject not into the reality it so steadfastly refuses, but rather into a peculiar dividedness wherein it (co)exists at two temporal moments simultaneously, forever between past and future, in a present that, as it were, is irremediably *untimely*.

"Suggestibility," as Freud is later to say of the superego itself, is in fact the persistent residue of infantile helplessness in the human subject.[146] "[W]hen a hypnotist gives the command to sleep," Freud tells us, "he is putting himself in the place of the subject's parents."[147] As much as that of the hypnotist's, then, the compelling power of the group leader is a re-edition of the archaic, omnipotent power of parental figures over their children. The power constitutive of the social is grounded in the prematurity of the human infant. For Freud, the roots of unquestioned authority are to be found in the unquestioned and unquestionable power of parental authority. Thus, the seductiveness of hypnosis captures not only he who, like Freud, finds himself in the flattering position of a no longer helpless miracle worker; it also simultaneously fascinates he who, like the hypnotized subject or the group-member, finds his helplessness alleviated in and through the reassuring presence of a miraculously omnipotent healer. The illusion of a powerful immortality that complements us permits us some respite from the helplessness of our vulnerable mortal condition. It is this helplessness that Freud seeks to work through or (re)cognize when he abandons hypnosis. Similarly, it is the unquestioned authority rooted in such helplessness that he seeks to challenge when he cajoles his analysands to encounter their transference—as much as when he refuses the magical concept of suggestion offered by the "authorities on group psychology."

By way of the helplessness of the human infant, Freud's opening investigations of the dynamics of hysterical phenomena in the "Preliminary Communication" of 1893 finally emerge as a theory of human nature. According to Freud, the prematurity of the human infant, along with the long period of dependence that the human child must traverse, is a fundamental component of a universally and distinctively human predisposition to neurosis.[148] "Becoming neurotic," Freud writes, is a uniquely "human privilege."[149] In fact, Freud relentlessly insists that "a healthy person, too, is virtually a neurotic."[150] At issue here is Freud's observation that the birth of a human infant initiates not only life itself, but simultaneously the operation of an intractable tendency running "counter to the movement of life."[151] For Freud, the human subject as such never fully manages to be born. Its subsequent, belated efforts to enter the field of temporality are fated to articulate themselves in the untimeliness of the Nachträglichkeit (retroactivity).[152]

Precisely because irremediably suspended at a crossroads between the claims of the dead and those of the living, Freud grasps the human subject as the field of a life-and-death struggle, the perennial twilight constitutive of its *interminable* journey to "real life." In this regard, the illusions Freud seeks to unmask are ill-fated contrivances that, in seeking an imaginary fullness, remove the subject from the struggle that forms the substance of its mortal life. The peculiarly human *right* Freud so insistently defends against the insidious intrusions of the hypnotic is none other than a subject's right to seek the fulfillment of its "first duty" to endure life—to find, as it were, its *own* path to death through the transience of life.

Thus, when mediated in and through Freud's analysis of the dynamics of the social in *Group Psychology*, the critique of illusion enunciated in "Thoughts for the Times" is simultaneously posed as a critique of unquestioned political authority. For Freud, illusions lie at the heart of earthly, temporal power. Once again, then, we reach the observation that the alternative attitude to death proposed in "Thoughts for the Times" is best grasped as a claim for the possibility of an alternative organization of the life and work of culture.

In *The Future of an Illusion*, Freud explicitly proposes such a possibility: he formulates the failure of hypnosis as a gigantic failure on the part of Western culture—a failure he witnessed in and through the Great War. On the one hand, as we shall see in the following chapter, *The Future of an Illusion* articulates the juncture of illusion and domination that Freud discerns at the heart of "all present-day cultures."[153] On the other, as we shall see in the concluding chapter, it propels Freud to explore the degree to which the retroactive mode of action he himself deployed therapeutically may itself be deployed at the level of culture. In that way, the "fateful question" Freud poses as he concludes *Civilization and Its Discontents* (re)finds its deepest and most ambitious of meanings.

NOTES

1. Sigmund Freud, *On the History of the Psycho-Analytic Movement*, in vol. 14 of *The Standard Edition of the Complete Psychological Works of Sigmund Freud*, ed. and trans. James Strachey et al. (London: Hogarth, 1953–1974), 16.

2. Sigmund Freud, *Introductory Lectures on Psycho-Analysis*, in vol. 16 of *The Standard Edition*, ed. and trans. James Strachey et al., 278.

3. Consider, for example, Philip Rieff's observation that "It is not so paradoxical as it at first appears that psychoanalysis encourages its subjects to live with a reduced burden of memory, closer to the surface of life, where tensions cannot take root and feed off the accumulated energies of the past. Though Freud is commonly thought to have measured neurosis against the ideal of an unimpaired sexual efficiency, it would be more accurate to say that he measured it against an ideal contemporaneity." Philip Rieff, *Freud: The Mind of the Moralist* (New York: Viking, 1959), 44. See also Herbert Marcuse, *Eros and Civilization: A Philosophical Inquiry into Freud* (Boston: Beacon, 1955), 18–19; Michael S. Roth, *Psycho-Analysis as History: Negation and Freedom in Freud* (Ithaca, N.Y.: Cornell University Press, 1987); and Steven E. Goldberg, *Two Patterns of Rationality in Freud's Writings* (Tuscaloosa: University of Alabama Press, 1988).

4. Freud, *Introductory Lectures*, 462.

5. Sigmund Freud, "'Civilized' Sexual Morality and Modern Nervous Illness," in vol. 9 of *The Standard Edition*, ed. and trans. James Strachey et al., 185.

6. Sigmund Freud and Josef Breuer, "On the Psychical Mechanism of Hysterical Phenomena: Preliminary Communication," in *Studies on Hysteria*, in vol. 2 of *The Standard Edition*, ed. and trans. James Strachey et al., 3.

7. Freud and Breuer, "Preliminary Communication," 6. For Breuer's description of the "chance observation" in question, see Freud and Breuer, *Studies on Hysteria*, 34. See also Sigmund Freud, *Five Lectures on Psycho-Analysis*, in vol. 11 of *The Standard Edition*, ed. and trans. James Strachey et al., 13–14.

8. Freud and Breuer, "Preliminary Communication," 7.

9. Freud and Breuer, "Preliminary Communication," 6.

10. For a useful illustration, see Freud, *Five Lectures*, 16–17.

11. Freud and Breuer, "Preliminary Communication," 8.

12. Laplanche and Pontalis note that "The neologism *'abreagieren'* seems to have been coined by Freud and Breuer from the verb *reagieren* in its transitive use and the prefix *ab–*, which has several meanings, particularly distance in time, the fact of separation, diminishment, suppression, etc." Jean Laplanche and Jean-Bertrand Pontalis, *The Language of Psycho-Analysis*, trans. Donald Nicholson-Smith (New York: Hogarth, 1973), 2.

13. Freud and Breuer, "Preliminary Communication," 10.

14. Freud and Breuer, "Preliminary Communication," 8 and 10–11.

15. Freud and Breuer, "Preliminary Communication," 9.

16. Laplanche and Pontalis, *Language of Psycho-Analysis*, 1.

17. Freud and Breuer, "Preliminary Communication," 11.

18. Freud and Breuer, "Preliminary Communication," 11.

19. Freud and Breuer, "Preliminary Communication," 9.

20. Freud and Breuer, "Preliminary Communication," 12.

21. Freud and Breuer, "Preliminary Communication," 12.

22. See Sigmund Freud, "A Note on the Unconscious in Psycho-Analysis," in vol. 12 of *The Standard Edition*, ed. and trans. James Strachey et al., 261.

23. Freud and Breuer, "Preliminary Communication," 13.

24. Freud and Breuer, "Preliminary Communication," 17.

25. Freud and Breuer, "Preliminary Communication," 17.

26. Sigmund Freud, *An Autobiographical Study*, in vol. 20 of *The Standard Edition*, ed. and trans. James Strachey et al., 30.

27. See Sigmund Freud, "The Psychotherapy of Hysteria," in Freud and Breuer, *Studies on Hysteria*, 285.

28. Freud, *On the History*, 11. See also Freud, *Autobiographical Study*, 22–23; and Freud, *Five Lectures*, 21–22. A brief and informative discussion of Freud's transition can be found in Laplanche and Pontalis, *Language of Psycho-Analysis*, 2 and 108.

29. Laplanche and Pontalis, *Language of Psycho-Analysis*, 104.

30. Freud, *Autobiographical Study*, 29.

31. Freud, "The Psychotherapy of Hysteria," 285.

32. Freud, *On the History*, 11.

33. Freud, *Five Lectures*, 22.

34. Freud, *Five Lectures*, 24.

35. Freud, *Five Lectures*, 24.

36. Freud, *Autobiographical Study*, 29.

37. Freud, *Five Lectures*, 24.

38. Sigmund Freud, "Repression," in vol. 14 of *The Standard Edition*, ed. and trans. James Strachey et al., 146.

39. Sigmund Freud, "Remembering, Repeating and Working-Through (Further Recommendations on the Technique of Psycho-Analysis, II)," in vol. 12 of *The Standard Edition*, ed. and trans. James Strachey et al., 152.

40. Freud, *Five Lectures*, 27.

41. Freud, *Introductory Lectures*, 278.

42. Freud, *Five Lectures*, 27.

43. Freud, *Introductory Lectures*, 433; see also 454.

44. Freud, *Autobiographical Study*, 30.

45. "According to Janet's view," Freud writes, "a hysterical woman was a wretched creature who, on account of a constitutional weakness, was unable to hold her mental acts together, and it was for that reason that she fell a victim to a splitting of her mind and to a restriction of the field of her consciousness. The outcome of psycho-analytic investigations, on the other hand, showed that these phenomena were the result of dynamic factors—of mental conflict and of repression." Freud, *Autobiographical Study*, 30–31. Elsewhere Freud insists that "[w]e do not derive the psychical splitting from an innate incapacity for synthesis on the part of the mental apparatus; we explain it dynamically, from the conflict of opposing mental forces and recognize it as the outcome of an active struggling on the part of the two psychical groupings against each other." Freud, *Five Lectures*, 25–26. See also Sigmund Freud, "A Short Account of Psycho-Analysis," in vol. 19 of *The Standard Edition*, ed. and trans. James Strachey et al., 193 and 196. Needless to say, Freud came to regard Breuer's 'hypnoid state' theory as itself "physiological." See the passage quoted above, note 28; and Freud, *Autobiographical Study*, 23.

46. "[O]n the one hand," Freud writes, "psycho-analysis has narrowed the region subject to the physiological point of view and on the other hand has brought a large section of pathology into the sphere of psychology." Sigmund Freud, "The Claims of Psycho-Analysis to Scientific Interest," in vol. 13 of *The Standard Edition*, ed. and trans. James Strachey et al., 166.

47. Freud, *Introductory Lectures*, 273.

48. Freud, *Introductory Lectures*, 275.

49. Freud, *Introductory Lectures*, 275.

50. Freud, *Introductory Lectures*, 275–76. In the same passage, speaking of the tempting "simple determinant" view, Freud writes: "Neurosis could then be equated with a traumatic illness and would come about owing to inability to deal with an experience whose affective colouring was excessively powerful. And this indeed was actually the first formula in which (in 1893 and 1895) Breuer and I accounted theoretically for our new observations."

51. Freud, *Introductory Lectures*, 359–60.

52. Freud, *Introductory Lectures*, 365.

53. Freud, *Introductory Lectures*, 358–61.

54. In "Creative Writers and Day-Dreaming," speaking of daydreams, Freud writes: "The relation of a phantasy to time is in general very important. We may say that it hovers, as it were, between three times—the three moments of time

which our ideation involves. Mental work is linked to some current impression, some provoking occasion in the present which has been able to arouse one of the subject's major wishes. From there it harks back to a memory of an earlier experience (usually an infantile one) in which this wish was fulfilled; and it now creates a situation relating to the future which represents a fulfillment of the wish. What it thus creates is a day-dream or phantasy, which carries about it traces of its origin from the occasion which provoked it and from the memory. *Thus past, present and future are strung together, as it were, on the thread of the wish that runs through them*" (emphasis added). Sigmund Freud, "Creative Writers and Day-Dreaming," in vol. 9 of *The Standard Edition*, ed. and trans. James Strachey et al., 147–48.

55. See Jacques Lacan, *The Seminar of Jacques Lacan: Book I, Freud's Papers on Technique, 1953–1954*, trans. John Forrester, ed. Jacques-Alain Miller (New York: Norton, 1988), 158.

56. Laplanche and Pontalis, *Language of Psycho-Analysis*, 112. The concept of retroactivity is present, albeit in rudimentary form, in the "Preliminary Communication" itself: "An attack will occur spontaneously, just as memories do in normal people; it is, however, possible to provoke one, just as any memory can be aroused in accordance with the laws of association. It can be provoked either by stimulation of a hysterogenic zone or by *a new experience which sets it going owing to a similarity with the pathogenic experience*" (emphasis added). Freud and Breuer, "Preliminary Communication," 16.

57. Madeleine Baranger, Willy Baranger, and Jorge Mario Mom, "The Infantile Psychic Trauma from Us to Freud: Pure Trauma, Retroactivity and Reconstruction," *International Journal of Psychoanalysis* 69 (1988): 115 and 116.

58. It is a matter of grasping the same phenomenon from different, complementary points of view. The—temporally construed—resignifying recovery of lost memories is simultaneously the resolution, by way of judgment, of the—spatially construed—dynamic conflict of opposing mental forces or layers of the personality. Thus, in "Remembering, Repeating and Working-Through," Freud tells us that the aim of the psychoanalytic procedure remains the same throughout: "*Descriptively* speaking, it is to fill in gaps in memory; *dynamically* speaking, it is to overcome resistances due to repression" (emphases added). Freud, "Remembering," 147–48.

59. Baranger et al., "The Infantile Psychic Trauma," 127. In 1925, speaking of the dynamic account of conflict at the root of his concept of repression, Freud writes: "[The] mutually opposing forces were described to begin with as the sexual instincts and the ego instincts. A later theoretical development changed them into Eros and the instinct of death or destruction." Sigmund Freud, "The Resistances to Psycho-Analysis," in vol. 19 of *The Standard Edition*, ed. and trans. James Strachey et al., 218.

60. Sigmund Freud, "On Psychotherapy," in vol. 7 of *The Standard Edition*, ed. and trans. James Strachey et al., 261.

61. Freud, *Autobiographical Study*, 17.

62. Freud, *Autobiographical Study*, 17.

63. Lacan, *Seminar*, 56.

64. Sigmund Freud, *Group Psychology and the Analysis of the Ego*, in vol. 18 of *The Standard Edition*, ed. and trans. James Strachey et al., 89.

65. Freud, "On Psychotherapy," 261.

66. Freud, *Introductory Lectures*, 450.

67. Jean Hyppolite writes: "If the psychoanalyst believes he can read the history of his patient by his symptoms and informs him of his discovery, he will fail. In fact, his patient would not recognize this truth, since it would be read to him, so to speak, without his reading it within himself. And by this very token, this truth would be an error." Jean Hyppolite, "Hegel's Phenomenology and Psychoanalysis," in *New Studies in Hegel's Philosophy*, ed. Warren E. Steinkraus (New York: Holt, Rinehart and Winston, 1971), 61.

68. Freud, *Introductory Lectures*, 451.

69. See Jean Paul Richter, ed. and comp., *The Literary Works of Leonardo da Vinci* (New York: Phaidon, 1970), 89 and 96.

70. Freud, "On Psychotherapy," 260–61.

71. Freud, *Introductory Lectures*, 450.

72. Freud, *Introductory Lectures*, 450–51.

73. For Freud's final image of the psychoanalyst as archaeologist rather than sculptor, see Sigmund Freud, "Constructions in Analysis," in vol. 23 of *The Standard Edition*, ed. and trans. James Strachey et al., 255–69. For an informative discussion of the role of "archaeology" in Freud's life and work, see Carl E. Schorske, "The Psychoarchaeology of Civilizations," in *The Cambridge Companion to Freud*, ed. Jerome Neu (Cambridge, UK: Cambridge University Press, 1991), 8–24. See also Carl E. Schorske, "Freud's Egyptian Dig," *New York Review of Books*, 27 May 1993, 35–40.

74. Freud, *Introductory Lectures*, 451.

75. Freud, "Remembering," 147.

76. Lacan, *Seminar*, 56 and 29.

77. G. W. F. Hegel, *Phenomenology of Spirit*, trans. A. V. Miller (New York: Oxford University Press, 1977), 47.

78. Hegel, *Phenomenology of Spirit*, 51.

79. Freud, "On Psychotherapy," 263–64.

80. Freud, *Introductory Lectures*, 450.

81. Sigmund Freud, "The Dynamics of Transference," in vol. 12 of *The Standard Edition*, ed. and trans. James Strachey et al., 106.

82. Sigmund Freud, "Negation," in vol. 19 of *The Standard Edition*, ed. and trans. James Strachey et al., 235.

83. Jean Hyppolite, "A Spoken Commentary on Freud's *Verneinung*," in Lacan, *Seminar*, 291.

84. Freud, "Negation," 235–36.

85. Freud, "Remembering," 155. "One must allow the patient," Freud continues, "time to become more conversant with this resistance with which he has now become acquainted, to *work through* it, to overcome it. . . ." (emphasis in original).

86. Sigmund Freud, "On Beginning the Treatment (Further Recommendations on the Technique of Psycho-Analysis, I)," in vol. 12 of *The Standard Edition*, ed. and trans. James Strachey et al., 142.

87. Freud, "On Beginning," 141. Regarding the intellectualist view of analysis, Freud goes on to say: "We thought it a special piece of good luck if we were able to obtain information about the forgotten childhood trauma from other

sources—for instance, from parents or nurses or the seducer himself—as in some cases it was possible to do; and we hastened to convey the information and the proofs of its correctness to the patient, in the certain expectation of thus bringing the neurosis and the treatment to a rapid end. It was a severe disappointment when the expected success was not forthcoming. How could it be that the patient, who now knew about his traumatic experience, nevertheless still behaved *as if he knew no more about it than before?"* (emphasis added).

88. Freud, "On Beginning," 142. In the same passage, Freud offers the following example: "In one particular case the mother of a hysterical girl had confided to me the homosexual experience which had greatly contributed to the fixation of the girl's attacks. The mother had herself surprised the scene; but the patient had completely forgotten it, though it had occurred when she was already approaching puberty. I was now able to make a most instructive observation. Every time I repeated her mother's story to the girl she reacted with a hysterical attack, and after this she forgot the story once more. There is no doubt that the patient was expressing *a violent resistance against the knowledge that was being forced upon her.* Finally, she simulated feeble-mindedness and a complete loss of memory in order to protect herself against what I had told her" (141–42; emphasis added).

89. Freud, "On Beginning," 141 and 142.

90. Freud, "On Beginning," 142.

91. Freud, "On Beginning," 142.

92. Laplanche and Pontalis, *Language of Psycho-Analysis,* 488.

93. If the wish for cure were in and of itself enough to get rid of the illness, there would not, of course, be an illness to begin with.

94. Freud, "On Beginning," 143.

95. Freud, *Introductory Lectures,* 445.

96. Freud, "On Psychotherapy," 260.

97. Freud, *Introductory Lectures,* 446.

98. Freud, *Introductory Lectures,* 448.

99. "[I]f a knife does not cut," Freud writes, "it cannot be used for healing either." Freud, *Introductory Lectures,* 463.

100. Freud, "Remembering," 155–56.

101. Freud, "Dynamics of Transference," 106.

102. Sigmund Freud, *An Outline of Psycho-Analysis,* in vol. 23 of *The Standard Edition,* ed. and trans. James Strachey et al., 175.

103. Freud, *Introductory Lectures,* 445–46.

104. Freud, *Introductory Lectures,* 451.

105. Freud, *Introductory Lectures,* 364. Elsewhere Freud writes: "In the majority of cases, indeed, a very early phase of life is chosen for the purpose—a period of their childhood or even, laughable as this may sound, of their existence as an infant at the breast." Freud, *Introductory Lectures,* 274.

106. Freud, "Repression," 148.

107. Sigmund Freud, *Inhibitions, Symptoms and Anxiety,* in vol. 20 of *The Standard Edition,* ed. and trans. James Strachey et al., 159–60.

108. Freud, *Introductory Lectures,* 455.

109. Freud, *Introductory Lectures*, 453.

110. See Sigmund Freud, "Formulations on the Two Principles of Mental Functioning," in vol. 12 of *The Standard Edition*, ed. and trans. James Strachey et al., 213–26. Freud speaks of an easier "imaginary satisfaction" occurring "in place of real satisfaction, which calls for effort and postponement" (223).

111. Freud, *Introductory Lectures*, 454.

112. Freud, *Introductory Lectures*, 453. Needless to say, it is this analysis of the transference that finally differentiates Freud's technique from the cathartic method.

113. Freud, "Dynamics of Transference," 108.

114. Jacques Lacan, *The Four Fundamental Concepts of Psycho-Analysis*, ed. Jacques-Alain Miller, trans. Alan Sheridan (New York: Norton, 1981), 133.

115. J.-B. Pontalis, "On Psychic Pain," in *Frontiers in Psychoanalysis: Between the Dream and Psychic Pain*, trans. Catherine Cullen and Philip Cullen (London: Hogarth, 1981), 205.

116. Freud, "Remembering," 154.

117. "Psychoanalysis," John Forrester writes, "is a pure culture of t[he] life instinct." John Forrester, *The Seductions of Psychoanalysis: Freud, Lacan, Derrida* (Cambridge, UK: Cambridge University Press, 1990), 7.

118. Freud, *Introductory Lectures*, 282.

119. See chapter 1.

120. Sigmund Freud, "Thoughts for the Times on War and Death," in vol. 14 of *The Standard Edition*, ed. and trans. James Strachey et al., 281.

121. Freud, "Thoughts for the Times," 283–84.

122. Freud, *Autobiographical Study*, 17.

123. Freud, "On Psychotherapy," 261.

124. Freud, *Group Psychology*, 89.

125. Freud, *Introductory Lectures*, 450.

126. Freud, *Group Psychology*, 88.

127. Freud, *Group Psychology*, 89–90.

128. Freud, *Group Psychology*, 69.

129. Freud, *Group Psychology*, 90.

130. Freud, *Group Psychology*, 95–96.

131. Freud, *Group Psychology*, 100.

132. See Freud, *Group Psychology*, passim, but especially chapter V.

133. Freud, *Group Psychology*, 97. In the same passage, Freud tells the following story: "A short time ago there came into my hands an English novel of Catholic origin, recommended by the Bishop of London, with the title *When It Was Dark*. It gave a clever and, as it seems to me, a convincing picture of such a possibility [i.e., the dissolution of a religious group] and its consequences. The novel, which is supposed to relate to the present day, tells how a conspiracy of enemies of the person of Christ and of the Christian faith succeed in arranging for a sepulchre to be discovered in Jerusalem. In this sepulchre is an inscription, in which Joseph of Arimathea confesses that for reasons of piety he secretly removed the body of Christ from its grave on the third day after its entombment and buried it in this spot. The resurrection of Christ and his divine nature are by this means disproved, and the

result of this archaeological discovery is *a convulsion in European civilization* and an extraordinary increase in all crimes and acts of violence, which only ceases when the forgers' plot has been revealed" (97–98; emphasis added).

134. Freud, *Group Psychology,* 115.

135. This aspiration is at the heart of Theodor Adorno's claim that "it is not an overstatement if we say that Freud, though he was hardly interested in the political phase of the problem, clearly foresaw the rise and nature of fascist mass movements in purely psychological categories." Theodor Adorno, "Freudian Theory and the Pattern of Fascist Propaganda," in *The Essential Frankfurt School Reader,* ed. Andrew Arato and Eike Gebhardt (New York: Continuum, 1982), 120. Of course, it is clear neither that Freud was "hardly interested" in the political, nor that his categories are "purely psychological" in any immediately self-evident sense. See, for example, Mikkel Borch-Jacobsen's deeply critical reading of *Group Psychology* in Mikkel Borch-Jacobsen, *The Freudian Subject,* trans. Catherine Porter (Stanford, Calif.: Stanford University Press, 1988), 137–239. Joel Kovel tells us that he "could never accept the limitation of psychoanalysis to the clinical realm, or its use as an ancilla to the social sciences, a way of getting at the 'unconscious factors' in the human situation. For the human situation itself had been called into question." Joel Kovel, *The Radical Spirit: Essays on Psychoanalysis and Society* (London: Free Association Press, 1988), 1.

136. Freud, *Inhibitions, Symptoms and Anxiety,* 154–55.

137. Freud, *Inhibitions, Symptoms and Anxiety,* 138.

138. Freud, *Inhibitions, Symptoms and Anxiety,* 137.

139. Freud, *Inhibitions, Symptoms and Anxiety,* 138.

140. Freud, *Inhibitions, Symptoms and Anxiety,* 146.

141. Freud, "Two Principles of Mental Functioning," 219.

142. Hegel, *Phenomenology,* 109.

143. Freud, "Two Principles of Mental Functioning," 219. Elsewhere, Freud writes: "And for however long it is fed at its mother's breast, it will always be left with a conviction after it has been weaned that its feeding was too short and too little." Freud, *Outline of Psycho-Analysis,* 189.

144. Freud, "Negation," 238.

145. Freud, "Two Principles of Mental Functioning," 222. "Since the later care of children is modelled on the care of infants," Freud writes elsewhere in the same text, "the dominance of the pleasure principle can really come to an end only when a child has achieved complete psychical detachment from its parents" (220).

146. Freud writes: "The long period of childhood, during which the growing human being lives in dependence on his parents, leaves behind it as a precipitate the formation in his ego of a special agency in which this parental influence is prolonged. It has received the name of *superego.* . . . This parental influence of course includes in its operation not only the personalities of the actual parents but also the family, racial and national traditions handed on through them, as well as the demands of the immediate social *milieu* which they represent. In the same way, the superego, in the course of an individual's development, receives contributions from later successors and substitutes of his parents, such as teachers and models in public life of admired social ideals" (emphases in original). Freud, *Outline of Psycho-Analysis,* 146.

147. Freud, *Group Psychology*, 127.

148. See Freud, *Inhibitions, Symptoms and Anxiety*, 154–56.

149. Sigmund Freud, *The Question of Lay Analysis*, in vol. 20 of *The Standard Edition*, ed. and trans. James Strachey et al., 211.

150. Freud, *Introductory Lectures*, 457. See also, for example, 358. In *The Question of Lay Analysis*, Freud notes "how neurotic our whole civilized life is, since ostensibly normal people do not behave very differently from neurotics." Freud, *The Question of Lay Analysis*, 207.

151. Freud, *Inhibitions, Symptoms and Anxiety*, 148.

152. I discuss this concept earlier in this chapter, in "From Hypnosis to Psychoanalysis." See also chapter 1, note 53, and accompanying text.

153. Sigmund Freud, *The Future of an Illusion*, in vol. 21 of *The Standard Edition*, ed. and trans. James Strachey et al., 12.

4

The Precarious Chances of Eros

You know that our therapeutic activities are not very far reaching. There are only a handful of us, and even by working very hard each one can devote himself in a year to only a small number of patients. Compared to the vast amount of neurotic misery there is in the world, and perhaps need not be, the quantity we can do away with is almost negligible.

—Sigmund Freud, "Lines of Advance in Psycho-Analytic Therapy"

THE HISTORICAL TASK OF PSYCHOANALYSIS

In the late spring of 1926, Theodor Reik, "a prominent non-medical member of the Vienna Psycho-Analytical Society," was charged "with a breach of an old Austrian law against 'quackery'—a law which made it illegal for a person without a medical degree to treat patients." The editors of *The Standard Edition* inform us that "Freud *at once intervened energetically*" (emphasis added).[1] His *The Question of Lay Analysis* was published in September 1926.

Freud's energetic intervention is rooted in his estimation of the profound stakes involved in the accusation against Reik. Following a history of widespread dismissal and derision, the requirement that psychoanalytic practitioners be medical doctors might be judged to contain a long-awaited recognition and authorization of the practice of psychoanalysis, at least as far as doctors are concerned. Freud tells us that interest in "*who* practices analysis" is far better than agreement that "*no one* should practise it." Yet, according to Freud, this apparent advance conceals a deeper draw-back: "[T]he demand that only doctors should analyze corresponds to a new and apparently more friendly attitude to analysis—if, that is, it can escape the suspicion of being after all only a slightly modified derivative of the earlier attitude" (emphases in original).[2] As *The Question of Lay Analysis* seeks definitively to establish, the demand that only doctors should analyze is in fact as anti-psychoanalytic as the prohibition of analysis. It denies psychoanalysis its status as an independent mode of investigation, a science in its own right, capable of defining its own domain and its own specific methodology for the investigation of that domain. For Freud, the submission of psychoanalysis to medicine, no matter how sympathetic, is in the end a tergiversation of psychoanalysis.

Another factor that contributes to Freud's profound estimation of the stakes at issue in the Reik case is Freud's insistence that, even if recognized as thoroughly autonomous and nonmedical, psychoanalysis is not only a therapeutic technique but also a cultural force[3]—a "movement," as he puts it in his *On the History of the Psycho-Analytic Movement* (1914). Accordingly, as he concludes his polemic on the problem of lay analysis, Freud raises the following question:

> Our civilization imposes an almost intolerable pressure on us and it calls for a corrective. Is it too fantastic to expect that psychoanalysis in spite of its difficulties may be destined to the task of preparing mankind for such a corrective?[4]

What could Freud have had in mind?

Just as, when he concludes *Civilization and Its Discontents*, Freud permits himself to "expect" that Eros might assert itself in the struggle with its "equally immortal adversary," so does he, in *The Question of Lay Analysis*, permit himself the "expectation" that psychoanalysis may be destined to play a pivotal role in the development of culture. The audacity of Freud's "fantastic" insinuation is truly remarkable: he ventures to link the destiny of the human species to the destiny of the discipline he brought into being. Thus, to ask for his understanding of the effort of self-assertion on the part of Eros is also to ask for his understanding of the position of psychoanalysis in regard to that effort. Freud's theory of culture diagnoses a particular historical situation in terms of which he understands the historical task of psychoanalysis.

I argued in chapter 1 that the question Freud leaves us with at the end of *Civilization and Its Discontents* is a question about the relation between war and death. Freud's theory of culture raises, as a matter of life and death, the possibility that we might, as a culture, learn to relate to death in some way other than that of war. In the second chapter, in addition to comparing Freud and Hegel, I interpreted Freud's analysis of the relation between war and death as a critique of the political thought of Thomas

Hobbes. My choice of Hobbes as the target of critique was not accidental. It followed C. B. Macpherson's insight that since Hobbes's thought is a paradigmatic statement of the political horizons of our culture, the critique of Hobbes is in fact a critique of those horizons.[5] This led me, in the third chapter, to investigate the mode of action that Freud claimed to have invented, a mode of action that, as distinct from hypnosis, he named "psychoanalysis." In that third chapter, a consideration of Freud's retroactive resignification of the onset of psychoanalysis—in *Group Psychology and the Analysis of the Ego*—allowed me to outline the conceptual movements whereby Freud's initial *therapeutic* protest against hypnosis transformed itself into Freud's subsequent *cultural* protest against a culture rooted in illusion. As regards the present chapter, the fundamental implication of that outline is that it places us in a position to grasp the emerging logic of psychoanalysis as the logic of a new culture.

In this chapter, then, I want to examine Freud's most audacious exploration of the possibility of a new culture—and of the role of psychoanalysis in it—as stated in *The Future of an Illusion* (1927). The essential claim I wish to make is that the logic of Freud's critique of culture leads to a recommendation for a humanization of the multifaceted spheres of authority. It is in *The Future of an Illusion* that the political content of the "fateful question" raised in *Civilization and Its Discontents* is most explicitly articulated.

To begin with, my argument shows that *The Future of an Illusion* frames the problem of culture as a fundamentally pedagogical problem, and that, in so doing, it presents itself as a reflection about the relation between politics and childhood. Yet for Freud, the pedagogical experiment of transformation envisioned in and through that reflection is by no means devoid of material—that is, economic—presuppositions. Accordingly, the consideration of these presuppositions leads him to an analysis of the dynamics whereby the psychical potentialities and vulnerabilities of the human infant, in the absence of such presuppositions, are deployed not pedagogically but oppressively, in the direction of the preservation of order rather than the cultivation of freedom. Thus, by the time *The Future of an Illusion* explicitly raises its central question—that of the relation between religion and culture—it does so in a context designed to articulate the helplessness of the human infant to the dynamics of political power. In this vein, I argue that Freud's intent is to seize the waning of religious belief in the modern world as a situation wherein, as it were, a *cultural* abandonment of hypnosis emerges as a concrete historical possibility. I conclude this chapter by connecting *The Future of an Illusion* to *Civilization and Its Discontents*, specifically by rendering the struggle between the religious and the irreligious in the former, not as one between religion and science, but rather as one between Death and Eros. As we shall see, this rendering is in fact a discussion of the political shapes of the new culture Freud permits himself to envision.

ECONOMICS AND PSYCHOLOGY

In the first chapter of *The Future of an Illusion*, Freud locates his speculations at the level of the "mental" as distinct from the "material."[6] His introductory intent is to shift the emphasis of discussion from the "economic field into the field of psychology."[7] His claim is that it is only on the basis of an adequate assessment of the "psychical inventory"[8] of civilization that we can hope to form an adequate judgment as to what may be expected or accomplished in the future. The shift from economics to psychology is a matter of defining the bounds of possibility.

Rather than give "way to the temptation to deliver an opinion on the probable future of our civilization," Freud tells us, he shall seek out a "small tract of territory" within which he shall circumscribe his reflection. This narrower region to be explored is the sphere of religion. To begin with, however, Freud sets out to determine the position of this small tract of territory in the "general scheme of things." This determination demands that he provide a brief description of culture as a whole.[9]

According to Freud, culture

> includes on the one hand all the knowledge and capacity that men have acquired in order to control the forces of nature and extract its wealth for the satisfaction of human needs, and, on the other hand, all the regulations necessary in order to adjust the relations of men to one another and especially the distribution of available wealth.[10]

These "two trends" of culture are not independent of one another, and Freud connects them in a threefold manner. First, "the mutual relations of men are profoundly influenced by the amount of instinctual satisfaction which the existing wealth makes possible." Second, "an individual man can himself come to function as wealth in relation to another one, in so far as the other person makes use of his capacity for work, or chooses him as a sexual object." And third, "every individual," Freud writes, "is virtually an enemy of civilization, though civilization is supposed to be an object of universal human interest."[11]

In this last regard, Freud repeatedly emphasizes the "remarkable" circumstance that "little as men are able to exist in isolation, they . . . nevertheless feel as a heavy burden the sacrifices which civilization expects of them in order to make a communal life possible." The paradox Freud has in mind is that the arrangements necessary for the production of wealth required to satisfy human needs wind up producing a dissatisfaction that in the end appears as a virtual hatred of civilization. Civilization inevitably produces a hostility that it then has to control. It "has to be defended against the individual, and its regulations, institutions and commands are directed to that task. They aim not only at effecting a certain distribution of wealth but at maintaining that distribution; indeed, they have to protect everything that contributes to the conquest of nature and the production of wealth against men's hostile impulses. Human creations are easily destroyed, and science and technology, which have built them up, can also be used for their annihilation."[12]

Freud then proceeds to consider the objection that these difficulties may be "not inherent in the nature of civilization itself but are determined by the imperfections of the cultural forms which have so far been developed."[13] These imperfections, he adds, are not "difficult to indicate."

> One would think that a re-ordering of human relations should be possible, which would remove the sources of dissatisfaction with civilization by renouncing coercion and the suppression of the instincts, so that, undisturbed by internal discord, men might devote themselves to the acquisition of wealth and its enjoyment.[14]

According to Freud, however, such a "golden age" cannot be realized. We must, he insists, face the "fact that there are present in all men destructive, and therefore anti-social and anti-cultural, trends and that in a great number of people these are strong enough to determine their behaviour in human society."[15]

For Freud, awareness of this "psychological fact" reframes the problem of civilization. Recognition of the individual's hostility to civilization shifts the emphasis of discussion "from the material to the mental" in that it forces us to abandon any perspective that holds that the "essence" of civilization "lies in controlling nature for the purpose of acquiring wealth and that the dangers which threaten it could be eliminated through a suitable distribution of that wealth among men." Rather, prefiguring the "fateful question" with which he will conclude *Civilization and Its Discontents,* Freud states that

> The *decisive question* is whether and to what extent it is possible to lessen the burden of the instinctual sacrifices imposed on men, to reconcile men to those which must necessarily remain and to provide a compensation for them.[16] (emphasis added)

This question fulfills a twofold purpose in the structure of Freud's reflection. On the one hand, it contains a recognition of the inevitability of frustration, regardless of the degree of material and organizational development that any particular culture might manage to reach. On the other, it permits Freud to begin to consider, now on the basis of a proposed minimization rather than an abolition of frustration, the possibilities truly available to human culture. The abandonment of the illusion of a golden age reopens the horizons of the future, horizons Freud understands as those of "reconciliation" and "compensation."

Freud grasps the implications of the "decisive question" he raises in political terms. Given the individual's hostility to civilization, he tells us, it is difficult to escape an "impression that civilization is something which was imposed on a resisting majority by a minority which understood how to obtain possession of the means to power and coercion."[17] Unabashedly, he proceeds, as Marx would put it, to divide "society into two parts, one of which is superior to society."[18] The passage is worth quoting at length:

> It is just as impossible to do without control of the mass by a minority as it is to dispense with coercion in the work of civilization. For masses are lazy and unintelligent; they have no love for instinctual renunciation, and they are not to be convinced by argument of its inevitability; and the individuals composing them support one another in giving free rein to their indiscipline. It is only through the influence of individuals who can set an example and whom masses recognize as their leaders that they can be induced to perform the work and undergo the renunciations on which the existence of civilization depends. All is well if these leaders are persons who possess superior insight into the necessities of life and who have risen to the height of mastering their instinctual wishes. But there is a danger that in order not to lose their influence they may give way to the mass more than it gives way to them, and it therefore seems necessary that they shall be independent of the mass by having means to power at their disposal. To put it briefly, there are two widespread human characteristics which are responsible for the fact that the regulations of civilization can only be maintained by a certain degree of coercion—namely, that men are not spontaneously fond of work and that arguments are of no avail against their passions.[19]

The "psychological fact" Freud claims to have unveiled in his movement from the material to the mental thus appears, politically, as the legitimation of an enlightened dictatorship of the superior and truly rational.

At this point Freud considers once again, in a move that at first seems unnecessarily repetitious, the objection that the situation he describes is a historical rather than an ontological predicament. His attitude to this objection, however, is now markedly different. The reason for Freud's change of attitude is highly instructive. Consider the following passage:

> It will be said that the characteristic of human masses depicted here, which is supposed to prove that coercion cannot be dispensed with in the work of civilization, is itself only the result of defects in the cultural regulations, owing to which men have become embittered, revengeful and inaccessible. New generations, who have been brought up in kindness and taught to have a

high opinion of reason, and who have experienced the benefits of civilization at an *early age*, will have a different attitude to it. They will feel it as a possession of their very own and will be ready for its sake to make the sacrifices as regards work and instinctual satisfaction that are necessary for its preservation. They will be able to do without coercion and will differ little from their leaders. If no culture has so far produced human masses of such a quality, it is because no culture has yet devised regulations which will influence men in this way, and in particular from *childhood* onwards.[20] (emphases added)

Although Freud goes on to tell us that such a possibility may be doubted and that its realization would presuppose the overcoming of great difficulties, he no longer dismisses it as yet another manifestation of the ill-fated wish for a golden age. On the contrary, Freud now explicitly insists that "[t]he experiment has not yet been made." Freud has changed his attitude toward the possibility of a new culture: *what differentiates the "experiment" he now has in mind from the ill-fated wish for a golden age is its psychoanalytically informed awareness of the profound weight of childhood experience.* "The grandeur of the plan and its importance for the future of human civilization," Freud writes, "cannot be disputed. It is *securely based* on the psychological discovery that man is equipped with the most varied instinctual dispositions, whose ultimate course is determined by the experiences of early childhood" (emphasis added).[21]

This appearance of the concept of childhood in Freud's reflection indicates that Freud's movement from economics to psychology is intended to pose the problem of culture as an essentially pedagogical rather than an exclusively material one. It is on the basis of a pedagogical transformation of the human being's remarkably hostile "attitude" to culture that Freud permits himself to envision a political horizon no longer bounded by a monopoly of the means of coercion on the part of an enlightened leadership. The "decisive question" Freud raises, as he himself puts it, is about "the limitations of man's capacity for education." The extent of these limitations—and not only the degree of technological and organizational development—is what requires investigation, even "experimentation." Accordingly, it is in terms of the expected results of such experimentation that Freud frames, ever so tentatively, the question of the possible: "Probably a certain percentage of mankind (owing to a pathological disposition or an excess of instinctual strength) will always remain asocial; but if it were feasible merely to reduce the majority that is hostile towards civilization to-day into a minority, a great deal would have been accomplished—perhaps all that *can* be accomplished" (emphasis in original).[22]

Freud's shift from the material to the mental, then, is not a shift from the alterable to the unalterable, from the realm of history to the realm of essence. Freud tells us that psychology, too, has a history, and that this history is the history of childhood. His distinction between the economic and the psychological presents itself as a distinction not between historicism and ahistoricism, but between different conceptions of the nature and the dynamics of culture.

The turning from the sphere of the material production of life to that of psychology neither does nor wishes to disregard the profound importance of the former. It is not a matter of seizing the 'subjective' at the expense of the 'objective.' At issue in Freud's distinction between the material and the mental, rather, is an effort to bring into relief the specific domain of psychoanalysis in the study of culture. The "remarkable" paradox Freud claims to discern in the core of culture permits him, first, to evoke that domain, and, second, to delimit the "small tract of territory" occupied by the sphere of religion within that domain. *The Future of an Illusion* is a reflection about the relation between religion—that is, "illusion"—and culture, and for Freud, this is but a way—albeit a central one—of talking about the relation between psychoanalysis and culture. This latter is the relation between politics and childhood, between the goals of culture and the psychical specificity of the human infant.

COMPULSION AND TRANSFORMATION

The recognition that every civilization rests on a compulsion to work and must therefore inevitably provoke opposition, then, carries with it the implication that civilization cannot be defined in solely economic terms—in other words, in terms of "wealth itself and the means of acquiring it and the arrangements for its distribution." Civilization must have constitutive features that transcend the sphere of the economic—on the one hand measures of coercion, and on the other "measures that are intended to reconcile men to [civilization] and to recompense them for their sacrifices." It is these latter measures that Freud calls the *"mental assets* of civilization" (emphasis added).[23]

The second chapter of *The Future of an Illusion* elaborates this concept of "mental wealth."[24] The purpose of this elaboration is to move us from psychology in general to religion in particular. Religion, Freud tells us, is the "most important item in the psychical inventory of a civilization."[25] Yet Freud once again postpones the problem of religion: before raising it explicitly, he returns to and complicates the relation between economics and psychology. It is only in and through such complication that he moves toward the "small tract of territory" to which he wishes to devote the rest of his reflection.

Freud begins his complication by defining his terminology. 'Frustration' is the "fact that an instinct cannot be satisfied." A 'prohibition' is "the regulation by which this frustration is established." And 'privation' is "the condition which is produced by the prohibition." Cultural prohibitions, then, establish frustrations that leave the participants in culture in a condition of privation to which they react with hostility.[26]

Not everyone, however, is subject to the same privations. Freud immediately distinguishes between "privations which affect everyone and privations which do not affect everyone but only groups, classes or even single individuals." Those that affect everyone are the earliest ones in the development of culture. According to Freud, the prohibitions that established them "began to detach man from his primordial animal condition."[27] For Freud, this earliest of detachments already involves a "psychological factor" that evidences the human being's susceptibility to both culture and historical development. Freud states unequivocally:

> It is not true that the human mind has undergone no development since the earliest times and that, in contrast to the advances of science and technology, it is the same to-day as it was at the beginning of history.[28]

The advances at the level of the mental involve the historical acculturation of the human psyche. "[E]xternal coercion," Freud writes, "gradually becomes internalized; for a special mental agency, man's superego, takes it over and includes it among its commandments. Every child presents this process of transformation to us; only by that means does it *become a moral and social being*." For Freud, this capacity of the psyche to receive culture deeply within itself is "a most precious cultural asset in the psychological field." Those in whom such a "strengthening of the superego" has taken place "are turned from being opponents of civilization into being its vehicles." Accordingly, "[t]he greater their number is in a cultural unit the more secure is its culture and the more it can dispense with external measures of coercion" (emphasis added).[29]

Freud poses the problem of the acculturation of the human being in terms of the developmental transformation of "elementary" human impulses or drives. This transformation is construed as a dialectic between two factors, one internal and the other external. Precisely as the inextricable convergence of both internal and external factors, culture cannot be adequately conceptualized by way of any simplistic distinction between inside and outside. The internal factor Freud has in mind is not only a nature over which culture imposes itself as if from the outside. Rather, it is also a capacity for sublimation; it is that about nature which makes culture possible. For Freud, this capacity for sublimation itself presupposes the presence in the human being of drives distinct from, yet as "elementary" as, those that are to be transformed. In "Thoughts for the Times on War and Death," for example, he tells us that the "admixture of *erotic* components" transforms "egoistic instincts" into "*social* ones." The elementary composition of the human being is neither entirely acultural nor entirely anticultural. Thus, as Freud puts it, culture avails itself of the "human need for love, taken in its widest sense" (emphases in original).[30]

To be sure, this internal factor is not in and of itself enough to transform the human being into a cultural being. Upbringing is the external factor, representing the "claims of our cultural environment." In "Thoughts for the Times," Freud tells us that

> Civilization has been attained through the renunciation of instinctual satis-
> faction, and it demands the same renunciation from each newcomer in turn.
> Throughout an individual's life there is a constant replacement of external by
> internal compulsion. The influences of civilization cause an ever-increasing
> transformation of egoistic trends into altruistic ones by an admixture of erotic
> elements.[31]

Like Freud's description of the transformation of the human infant into a moral and social being in *The Future of an Illusion*,[32] this passage places before us an ambiguity of crucial importance. On the one hand, Freud speaks as though culture were something external to the "admixture" at issue. The influences of culture "cause" this admixture as if from the outside. On the other hand, he insists in the same breath that culture is in fact nothing other than the very admixture it itself somehow causes. Thus, he simultaneously refers to culture both as "compulsion" and as "transformation." Of course, the ambiguity lies in that Freud grasps the "replacement of external by internal compulsion" as a process of "transformation." As we noted in chapter 2, then, Freud moves beyond Hobbes to the degree to which he grasps social relations not only as externally compulsive but also as internally constitutive of the human subject as such. Yet he simultaneously stops short of Hegel to the degree to which he refuses to grasp the relational constitution of the human subject as exhaustive of that subject's identity.

To attempt to resolve this ambiguity is to miss the central thrust of Freud's theory of culture. The observation that for Freud, the elementary composition of human beings is not entirely anticultural by no means intends to suggest that the Freudian dialectic of culture is in some sense unproblematic. The point, rather, is to grasp the crucial paradox that the unhappiness constitutive of the human subject is itself the result of acculturation. The discontents of culture evidence not only the human subject's refusal of culture but simultaneously its capacity to develop as a cultural being. They presuppose a natural openness to culture precisely as the condition of their very possibility. 'Susceptibility to culture' is the name Freud gives to this openness.[33] The central question raised by Freud's theory of culture is that of the prospects of a maximization of this susceptibility.

Thus, it is on the basis of this susceptibility that, in *The Future of an Illusion*, Freud raises the pedagogical question of the "limitations of man's capacity for education."[34] The internalization of cultural prohibitions is profoundly negative in that it amounts to the institutionalization of coercion at the deepest of internal levels. At the same time, however, this negative movement entails a profoundly positive dimension in that it evidences a movement in the direction of humanization. The painful insertion of the "No" into the human psyche is simultaneously its accession into the field of intersubjectivity. Fundamentally, this is why *The Future of an Illusion* envisions not an elimination of cultural frustration but rather a "different *attitude*" to culture. The members of Freud's envisioned culture shall have been "brought up in kindness," shall have been "taught to have a high opinion of reason," and shall have "experienced the benefits of civilization." They will thus experience culture as "a possession of their very own" (emphasis added).[35] Freud's is a "reconciliation" to culture effected on the basis of both minimization of frustration and "compensation."[36]

It is in terms of the benefits of culture—which are material as well as mental—that Freud proceeds to discuss the privations that do not affect everyone. In regard to "those restrictions that apply only to certain classes of society," Freud writes, the "state of things . . . is flagrant and . . . has always been recognized."

> It is to be expected that these underprivileged classes will envy the favoured ones their privileges and will do all they can to free themselves from their own *surplus of privation.*[37] (emphasis added)

The results of underprivilege are a "permanent measure of discontent" and the ever-present possibility of "dangerous revolts." Once again, Freud speaks unequivocally:

> If . . . a culture has not gone beyond a point at which the satisfaction of one portion of its participants depends upon the suppression of another, and perhaps larger, portion—and this is the case in all present-day cultures—it is *understandable* that the suppressed people should develop an intense hostility towards a culture whose existence they make possible by their work, but in whose wealth they have too small a share. *In such conditions an internalization of the cultural prohibitions among the suppressed people is not to be expected.* On the contrary, they are not prepared to acknowledge the prohibitions, they are intent on destroying the culture itself, and possibly even on doing away with the postulates on which it is based.[38] (emphasis added)

Whatever the degree of constitutive "laziness" attributable to the human being, the problematics of culture are by no means exhausted in and through the simplistic assertion that the great mass of the oppressed refuses to do the work culture requires for its preservation. Their hostility to culture is rooted not only in the "remarkable" universal hostility of the human being to culture as such, but also in a thoroughly "understandable" and historically produced hostility to a culture flagrantly rooted in injustice. "It goes without saying," Freud writes, "that a civilization which leaves so large a number of its participants unsatisfied and drives them into revolt neither has nor deserves the prospect of a lasting existence."[39]

Freud's "decisive question," then, transcends the limits of exclusively psychological modes of "compensation" and "reconciliation." Human beings can approach the experience of culture as a "possession of their very own" only on the basis of particular material conditions. Short of these conditions, Freud tells us, success in the pedagogical experiment whereby human beings are to be transformed from enemies into vehicles of culture is, quite simply, "not to be expected." A culture rooted in injustice is in principle incapable of transforming its participants into "social and moral beings." Strictly speaking, it is not a culture but a historically constructed *oppressive order*. Its prohibitions do not catalyze but rather preclude the truly cultural, pedagogical movement of humanization. As Herbert Marcuse well knew, few endeavours are as deeply anti-Freudian as the cruel attempt to demand and effect a psychical reconciliation to a 'reality' where flagrantly "surplus privation" is prevalent.[40]

If, on the one hand, the realization of Freud's proposed pedagogical experiment of reconciliation presupposes a transformation of the sphere of the economic, it provides us, on the other, with an analysis of the psychical dynamics whereby a culture rooted in surplus privation can manage to sustain itself in spite of the widespread and "intense" hostility it generates. "The extent to which a civilization's precepts have been internalized," Freud writes, "is not the only form of mental wealth that comes into consideration in estimating a civilization's value." A culture's psychical assets also include the satisfactions that can be derived from "ideals and artistic creations."[41] According to Freud, the former are especially important in the maintenance of an oppressive order. A particular culture's ideals do not determine but are determined by its achievements. Cultures value that which their specific "internal gifts" and "external circumstances" have allowed them to achieve. A culture's ideals are a monument to its "pride in what has already been successfully achieved." In regard to the management of hostility within a particular cultural unit, Freud's point is that this pride "calls for a comparison with other cultures which have aimed at different achievements and have developed different ideals." For Freud, this outward direction of the hostility of the suppressed masses fulfills a twofold function of integration. On the one hand, the satisfaction "can be shared not only by the favoured classes, which enjoy the benefits of the culture, but also by the suppressed ones, since the right to despise the people outside it compensates them for the wrongs they suffer within their own unit":

No doubt one is a wretched plebeian, harassed by debts and military service; but, to make up for it, one is a Roman citizen, one has one's share in the task of ruling other nations and dictating their laws.[42]

On the other hand, in addition to the integrating function that war and conquest can and do serve, Freud tells us that the outward direction of internally produced hostility opens the way for an attachment to their masters on the part of the oppressed:

> [T]he suppressed classes can be emotionally attached to their masters; in spite of their hostility to them they may see in them their ideals; *unless such relations of a fundamentally satisfying kind subsisted, it would be impossible to understand how a number of civilizations have survived so long in spite of the justifiable hostility of large human masses.*[43] (emphasis added)

Thus the sphere of substitutive psychical satisfactions is constitutive of the very possibility of injustice.[44]

Freud's complication of the relation between economics and psychology indicates that his critique of surplus privation follows the prescriptions not only of moral indignation but also those of his theorization of the dynamics of mourning. For Freud, the pedagogical transformation of human beings from enemies into vehicles of culture coincides with the construction of an alternative superego, of a superego whose commands are in accordance with the erotic claims of our "first duty" as living beings. As we saw in chapter 1, it is precisely in terms of the dynamics of mourning that Freud posits the possibility of such a construction. Accordingly, it is only in terms of those dynamics that the psychological depth of Freud's critique of the injustice he discerns at the root of "all present-day cultures" can be adequately broached.

"Mourning," Freud tells us, "occurs under the influence of reality-testing; for the latter function demands categorically from the bereaved person that he should separate himself from the object, since it no longer exists."[45] At issue is a struggle of life and death, an encounter in and through which "the libido's attachment to the lost object is met by the verdict of reality that the object no longer exists."[46] According to Freud, this struggle is as fateful as it is decisive, since it raises the ominous possibility of an "overcoming of the instinct which compels every living thing to cling to life."[47] Alternatively, "the ego, confronted as it were with the [fateful] question whether it shall share this fate [of the dead object], is persuaded by the sum of the narcissistic satisfactions it derives from being alive to sever its attachment to the object that has been abolished." In this way, mourning "impels the ego to give up the object by declaring the object to be dead and offering the ego the inducement of continuing to live."[48]

Freud's complication of the relation between economics and psychology obeys his insight that the context of surplus privation minimizes the chances of Eros: it can offer not reality but only deathly illusions as an ultimately ill-fated inducement to live.[49] The material presuppositions of Freud's proposed pedagogical experiment are indeed part and parcel of the psychical composition of the dynamics of mourning, just as the infant's nourishment at the breast is literally inseparable from its experience of life and love. For Freud, surplus privation typifies a situation in which human beings are at best unlikely to bring each other to life.

Needless to say, this is not a matter of allowing ourselves to believe that the absence of surplus privation in any way guarantees an alternative attitude to life. By no means: the human being's existential predicament cannot be dissolved into the vicissitudes of the sociohistorical. The point, rather, is to grasp that Freud's critique of surplus privation is rooted in an exposure of a sociohistorical situation that manages to articulate the premature birth of the human infant, along with its attendant vulnerability and propensity to illusion, with the production and reproduction of injustice. Freud's refusal to enter the sphere of religion without having first attempted such an exposure reveals its crucial importance. Freud's critique of religion is an effort to theorize the connectedness of our existential predicament with the vicissitudes of political power in the modern world.

THE CULTURAL ABANDONMENT OF HYPNOSIS

Specific about "religious ideas in the widest sense"[50] is that they seek to reconcile human beings not only to the sufferings imposed by culture, but simultaneously to "the cruelty of Fate, particularly as it is shown in death."[51] Freud writes:

> We know already how the individual reacts to the injuries which civilization and other men inflict on him: he develops a corresponding degree of resistance to the regulations of civilization and of hostility to it. But how does he defend himself against the superior powers of nature, of Fate, which threaten him as they threaten all the rest?[52]

Even in the face of the advances of civilization, natural disasters, disease, and the "painful riddle of death" continue to insist upon our "weakness and helplessness." Life, Freud tells us once again, is "hard to bear," and our injured self-regard "calls for consolation": it seeks to rob life and the universe of their "terrors."[53] Religious ideas permit us to "breathe freely," to "feel at home in the uncanny," to "deal by psychical means with our senseless anxiety."[54]

For Freud, the situation of the adult human being faced with the "terrors" of life and the universe is in fact "only the continuation" of the "state of helplessness" in which he found himself as a child. Thus, on the basis of this "infantile prototype," he transforms the overpowering forces of nature and Fate into gods, at once awesome and protective, dangerous yet benevolent:[55]

> When the growing individual finds that he is destined to remain a child for ever, that he can never do without protection against strange superior powers, he lends those powers the features belonging to the figure of his father; he creates for himself the gods whom he dreads, whom he seeks to propitiate, and whom he nevertheless entrusts with his own protection. Thus his longing for a father is a motive identical with his need for protection against the consequences of his human weakness. The defence against childish helplessness is what lends its characteristic features to the adult's reaction to the helplessness which *he* has to acknowledge—a reaction which is precisely the formation of religion.[56] (emphasis in original)

Psychologically speaking, then, religious ideas are fulfillments of infantile longings for parental protection. They are "born from man's need to make his helplessness tolerable and built up from the material of memories of the helplessness of his own childhood. . . ."[57]

Freud's claim that the psychic origins of religious ideas are to be found in infantile helplessness permits him both to raise and to resolve what he calls a "fresh psychological problem."[58] It is "remarkable," he observes, "that of all the information provided by our cultural assets it is precisely the elements which might be of the greatest importance to us and which have the task of solving the riddles of the universe and of reconciling us to the sufferings of life—it is precisely those elements that are the least well authenticated of any."[59] For Freud, religious ideas claim to rise above the "jurisdiction of reason"; they "appeal to a court above that of reason."[60] Their specificity as teachings lies precisely in their being "teachings and assertions about facts and conditions of external (or internal) reality which tell one something one has not discovered for oneself and which lay claim to one's belief."[61] They are neither the results of observation or experience, nor the culmination of sustained processes of thought. In spite of this, however, religious ideas "have exercised the strongest possible influence on mankind." Accordingly, the fresh psychological problem Freud has in mind is that of the "inner force of those doctrines" and of the roots of their efficacy, "independent as it is of recognition by reason."[62]

Illusions, Freud tells us, are to be distinguished from mere "errors." Unlike errors, "illusions need not necessarily be false—that is to say, unrealizable or in contradiction to reality." Thus, whereas "Aristotle's belief that vermin are developed out of dung . . . was an error," it was an illusion of Columbus's to have believed that "he had discovered a new sea-route to the Indies." Freud's point is that, regardless of their relation to reality, what characterizes illusions is that "they are derived from human wishes." A belief is an illusion "when a wish-fulfilment is a prominent factor in its motivation."[63]

Freud is aware that his psychological derivation of religious ideas from infantile helplessness entails little in regard to the truth-value of those ideas.[64] Nonetheless, rooted as it is in the assumption that religious ideas cannot be accounted for rationally, his concept of illusion permits him to state that the strength of those ideas is less a measure of their truth than of the depth of the "terrifying impressions of helplessness in childhood." The power of their influence is a function of the "enormous relief" they offer.[65] According to Freud, this is why religious ideas are prized "as the most precious possessions of civilization, as the most precious things it has to offer its participants." The high esteem in which they are held lies in that "[p]eople feel that *life would not be tolerable* if they did not attach to those ideas the value that is claimed for them" (emphasis added).[66]

This appearance of the problematics of tolerating or enduring life places us squarely in the wake of Freud's paradigmatic statement, in "Thoughts for the Times on War and Death," that "illusion can have no value" if its truth is ultimately that it makes our "first duty" to endure life more difficult to come to terms with. For Freud, it is not the condition of helplessness or loss as such, but rather the illusory attempt to remedy or deny it, that is the hallmark of religion:

> Critics persist in describing as "deeply religious" anyone who admits to a sense of man's insignificance or impotence in the face of the universe, although what constitutes the essence of the religious attitude is not this feeling but only the next step after it, the reaction which seeks a remedy for it. The man who goes no further, but humbly acquiesces in the small part which human beings play in the great world—such a man is, on the contrary, irreligious in the truest sense of the word.[67]

In this way, Freud positions the struggle between the religious and the irreligious in the face of helplessness alongside his conception of the struggle between illusion and (re)cognition in the face of the death of loved ones, between hypnotic suggestion and analytic working-through in the face of the primordial ambivalence of human drives.[68] Freud interprets religion as the cultural shape of a universal refusal to mourn, a universal denial of death.[69] Its mode of acculturation is hypnotic rather than analytic. It seeks subjection to authority rather than analysis of the roots of obedience and disobedience. Fundamentally, this is because it conceives the problematics of culture at the level of *order* rather than that of *pedagogy*. Like hypnosis, it in the long run inadvertently strengthens what it is attempting to subdue—it plays into the hands of Death precisely as it attempts to offer an inducement to live.

The explicitly political dimension of Freud's critique of religion unfolds in a context that we might call, borrowing a phrase from Michael Harrington, "the politics at God's funeral."[70] For Freud, religious ideas fulfill the political function of investing cultural prohibitions "with a quite special solemnity."[71] They take possession of the human longing for protection in terms of a mystification of authority. Accordingly, it is at this juncture of his reflection that, having evoked the horizon of an alternative mode of dealing with helplessness, Freud deploys his conception of the possibility of an alternative culture against the objection that the decline of religion in the modern world necessarily augurs the collapse of culture as such. He seeks to seize the waning of religion as an opportunity to be celebrated rather than a loss to be regretted. He seeks to mourn the death of God as a renewed invitation to live.

Freud ascribes the objection in question to an imaginary interlocutor:

> "Archaeological interests are no doubt most praiseworthy, but no one undertakes an excavation if by doing so he is going to undermine the habitations of the living so that they collapse and bury people under their ruins. The doctrines of religion are not a subject one can quibble about like any other. Our civilization is built up on them, and the maintenance of human society is based on the majority of men's believing in the truth of those doctrines. If men are taught that there is no almighty and all-just God, no divine world-order and no future life, they will feel exempt from all obligation to obey the precepts of civilization. Everyone will, without inhibition or fear, follow his asocial, egoistic instincts and seek to exercise his power; Chaos, which we have banished through many thousands of years of the work of civilization, will come again."[72]

In response, Freud announces that he shall "assert the view that civilization runs a greater risk if we maintain our present attitude to religion than if we give it up."[73] For Freud, the present situation of European Christian civilization is such that "religion no longer has the same influence on people that it used to." At issue in this historic waning of the power of religion is "the increase of the scientific spirit in the higher strata of human society."[74] "The greater the number of men to whom the treasures of knowledge become accessible," Freud writes, "the more widespread is the falling-away from religious belief."[75] As regards the "uneducated and oppressed" masses who "have every reason for being enemies of civilization," then, all is well "[s]o long as they do not discover that people no longer believe in God." But, Freud warns his interlocutor, "they will discover it, infallibly."[76]

Freud's point is that the waning of religious belief cannot be forestalled by way of a nostalgic appeal to authority structures that have been outmoded, that no longer hold. Once the sphere of cultural prohibition has lost its "solemnity," the problem of legitimacy arises in such a way that the roots of "the obligation to obey the precepts of civilization" must of necessity undergo a fundamental transformation. "If the sole reason why you must not kill your neighbour," Freud writes, "is because God has forbidden it and will severely punish you for it in this or the next life—then, when you learn that there is no God and that you need not fear His punishment, you will certainly kill your neighbour without hesitation, and you can only be prevented from doing so by mundane force." Thus, Freud claims to have grasped a historical situation that of itself poses two distinct, yet intimately related, political alternatives:

> Thus either these dangerous masses must be held down most severely and kept most carefully away from any chance of intellectual awakening, or else the relationship between civilization and religion must undergo a fundamental revision.[77]

Violence, for Freud, is the price of nostalgia. Not only the "severe" violence of "mundane force," but also the "careful" hypnotic violence designed to preclude the chances of "intellectual awakening." Such is the concrete political meaning of the fatefully "decisive question" that traverses Freud's work as a whole. In *The Future of an Illusion*, then, Freud articulates his "fateful question" about the relation between war and death in terms of a specific historical juncture in and through which we must come to choose between religion and psychoanalysis. Freud speaks with the truly audacious and "fantastic" boldness of one who deems himself a founder. He hopes to have unveiled an opportunity wherein his own abandonment of hypnosis emerges as a concrete historical possibility for Western culture as a whole.

This image of a cultural abandonment of hypnosis guided and supported by an "intellectual awakening" is Freud's response to his less pleasing image of a truly rational and enlightened political dictatorship necessitated by the purportedly congenital stupidity of human masses. In the new culture Freud envisions, the hierarchical division of society into two parts is to be transcended. Freud tells us unambiguously that the imaginary inhabitants of his proposed irreligious culture "will be able to do without coercion and will differ little from their leaders."[78] The heart of Freud's proposal is a transformation of the nature of authority, a replacement of the "affective" basis of obedience by a "rational" one.[79]

Freud's hope obeys the expectation that "honestly" admitting "the purely human origin of all the regulations and precepts of civilization" might strengthen rather than weaken its prospects:

Along with their pretended sanctity, these commandments and laws would lose their rigidity and unchangeableness as well. People could understand that they are made, not so much to rule them as, on the contrary, to serve their interests; and they would adopt a more friendly attitude to them, and instead of aiming at their abolition, would aim only at their improvement. *This would be an important advance along the road which leads to becoming reconciled to the burden of civilization.*[80] (emphasis added)

Such remolding of the basis of culture, of course, would by no means "stop at renouncing the solemn transfiguration of cultural precepts." On the contrary, "a general revision of them will result in many of them being done away with." It is this revision that, Freud hopes, will to a great extent achieve "our appointed task of reconciling men to civilization."[81]

The obvious corollary of Freud's vision of reconciliation is a historicization of the stupidity of human masses. The project of an "intellectual awakening" evidently contradicts any conception of human nature as thoroughly impervious to the power of reason. Once again, we reach the pedagogical dimension of Freud's reflection. The "decisive question" of whether human beings can, in the absence of religion, construct their own reconciliation to the necessary burdens of life and culture is a question about the extent of the limitations of their "susceptibility to culture." In *The Future of an Illusion*, Freud's treatment of this problematic takes place at two levels. The first concerns an evolutionist view of the dynamics of history, themselves thus framed in terms of a linear conception of temporality alarmingly distant from Freud's own central hypothesis of the unconscious. The second, far closer to the core of Freud's own thought and not necessarily dependent on the first, concerns Freud's claim that the atrophy of the intellectual potentialities of human beings is itself to be understood as a result of the shortcomings of the religious mode of acculturation.

Freud's evolutionist speculations render religion as a stage in the development of the human species—a stage destined to be surmounted.[82] To the objection that "[e]ven in present-day man purely reasonable motives can effect little against passionate impulses," Freud responds by way of an "analogy" between individual and cultural development.[83] In the maturation of the human individual as a social and cultural being, affective—as distinct from rational—forces cannot be dispensed with due to the weakness of the child's intellect. The premature birth of the human infant means that "many instinctual demands which will later be unserviceable cannot be suppressed by the rational operation of the child's intellect but have to be tamed by acts of repression, behind which, as a rule, lies the motive of anxiety."[84] Thus, on the one hand, "a human child cannot successfully complete its development to the civilized stage without passing through a phase of neurosis sometimes of greater and sometimes of less distinctness."[85] But, on the other, "most of these infantile neuroses are overcome spontaneously in the course of growing up . . . [and] [t]he remainder can be cleared up later still by psycho-analytic treatment."[86]

Freud proposes that we "might assume," analogically, that this spontaneous process of overcoming is destined to take place for "humanity as a whole." He writes:

> If this view is right, it is to be supposed that a turning-away from religion is bound to occur with the fatal inevitability of a process of growth, and that we find ourselves at this very juncture in the middle of that phase of development.[87]

His claim, then, is that as regards humanity as a whole "the time has probably come, as it does in analytic treatment, for replacing the effects of repression by the results of the rational operation of the intellect."[88]

Most unsettling about Freud's evolutionist speculations is their teleological structure. In the midst of their linearity, the concept of the unconscious—which must of necessity break the spell of teleology—appears to be forgotten. Freud speaks no longer of a fateful or decisive *question* to be taken up, of an uncertain and "interminable" *struggle* constitutive of the human predicament. The unconscious appears at best as the temporary darkness of a stage to be spontaneously transcended, not as the haunting emblem of a helplessness that is forever to be dealt with. It is almost as if Freud permits himself to invite us to the bittersweet daylight of the Reason of Enlightenment. Freud's fundamental concept of the Death drive is conspicuously absent from this aspect of *The Future of an Illusion*. Thus, the difficult and uncertain *task* of mourning, along with the delicate twilight of a *duty* to endure life, is lost in the consoling "inevitability of a process of growth," of a virtually rationalistic unfolding that cannot help but evoke the optimistic safety of a Providential maturation. The precarious chances of Eros are lost in the deathly ruse of a guaranteed victory.[89]

It is only at the second level of his treatment of the historical specificity of the so-called stupidity of human masses that Freud remains close to the "experimental" texture of his reflection, to the conception of a struggle that retains the full dignity of its uncertain and complex, open historicity. "It is true that men *are* like this," Freud writes,

> but have you asked yourself whether they *must* be like this, whether their innermost nature necessitates it? Can an anthropologist give the cranial index of a people whose custom it is to deform their children's heads by bandaging them round from their earliest years? Think of the depressing contrast between the radiant intelligence of a healthy child and the feeble intellectual powers of the average adult. Can we be quite certain that it is not precisely religious education which bears a large share of the blame for this relative atrophy?[90] (first emphasis added)

Accordingly, Freud stakes the prospects of his proposed pedagogical experiment on the envisaged results of an alternative mode of acculturation.

"[Y]ou must admit," he tells his skeptical interlocutor, "that here we are justified in having a hope for the future—that perhaps there is a treasure to be dug up capable of enriching civilization and that it is worth making the experiment of an *irreligious education*." "Should the experiment prove unsatisfactory," he concedes, "I am ready to give up the reform and to return to my earlier, purely descriptive judgment that man is a creature of weak intelligence who is ruled by his instinctual wishes" (emphasis added).[91]

The "sole purpose" of *The Future of an Illusion*, Freud writes, "is to point out the necessity for this forward step." On the one hand, the proposed *"education to reality"* requires that human beings "admit to themselves the full extent of their helplessness and their insignificance in the machinery of the universe" (emphasis in original).[92] It is a matter of learning to "endure" the great necessities of Fate "with resignation." And on the other, Freud insists that

> As honest smallholders on this earth they will probably know how to culti-
> vate their plot in such a way that it supports them. By withdrawing their ex-
> pectations from the other world and concentrating all their liberated energies
> into their life on earth, they will probably succeed in achieving a state of
> things in which life will become tolerable for everyone and civilization no
> longer oppressive to anyone.[93]

With this crucial distinction between the toleration of life and that of oppression, *The Future of an Illusion* restates Freud's intertwining of resignation and critique: the fulfillment of our "first duty" as living beings entails the transformation of a culture that denies it. Freud's resigned submission to the superior powers of Fate is at the same time a liberation from the illusory seductions of the immortal.

EROS AND LOGOS

At the level of the political, the opposition between the religious and the irreligious appears as an opposition between cultural units that divide society into two parts, on the one hand, and cultural units whose members, as Freud has it, "differ little from their leaders," on the other. Yet scarcely five years after the publication of *The Future of an Illusion*, Freud returns quite unequivocally to the hierarchical conception of the political. In "Why War" (1932), he writes:

> One instance of the innate and ineradicable inequality of men is their ten-
> dency to fall into the two classes of leaders and followers. The latter consti-
> tute the vast majority; they stand in need of an authority which will make
> decisions for them and to which they for the most part offer an unqualified

submission. This suggests that more care should be taken than hitherto to educate an upper stratum of men with independent minds, not open to intimidation and eager in the pursuit of truth, whose business it would be to give direction to the dependent masses.[94]

It is as if, already by 1932, Freud has lost his conviction that the experiment of an alternative education "has not yet been made," and hence returns to his earlier judgment that human beings are on the whole creatures of "weak intelligence." That which Freud wished to dismiss in 1927 (i.e., in *The Future of an Illusion*), no longer puts up with its dismissal in 1932 (i.e., in "Why War?").

To be sure, one way out of this contradiction is to point out that in "Why War?" Freud adds that "[t]he ideal condition of things would of course be a community of men who had subordinated their instinctual life to the *dictatorship of reason*," (emphasis added)[95] a move possibly closer to the claims of *The Future of an Illusion*. Nonetheless, even if posited as universally shared and accepted, this conception of a rational dictatorship at best translocates the hierarchical division of the social so as to (re)place it at the heart of each, as it were self-led, individual. Of course, the problem with this translocation is not that it correctly posits *division* at the heart of the human subject, but that it does so in a manner that seems to retain a preoccupyingly pre-Freudian understanding of the relation between "passion" and "reason." Thus, it cannot help but cast the central opposition between the religious and the irreligious as an opposition between the "affective" and the "rational," between the claims of the body and those of a peculiarly disembodied Reason. Such a Reason would, as it were, presumably hover rootlessly above the rest of the individual, just like a political dictatorship of the truly rational would hover, either impotent or authoritarian, above the part of society to which it is deemed superior. Such a Reason, to put it otherwise, would reproduce what Freud himself grasped and criticized as the predicament of hypnosis.

In fact, when speaking of the ways in which "psycho-analysis has sought to educate the ego," Freud admonishes the pre-Freudian "intelligence" not yet informed that "*the ego is not master in its own house*":

> You behave yourself like an absolute ruler who is content with the information supplied him by his highest officials and never goes among the people to hear their voice.[96] (emphasis in original)

Thus, by way of conclusion to this chapter, I wish to render the problem of the political shape of Freud's pedagogical vision not in terms of the question of whether the dictatorship of reason is or is not to be self-imposed, but rather in terms of the very way in which we are to conceive the "intelligence" Freud so urgently seeks to "awaken." At stake here is the relation between the *Logos* Freud seeks to liberate in the *Future of an Illusion*, and the *Eros* whose self-assertion he permits himself to expect as he concludes *Civilization and Its Discontents*.

Needless to say, much has been said about Freud's scientism, or, alternatively, about his purported adherence to the Reason of Enlightenment. Joel Kovel, for example, concludes an analysis of *The Future of an Illusion* with the claim that Freud is "no humanist," but

> a latter-day Calvinist who had lost faith in the spirit and tried to replace this with faith in scientific rationality, or what he called Logos. I think it is time to call this attitude the disaster it in fact is. Perhaps we can exonerate Freud for not knowing better, in 1927, than "civilization has little to fear from educated people and brain workers"—although one would have thought that World War I would have given him more pause than it seems it did. Sixty years later, with systematic ruination of the globe visible all about us as the fruit of these brains, we are obliged to reject Freud's uncritical adulation of science. This is, it must be emphasized, not the same thing as rejecting science, but it does mean reintegrating science with those spiritual elements that were split off at the beginning of the modern era, when the soul became the isolated and driven ego. Unless there is a radical transformation of society grounded in the sense of universal interconnectedness, we are all quite doomed.[97]

The naiveté of Freud's statement about "educated people and brain workers" is indeed truly striking, especially if we recall that in *The Future of an Illusion*, Freud is deeply preoccupied with "men's hostile impulses," and therefore with the fact that "[h]uman creations are easily destroyed, and science and technology, which have built them up, can also be used for their annihilation."[98] All the same, the fact that Freud utters this warning in the context of his discussion of the imminent anticultural rebellion of "dangerous masses," not of "educated people," appears to confirm Kovel's claim about Freud's "uncritical adulation of science."

Most problematic about such adulation is that it flatly contradicts the exquisite awareness of the juncture between civilization and barbarism, reason and violence, that informs Freud's work as a whole. One might say, in this vein, that Freud's uncritical posture toward science evidences an instance of profound forgetfulness. In the very first lines of "Thoughts for the Times on War and Death," for example, it is precisely the crucial participation of educated people in World War I, of distinguished and accredited scientists, that gives Freud reason to pause and observe:

> We cannot but feel that no event has ever destroyed so much that is precious in the common possessions of humanity, *confused so many of the clearest intelligences,* or so thoroughly debased what is highest. Science herself has lost her passionless impartiality; her deeply embittered servants seek for weapons

from her with which to contribute towards the struggle with the enemy. An-
thropologists feel driven to declare him inferior and degenerate, psychiatrists
issue a diagnosis of his disease of mind or spirit.[99] (emphasis added)

Indeed, the passage in the *Future of an Illusion* in which Freud exonerates
"brain workers" does corroborate his ambivalent attitude toward the "uneducated," *but not without informing us a great deal about what Freud has in
mind when he speaks of "scientific thinking."* This is the passage in question:

> Civilization has little to fear from educated people and brain-workers. In
> them the replacement of religious motives for civilized behaviour by other,
> secular motives would proceed unobtrusively; moreover, such people are to
> a large extent themselves *vehicles of civilization.* But it is another matter with
> the great mass of the uneducated and oppressed, who have every reason for
> being enemies of civilization. So long as they do not discover that people no
> longer believe in God, all is well. But they will discover it, infallibly, even if
> this piece of writing of mine is not published. And they are ready to accept
> the results of scientific thinking, but without *the change having taken place in
> them which scientific thinking brings about in people.*[100] (emphases added)

As deployed in *The Future of an Illusion*, Freud's *concept* of science cannot
by any means be divorced from the profound ethical content it carries. It
eo ipso contains the pedagogical construction of a superego genuinely ev-
idencing a transformation of human beings into "vehicles of civilization."
Reason, for Freud, transcends the sphere of technical knowledge.

It is not by chance that Freud viewed psychoanalysis as a "*special* branch
of knowledge," deeply at odds with the "representatives of official science"
to whom he repeatedly referred as the "*so-called* scientific opponents" of psychoanalysis and against whom he never tired of directing his disdain (emphases added).[101] Consider, for example, Freud's nuanced characterization
of the pre-psychoanalytic physician when confronted with hysteria:

> But all his knowledge—his training in anatomy, in physiology, and in
> pathology—leaves him in the lurch when he is confronted by the details of
> hysterical phenomena. He cannot understand hysteria, and in the face of
> it he is himself a layman. This is not a pleasant situation for anyone who
> as a rule sets so much store by his knowledge. So it comes about that hys-
> terical patients forfeit his *sympathy.* He regards them as people who are
> transgressing the laws of his science—like heretics in the eyes of the or-
> thodox. He attributes every kind of wickedness to them, accuses them of
> exaggeration, of deliberate deceit, of malingering. And he punishes them
> by withdrawing his interest from them.[102] (emphasis added)

For Freud, psychoanalysis first arises as a mode of knowledge that no
longer regards that which is other than itself with contempt rather than

"sympathy," with the ease of horror rather than the painstaking difficulty of a hermeneutic effort.[103]

Precisely as the paradoxical "science of the mental unconscious,"[104] Freud places psychoanalysis itself in the position of the outlawed hysteric.[105] He repeatedly speaks of the "indignation, derision and scorn which, in disregard of every standard of logic and good taste, have characterized the controversial methods of its opponents."[106] The "original outlawing of psycho-analysis by scientific circles," he writes, has at best become "a sort of buffer-layer . . . in scientific society between analysis and its opponents."[107] Speaking of the early days of psychoanalysis, Freud likens the situation to

> what was actually put into practice in the Middle Ages when an evil-doer, or even a mere political opponent, was put in the pillory and given over to maltreatment by the mob. You may not realize clearly, perhaps, *how far upwards* in our society mob-characteristics extend, and what misconduct people will be guilty of when they feel themselves part of a crowd and relieved of personal responsibility.[108] (emphasis added)

Nor is Freud at all unaware of the decidedly political content of the derision which, he feels, his science inevitably provokes:

> Such a display of unfairness and lack of logic cries out for an explanation. Its origin is not hard to find. Human civilization rests upon two pillars, of which one is the control of natural forces and the other the restriction of our instincts. The ruler's throne rests upon fettered slaves. Among the instinctual components which are thus brought into service, the sexual instincts, in the narrower sense of the word, are conspicuous for their strength and savagery. Woe, if they should be set loose! The throne would be overturned and the ruler trampled underfoot. Society is aware of this—and will not allow the topic to be mentioned.[109]

For Freud, these 'resistances' oppose themselves precisely to the ethical content of psychoanalysis. They are but the manifestation of what Freud regards as a socially maintained "condition of *cultural hypocrisy*," a condition "which is bound to be accompanied by a sense of insecurity and a necessity for guarding what is an undeniably precarious situation by forbidding criticism and discussion" (emphasis in original).[110] At issue is the fact that "psychoanalysis has revealed the weakness of this system and has recommended that it should be altered":

> It proposes that there should be a reduction in the strictness with which instincts are repressed and that correspondingly more play should be given to *truthfulness*. Certain instinctual impulses, with whose suppression society has gone too far, should be permitted a greater amount of satisfaction; in the

case of certain others the inefficient methods of suppressing them by means of repression should be replaced by a better and securer procedure.[111] (emphasis added)

Thus, the admittedly important question of whether Freud is correct in connecting the ethical dimension of his conception of science to scientific reason as we have come to know it since the beginning of the modern era need not obscure the fact that, as an alternative to what he took to be the illusory claims of religion, Freud is seeking to specify a mode of (re)cognition, a "kind of knowledge" informed by his eminently psychoanalytic conviction that

> anyone who has succeeded in educating himself to truth about himself is permanently defended against the danger of immorality, even though his standard of morality may differ in some respect from that which is customary in society.[112]

Freud's conception of the search for truth is irretrievably ethical: it necessarily entails an acceptance of death that, in accordance with our "first duty" as living beings, both posits and presupposes the transformation of Death into Eros. The science of which Freud speaks in *The Future of an Illusion* designates a particular attitude to life corresponding to the alternative attitude to death proposed in "Thoughts for the Times on War and Death."

Accordingly, the central opposition of *The Future of an Illusion* is best grasped not as one between "passion" and "reason," but as one between religion and psychoanalysis.[113] It is of crucial importance in this regard to note that *The Future of an Illusion* understands the restrictiveness of "all present-day cultures" not as a suppression of the body on the part of the mind, but rather as an inhibition of the intelligence. It is intelligence that Freud seeks to awaken from the fetters of culture, and it is the enfeeblement of intellectual powers that he directly and explicitly connects to the repression of sexuality:

> [W]e have no other means of controlling our instinctual nature but our intelligence. How can we expect people who are under the dominance of prohibitions of thought to attain the psychological ideal, the primacy of the intelligence? You know, too, that women in general are said to suffer from "physiological feeble-mindedness"—that is, from a lesser intelligence than men. The fact itself is disputable and its interpretation doubtful, but one argument in favour of this intellectual atrophy being of a secondary nature is that women labour under the harshness of an early prohibition against turning their thoughts to what would most have interested them—namely, the problems of sexual life. So long as a person's early years are influenced not only by a sexual inhibition of thought but also by a religious inhibition and by a loyal inhibition derived from this, we cannot really tell what in fact he is like.[114]

Freud neither can nor does proceed from a point of view that opposes mind to body in the sense of reason and unreason. Essential to psychoanalysis is the discovery that what ordinary modes of thinking and living take to be irrational is in fact deeply meaningful. The truth of the matter is that the entire thrust of Freud's proposal to "awaken" the intelligence is irretrievably lost if grasped in terms of a "reason" at odds with the "passions," a bodyless ego intent on "mastering" the claims of the id. The fundamental loss Freud discerns at the heart of the culture he wishes to transform is precisely that of the possibility of a *dialogue* between ego and id, a dialogue that, for him, is the only chance we have of educating ourselves, of maximizing our ineradicably limited susceptibility to culture.[115] 'Psychoanalysis' is the name Freud gave to this dialogue. At its center, he located the dynamics of mourning, of a fateful struggle between Death and Eros, between our narcissistic longing for immortality and the irreducibly intersubjective law of death.

The return to and of life from the womb of death can be adequately described as a "dictatorship" on the part of a disembodied reason, whether at the political or at the individual level, as little as the claims of Eros can be reduced to the exclusively bodily. No dictatorship can hope to escape the necessarily ill-fated dialectic of hypnosis, the identity of authoritarianism and impotence that hypnotic suggestion carries at its core. This is why, contrary to an unfortunately widespread impression, it is not in *The Future of an Illusion* but in *Civilization and Its Discontents* that Freud comes closest to grounding his insistence upon the possibility of a new culture.[116] By way of its conception of an open-ended struggle between Eros and Death, Freud's theory of culture manages to ground the chances of Eros immanently within us. Our "first duty" as living beings is not devoid of profound bodily roots. The "primacy of the intelligence" Freud seeks is best conceived as the precarious and difficult primacy of Eros. "Where *sympathy* is lacking," Freud tells us, "*understanding* will not come very easily" (emphases added).[117] Devoid of Eros, Logos is not truly itself.

In the chapter that follows, then, I shall explore by way of conclusion Freud's problematic articulation of our "hopes for the future"[118] in terms of a psychoanalytically informed pedagogy—a pedagogy deeply sympathetic to the helplessness of the human infant and to the vicissitudes of childhood experience.

NOTES

1. James Strachey, editor's note to *The Question of Lay Analysis,* in vol. 20 of *The Standard Edition of the Complete Psychological Works of Sigmund Freud,* ed. and trans. James Strachey et al. (London: Hogarth, 1953–1974), 180.

2. Sigmund Freud, *The Question of Lay Analysis,* in vol. 20 of *The Standard Edition,* ed. and trans. James Strachey et al., 183.

3. "The use of analysis for the treatment of the neuroses," Freud writes, "is only one of its applications; the future will perhaps show that it is not the most important one. In any case it would be wrong to sacrifice all the other applications to this single one, just because it touches on the circle of medical interests." Freud, *The Question of Lay Analysis,* 248. In the *New Introductory Lectures,* Freud speaks of what he calls an "exceedingly important" topic, "rich in hopes for the future, perhaps the most important of all the activities of analysis." "What I am thinking of," he specifies, "is the application of psychoanalysis to education, to the upbringing of the next generation." Sigmund Freud, *New Introductory Lectures on Psycho-Analysis,* in vol. 22 of *The Standard Edition,* ed. and trans. James Strachey et al., 146.

4. Freud, *The Question of Lay Analysis,* 249–50.

5. The *locus classicus* of Macpherson's position is C. B. Macpherson, *The Political Theory of Possessive Individualism: From Hobbes to Locke* (Oxford, UK: Oxford University Press, 1962). See also Macpherson's introduction to his edition of *Leviathan;* and C. B. Macpherson, "Hobbes's Bourgeois Man," in *Democratic Theory: Essays in Retrieval* (Oxford, UK: Clarendon, 1973), 238–50.

6. Sigmund Freud, *The Future of an Illusion,* in vol. 21 of *The Standard Edition,* ed. and trans. James Strachey et al., 7.

7. Freud, *Future of an Illusion,* 10.

8. Freud, *Future of an Illusion,* 14.

9. Freud, *Future of an Illusion,* 5.

10. Freud, *Future of an Illusion,* 6.

11. Freud, *Future of an Illusion,* 6.

12. Freud, *Future of an Illusion,* 6.

13. Freud, *Future of an Illusion,* 6.

14. Freud, *Future of an Illusion,* 7.

15. Freud, *Future of an Illusion,* 7.

16. Freud, *Future of an Illusion,* 7.

17. Freud, *Future of an Illusion,* 6.

18. Karl Marx, "Theses on Feuerbach," in *The Marx-Engels Reader,* ed. Robert C. Tucker (New York: Norton, 1978), 144.

19. Freud, *Future of an Illusion,* 7–8.

20. Freud, *Future of an Illusion,* 8.

21. Freud, *Future of an Illusion,* 9.

22. Freud, *Future of an Illusion,* 8-9.

23. Freud, *Future of an Illusion,* 10. For a discussion of the relation between the spheres of economics and psychology in the context of Herbert Marcuse's reading of Freud, see Gad Horowitz, *Repression: Basic and Surplus Repression in Psychoanalytic Theory: Freud, Reich and Marcuse* (Toronto: University of Toronto Press, 1977), 173–77 and 185–95.

24. Freud, *Future of an Illusion,* 12.

25. Freud, *Future of an Illusion,* 14.

26. Freud, *Future of an Illusion,* 10.

27. Freud, *Future of an Illusion,* 10.

28. Freud, *Future of an Illusion,* 11.

29. Freud, *Future of an Illusion*, 11.

30. Sigmund Freud, "Thoughts for the Times on War and Death," in vol. 14 of *The Standard Edition*, ed. and trans. James Strachey et al., 282.

31. Freud, "Thoughts for the Times," 282.

32. See the passage cited above, note 29.

33. Freud, "Thoughts for the Times," 283. See also Freud, *Future of an Illusion*, 38.

34. Freud, *Future of an Illusion*, 9.

35. Freud, *Future of an Illusion*, 8.

36. Freud, *Future of an Illusion*, 7. See also 41 and 44.

37. Freud, *Future of an Illusion*, 12.

38. Freud, *Future of an Illusion*, 12.

39. Freud, *Future of an Illusion*, 12.

40. This insight is at the root of Herbert Marcuse's reading of Freud. See especially Herbert Marcuse, "Critique of Neo-Freudian Revisionism," published as the epilogue to *Eros and Civilization: A Philosophical Inquiry into Freud* (Boston: Beacon, 1965), 238–74. See also Russell Jacoby, *Social Amnesia: A Critique of Conformist Psychology from Adler to Laing* (Boston: Beacon, 1975); and Russell Jacoby, *The Repression of Psychoanalysis: Otto Fenichel and the Political Freudians* (New York: Basic, 1983).

41. Freud, *Future of an Illusion*, 12.

42. Freud, *Future of an Illusion*, 13. "In this way," Freud adds, "cultural ideals become a source of discord and enmity between different cultural units, as can be seen most clearly in the case of nations."

43. Freud, *Future of an Illusion*, 13.

44. As regards the satisfactions to be derived from the sphere of art, Freud writes that, as a rule, they "remain inaccessible to the masses, who are engaged in exhausting work and have not enjoyed any personal education." Freud, *Future of an Illusion*, 13.

45. Sigmund Freud, *Inhibitions, Symptoms and Anxiety*, in vol. 20 of *The Standard Edition*, ed. and trans. James Strachey et al., 172.

46. Sigmund Freud, "Mourning and Melancholia," in vol. 14 of *The Standard Edition*, ed. and trans. James Strachey et al., 255.

47. Freud, "Mourning and Melancholia," 246.

48. Freud, "Mourning and Melancholia," 257.

49. Freud writes: "We shall probably discover that the poor are even less ready to part with their neuroses than the rich, because the hard life that awaits them if they recover offers them no attraction, and illness gives them more claim to social help." Sigmund Freud, "Lines of Advance in Psycho-Analytic Therapy," in vol. 17 of *The Standard Edition*, ed. and trans. James Strachey et al., 167.

50. Freud, *Future of an Illusion*, 14.

51. Freud, *Future of an Illusion*, 18.

52. Freud, *Future of an Illusion*, 16.

53. Freud, *Future of an Illusion*, 16.

54. Freud, *Future of an Illusion*, 17.

55. Freud, *Future of an Illusion*, 17.

56. Freud, *Future of an Illusion*, 24.

57. Freud, *Future of an Illusion*, 18.

58. Freud, *Future of an Illusion*, 29.

59. Freud, *Future of an Illusion*, 27.

60. Freud, *Future of an Illusion*, 28.

61. Freud, *Future of an Illusion*, 25.

62. Freud, *Future of an Illusion*, 29. Cf. Sigmund Freud, *Group Psychology and the Analysis of the Ego*, in vol. 18 of *The Standard Edition*, ed. and trans. James Strachey et al., 90: "But there has been no explanation of the nature of suggestion, that is, of the conditions under which influence without adequate logical foundation takes place."

63. Freud, *Future of an Illusion*, 30–31.

64. All the same, he writes that, given the psychological derivation, "our attitude to the problem of religion will undergo a marked displacement." Freud, *Future of an Illusion*, 33.

65. Freud, *Future of an Illusion*, 30.

66. Freud, *Future of an Illusion*, 20.

67. Freud, *Future of an Illusion*, 32–33.

68. Joel Kovel is clearly correct in observing that "it is as though religion and psychoanalysis hover above the same place on the human landscape, and map it in different ways." Joel Kovel, "Beyond *The Future of an Illusion*: Further Reflections on Freud and Religion," *Psychoanalytic Review* 77 (Spring 1990): 72.

69. "Religion," Freud writes, "would thus be the universal obsessional neurosis of humanity. . . ." Freud, *Future of an Illusion*, 43.

70. See Michael Harrington, *The Politics at God's Funeral* (Middlesex, UK: Penguin, 1983).

71. Freud, *Future of an Illusion*, 41.

72. Freud, *Future of an Illusion*, 34.

73. Freud, *Future of an Illusion*, 35.

74. Freud, *Future of an Illusion*, 38. The intriguing value of Freud's insistence upon the passivity of the oppressed is that it permits him to account for the dynamics whereby a cultural unit rooted in surplus privation can manage to sustain itself. But we need not lose the conditions for the possibility of theorizing domination if we note that, ironically enough, Freud's very conception of the roots of the crisis of authority he wishes to analyze cannot help but underscore his ambivalence about the "uneducated and oppressed" masses whose eminently "justifiable hostility" to culture—as the historical record amply shows—in fact actively articulates itself as intelligent participation in the struggle against arbitrary authority. See, for example, Macpherson's nuanced and insightful comments on the ambiguities of liberal democracy in C. B. Macpherson, *The Real World of Democracy* (Toronto: CBC Enterprises, 1965), 1–11.

75. Freud, *Future of an Illusion*, 38.

76. Freud, *Future of an Illusion*, 39.

77. Freud, *Future of an Illusion*, 39.

78. Freud, *Future of an Illusion*, 8.

79. Freud, *Future of an Illusion*, 46.

80. Freud, *Future of an Illusion*, 41.

81. Freud, *Future of an Illusion*, 44.

82. Thus, for example, Philip Rieff begins his treatment of *The Future of an Illusion* with the claim that "confronting religion, psychoanalysis shows itself for what it is: the last great formulation of nineteenth-century secularism, complete with substitute doctrine and cult—capacious, all-embracing, similar in range to the social calculus of the utilitarians, the universal sociolatry of Comte, the dialectical historicism of Marx, the indefinitely expandable agnosticism of Spencer." Philip Rieff, *Freud: The Mind of the Moralist* (New York: Viking, 1959), 257.

83. Freud, *Future of an Illusion*, 42.

84. Freud, *Future of an Illusion*, 42–43.

85. Freud, *Future of an Illusion*, 42.

86. Freud, *Future of an Illusion*, 43.

87. Freud, *Future of an Illusion*, 43. Still, Freud does not fail to add: "But these are only analogies, by the help of which we endeavour to understand a social phenomenon; the pathology of the individual does not supply a fully valid counterpart." For a discussion of this point, see Robert A. Paul, "Freud's Anthropology: A Reading of the 'Cultural Books,'" in *The Cambridge Companion to Freud*, ed. Jerome Neu (Cambridge, UK: Cambridge University Press, 1991), 267–86. See also Michael S. Roth, *Psycho-Analysis as History: Negation and Freedom in Freud* (Ithaca, N.Y.: Cornell University Press, 1987), section III, "The Analogy with the Group," 135–92; and Richard J. Bernstein, *Freud and the Legacy of Moses* (Cambridge, UK: Cambridge University Press, 1998), chapter 2, "Tradition, Trauma, and the Return of the Repressed," 27–74.

88. Freud, *Future of an Illusion*, 44.

89. It is fitting here to recall Walter Benjamin's warning, in "Theses on the Philosophy of History," regarding the pitfalls of a progressivist, linear conception of the historical process: "One reason why Fascism has a chance is that in the name of progress its opponents treat it as a historical norm. The current amazement that the things we are experiencing are 'still' possible in the twentieth century is *not* philosophical. This amazement is not the beginning of knowledge—unless it is the knowledge that the view of history which gives rise to it is untenable" (emphasis in original). Walter Benjamin, "Theses on the Philosophy of History," in *Illuminations*, trans. Harry Zohn, ed. Hannah Arendt (New York: Schocken, 1969), 257. For a reading of Benjamin's "Theses," see Rebecca Comay, "Redeeming Revenge: Nietzsche, Benjamin, Heidegger," in *Nietzsche as Postmodernist: Essays Pro and Contra*, ed. Clayton Koelb (Albany: State University of New York Press, 1990), 21–38. See also Rebecca Comay, "Mourning Work and Play," *Research in Phenomenology* 23 (1993): 105–30.

90. Freud, *Future of an Illusion*, 47.

91. Freud, *Future of an Illusion*, 48–49.

92. Freud, *Future of an Illusion*, 49.

93. Freud, *Future of an Illusion*, 50.

94. Sigmund Freud, "Why War?" in vol. 22 of *The Standard Edition*, ed. and trans. James Strachey et al., 212.

95. Freud, "Why War?" 213.

96. Sigmund Freud, "A Difficulty in the Path of Psycho-Analysis," in vol. 17 of *The Standard Edition*, ed. and trans. James Strachey et al., 143.

97. Joel Kovel, "Further Reflections on Freud and Religion," 83–84.

98. Freud, *Future of an Illusion*, 6.
99. Freud, "Thoughts for the Times," 275.
100. Freud, *Future of an Illusion*, 39.
101. Freud, *New Introductory Lectures*, 137 and 140. In *The Question of Lay Analysis*, a book concerned with the specificity of psychoanalysis as a "kind of knowledge," Freud writes that, when talking to a newcomer about psychoanalysis, "[t]here are unmistakable signs that he is trying to understand psycho-analysis with the help of his previous knowledge, that he is trying to link it up with something he already knows. The difficult task now lies ahead of us of making it clear to him that he will not succeed in this: that analysis is a procedure *sui generis*, something novel and special, which can only be understood with the help of *new* insights—or hypotheses, if that sounds better" (emphases in original). Freud, *The Question of Lay Analysis*, 218 and 189–90.
102. Sigmund Freud, *Five Lectures on Psycho-Analysis*, in vol. 11 of *The Standard Edition*, ed. and trans. James Strachey et al., 12.
103. A "medical education," Freud insists, carries the danger of diverting the doctor's "interest and his *whole mode of thought* from the understanding of psychical phenomena" (emphasis added). Freud, *The Question of Lay Analysis*, 252. "[A]nalytic instruction," he writes, "would include branches of knowledge which are remote from medicine and which the doctor does not come across in his practice: the history of civilization, mythology, the psychology of religion and the *science* of literature. Unless he is well at home in these subjects, an analyst can make nothing of a large amount of his material" (emphasis added). Freud, *The Question of Lay Analysis*, 246. "I still feel some doubts," Freud adds polemically, whether the doctors presently wooing psychoanalysis "wish to take possession of their object for the purpose of destroying or of preserving it." Freud, *The Question of Lay Analysis*, 253.
104. Freud, *The Question of Lay Analysis*, 231.
105. Daphne de Marneffe writes that Freud's "desire to discover scientific truths compelled him to humble himself before what he heard and to identify his patients' utterances as a primary source of clinical knowledge." On the basis of her reading of Freud's "listening," she proceeds to observe that "Freud's early work develops something of a 'feminist' science." Unfortunately, though not without the usual caveats, de Marneffe concludes with the claim that the late Freud betrayed the insights of the "short-lived . . . early phase of Freud's work." Daphne de Marneffe, "Looking and Listening: The Construction of Clinical Knowledge in Charcot and Freud," in *Signs: Journal of Women in Culture and Society* 17 (Autumn 1991): 104 and 108. Jacqueline Rose notes the irony that the repudiation of psychoanalysis on the part of feminism "can be seen as linking up with the repeated marginalization of psychoanalysis within our general culture, a culture whose oppressiveness for women is recognized by us all." Jacqueline Rose, "Femininity and Its Discontents," in *Sexuality: A Reader*, ed. *Feminist Review* (London: Virago, 1987), 177. Nancy Chodorow's "Freud on Women" is a particularly clear and forceful discussion of women and femininity in Freud's work. Nancy Chodorow, "Freud on Women," in *The Cambridge Companion to Freud*, 224–48. For more recent discussion, see Anthony Elliot, "Freud, Feminism and Postmodernism," in *Freud 2000*, ed. Anthony Elliot (New York: Routledge, 1999), 88–109; and Jessica Benjamin,

"The Primal Leap of Psychoanalysis, From Body to Speech: Freud, Feminism and the Vicissitudes of the Transference," in *Freud 2000*, ed. Anthony Elliot (New York: Routledge, 1999), 110–38.

106. Sigmund Freud, "The Resistances to Psycho-Analysis," in vol. 19 of *The Standard Edition*, ed. and trans. James Strachey et al., 217.

107. Freud, *New Introductory Lectures*, 138.

108. Freud, *New Introductory Lectures*, 137.

109. Freud, "Resistances to Psycho-Analysis," 219.

110. Freud, "Resistances to Psycho-Analysis," 219.

111. Freud, "Resistances to Psycho-Analysis," 220.

112. Sigmund Freud, *Introductory Lectures on Psycho-Analysis*, in vol. 16 of *The Standard Edition*, ed. and trans. James Strachey et al., 434.

113. "Progress in scientific work," Freud writes, "is just as it is in an analysis." Freud, *New Introductory Lectures*, 174.

114. Freud, *Future of an Illusion*, 48.

115. André Green writes: "The opposition between the primary and secondary processes should not be described in terms of the primary processes being irrational and the secondary processes rational. Rather, they are competitive and complementary processes which obey different types of reason. We can draw two important conclusions from this. First, the psychical unity of man is fallacious. The validity of the equation psychical-conscious was contested by the idea of the unconscious. The subject was no longer One but Two; or, put another way, the unity was that of a couple living together in tolerable conflict or relative harmony. The second idea, proceeding from the first, is that the existence of two conflicting terms tends toward the creation of compromise formations which endeavour to build a bridge between them." André Green, "Psychoanalysis and Ordinary Modes of Thought," trans. Pamela Tyrell, in *Private Madness* (London: Hogarth Press and Institute of Psychoanalysis, 1986), 18.

116. Cf. John Deigh, "Freud's Later Theory of Civilization: Changes and Implications," in *The Cambridge Companion to Freud*, 287–308.

117. Freud, "A Difficulty in the Path of Psycho-Analysis," 137.

118. Freud, *New Introductory Lectures*, 146.

5

Pedagogical Hopes
for the Future

A moment's reflection tells us that hitherto education has fulfilled its task very badly and has done children great damage.

—Sigmund Freud, *New Introductory Lectures on Psycho-Analysis*

AFFAIRS IN A CHILD'S WORLD

Few communications in the history of Western thought are as compassionate as Freud's brief text "Two Lies Told by Children." "A number of lies told by well-brought-up children," Freud tells us, "have a particular significance and should cause those in charge of them to *reflect rather than be angry.*" "These lies," he continues, "occur under the influence of excessive feelings of love, and become momentous when they lead to a misunderstanding between the child and the person it loves" (emphasis added).[1]

One of the stories Freud shares with us in "Two Lies Told by Children" concerns a child of seven for whom taking money from anyone had "early come to mean . . . a physical surrender, an erotic relation"[2]:

When she was three and a half she had a nursemaid of whom she was extremely fond. This girl [i.e., the nursemaid] became involved in a love affair with a doctor whose surgery she visited with the child. It appears that at that time the child witnessed various sexual proceedings. It is not certain whether she saw the doctor give the girl money; but there is no doubt that, to make sure of the child's keeping silence, the girl gave her some small coins, with which purchases were made (probably of sweets) on the way

141

home. It is possible too that the doctor himself occasionally gave the child money. Nevertheless the child betrayed the girl to her mother out of jealousy. She played so ostentatiously with the coins she had brought home that her mother could not help asking: 'Where did you get that money?' The girl was dismissed.[3]

Some years later, now a girl of seven attending her second year at school, the child "asked her father for some money to buy colours for painting Easter eggs." The father denied the request, saying, as adults are wont to say, that he had no money. Not long thereafter, however, the child once again asked her father for some money, this time for

> a contribution towards a wreath for the funeral of their reigning princess, who had recently died. Each of the schoolchildren was to bring fifty pfennigs [sixpence]. Her father gave her ten marks [ten shillings]; she paid her contribution, put nine marks on her father's writing-table, and with the remaining fifty pfennigs bought some paints, which she hid in her toy cupboard.[4]

When confronted by her father about the missing fifty pfennigs, and about "whether she had not bought paints with them after all," the child denied the accusation. But the child's brother, "two years her elder and with whom she had planned to paint the eggs, betrayed her." Having found the paints in the cupboard, "the angry father handed the culprit over to her mother for punishment, and it was severely administered. Afterwards her mother was herself much shaken, when she saw how great the child's despair was. She caressed the little girl after the punishment, and took her for a walk to console her."[5]

Yet the "effects of the experience," Freud tells us, "proved to be ineradicable." Up to then the little girl "had been a wild, self-confident child, afterwards she became shy and timid."[6] According to Freud, "the appropriation of the fifty pfennigs in her childhood had had a significance which her father could not guess."[7] On the basis of the association that had earlier been established in the child's mind between the taking of money and erotic relations, the subsequent appropriation of her father's money had been, for the child, "equivalent to a declaration of love." The child, however, "could not admit . . . that she had appropriated the money; she was obliged to disavow it, because her motive for the deed, which was unconscious to herself, could not be admitted." "Her father's punishment," Freud concludes, "was thus a rejection of the tenderness she was offering him—a humiliation—and so it broke her spirit."[8] The child's early experience involving the nursemaid of whom she was so fond had come to attain, retroactively, a traumatic significance.

In this concluding chapter, I wish to examine Freud's attempt to conceptualize the transformation of culture as a transformation of pedagogical practices. Even in the wake of *Civilization and Its Discontents*, Freud roots the precarious chances of Eros in a "psycho-analytically enlightened education,"[9] in "people," he tells us, "who are not ashamed to concern themselves with the affairs in a child's world, and who understand how to find their way into a child's mental life."[10] For Freud, psychoanalysis provides us with a novel and unprecedented access to the vicissitudes of childhood experience. Accordingly, it is from the viewpoint of such access that Freud derives the crucial participation of psychoanalysis in the pedagogical construction of a new superego instantiating the ethical demands of culture in accordance with our "first duty" as living beings.

POLITICS AND PEDAGOGY

Toward the conclusion of *Civilization and Its Discontents*, Freud raises the question of whether "some civilizations, or some epochs of civilization—possibly the whole of mankind—have become 'neurotic'?"[11] "An analytic dissection of such neuroses," Freud tells us, "might lead to therapeutic recommendations which could lay claim to great practical interest." Nonetheless, Freud immediately adds that the "therapeutic application" of knowledge garnished in and through a psychoanalytic "pathology of cultural communities" is at best doubtful. "What would be the use," he asks, "of the most correct analysis of social neuroses, since no one possesses the authority to impose such a therapy upon the group?"[12]

The familiar impasse Freud here alludes to—that of a knowledge devoid of power—is by no means exclusively practical. On the contrary, the very way in which psychoanalysis frames the problem of knowledge should alert us to the theoretical dimension of the predicament Freud has in mind. For, strictly speaking, the crucial question is not that of whether psychoanalysis may somehow seize the reins of political power, but rather that of the extent to which a mode of investigation that insistently defines the possibility of knowledge in opposition to the imposition of external authority can consistently long to place itself in the authoritative position from which, alone, it may hope to implement *its* knowledge. At the level of the therapeutic, Freud attempts to negotiate this impasse in terms of both the deployment and the resolution of transference, relating the former to the affective forces accounting for the movement of analysis, and the latter to its goal.[13] Yet regardless of how confident one might choose to feel about the prospects of resolving the transference at the level of the therapeutic, it is by no means clear whether such prospects are in fact prospects *at all* at the level of culture—in regard, that is, not to a psychoanalyst but to a political leader.

The dilemmas of a psychoanalysis seeking to make an appearance in the field of political action are visible in Freud's own statement, in *Civilization and Its Discontents*, that

> The superego of an epoch of civilization has an origin similar to that of an individual. It is based on the impression left behind by the personalities of great leaders—men of overwhelming force of mind or men in whom one of the human impulsions has found its strongest and purest, and therefore often its most one-sided, expression.[14]

This passage contains the clue to a profound continuity between *Group Psychology* and *Civilization and Its Discontents*. Having written the latter, Freud reformulates—in the *New Introductory Lectures on Psycho-Analysis*—the thesis developed in the former: "a psychological group," he writes, "is a collection of individuals who have introduced the same person into their *superego* and, on the basis of this common element, have identified themselves with one another in their ego" (emphasis added).[15] Important about this continuity is that it permits us to ascertain that, *even in the absence of a physically present leader*, Freud insists upon grasping social relations as hypnotically constituted. In *Civilization and Its Discontents*, his claim is that human infants become members of a culture—i.e., cultural beings—by way of the institution, in the shape of the superego, of the hypnotist *within* them.

To be sure, it is true that for Freud, such institution is mediated in and through the power of parental figures over their children. According to Freud, an individual's superego in fact prolongs into adulthood the "parental influence" to which he was subject as a child, so that "the details of the relation between the ego and the superego [in the adult] become completely intelligible when they are traced back to the child's attitude to its parents."[16] But at the same time, Freud tells us that the analytical disclosure of the demands of an *individual's* superego as a rule reveals that those demands "coincide with the precepts of the prevailing *cultural* superego" (emphasis added).[17] In this way, Freud renders a particular culture's superego as the emblem of a shared subjection to the mythical, hypnotic power of its founder's "overwhelming force of mind"—a founder whose presence reproduces itself by way of the repeatedly renewed commemoration of his power and his deeds in and through that culture's social and political institutions. Through the analysis of both the bonding power of the hypnotic leader in *Group Psychology* and of the intellectually inhibiting power of religion in *The Future of an Illusion*, Freud's initial critique of the ill-fated therapeutic ambitions of the hypnotist thus culminates in his formulation of the discontents of culture, of the nucleus of the superego in *Civilization and Its Discontents*. The struggle against the fascinations of hypnosis thereby reveals itself as the overarching thematic thread traversing

Freud's lifework as a whole.

In such a context, it is clear that Freud's effort to imagine a politics of cultural change must heed the irreducible lesson drawn from the psychoanalytic critique of hypnotic suggestion. The removal or transformation of the particular precepts of a given culture can neither succeed nor be adequately conceived as the mere insertion of alternative contents into that culture's superego. Thus, for Freud, the problem of cultural transformation can scarcely be resolved in terms of the political victory of yet another—albeit psychoanalytically informed—"great leader" or prophet. Psychoanalysis is, in its essence, itself a critique of the shortcomings of such leadership. The only kind of cultural foundation it can hope to lay claim to is one that, paradoxically, must posit both the possibility and the necessity of its own dissolution. A psychoanalytic politics of cultural transformation, in other words, must oppose what we might call the hypnotic politics of foundation. Indeed, one can hardly deem it to be accidental that, in the wake of his suggestion that a "therapy" might be "imposed upon the group," Freud delivers the following warning:

> Thus I have not the courage to rise up before my fellow-men as a prophet, and I bow to their reproach that I can offer them no consolation: for at bottom that is what they are all demanding—the wildest revolutionary no less passionately than the most virtuous believers.[18]

At issue here—to borrow a formulation of Leo Bersani's—is a possibly irresolvable "tension between certain radical speculative movements and the wish to practice and even to institutionalize the speculative process itself."[19] The truth of the matter is that, as Freud well knew, *nothing necessarily secures us against the irony of a psychoanalytical religion.*[20]

I need not state at this point that my wish is not to resolve but rather to explore the pedagogical dimension of Freud's work in the light of that most delicate of tensions. Freud's movement away from the temptations of political power is also his movement into the sphere of pedagogy. Thus, in the midst of a cursory discussion of the applications of psychoanalysis in the *New Introductory Lectures,* he writes:

> But there is one topic which I cannot pass over so easily—not, however, because I understand particularly much about it or have contributed very much to it. Quite the contrary: I have scarcely concerned myself with it at all. *I must mention it because it is so exceedingly important, so rich in hopes for the future, perhaps the most important of all the activities of analysis.* What I am thinking of is the application of psycho-analysis to education, to *the upbringing of the next generation.*[21] (emphases added)

Not the details of Freud's practical recommendations—which, in any case, are at best scanty—but the way in which, in and through his pedagogical speculations, Freud attempts to negotiate the impasse he ascertains, is here of interest.

RELATIONS BETWEEN GENERATIONS

An early paper of Freud's, entitled "The Sexual Enlightenment of Children," concludes with the sobering thought that "here, once again, we see the unwisdom of sewing a single silk patch on to a tattered coat—the impossibility of carrying out an isolated reform without altering the foundations of the whole system."[22] At the same time, however, Freud's subsequent pedagogical reflections appear to wield this same systematic interconnectedness of the social in a context no longer dependent upon the need for a totalizing transformation presumably guided—as it were from the outside—by a "great leader" or prophet. The concept of culture as the field of a continuous and interminable struggle not only debunks the image of the social as a fully sutured, systematic totality. In so doing, it simultaneously intimates, at least in principle, the existence of points of rupture that would, as such, evoke the possibility for an intervention.[23]

What seeks to emerge in and through the concept of struggle is the image of a wisdom that aims at a protracted effort of (self-)reconstitution whose eventual outcome, it is true, is at best uncertain—yet whose strategic hopes are no longer framed in terms of the ill-fated dialectic of hypnosis. The difficult and thoroughly unavoidable challenge presented by Freud's theory of culture is that of seizing his pedagogical speculations as an effort to visualize, against the hypnotic fascinations of political power, the operations of the precarious mode of action he named 'psychoanalysis'—i.e., of the logic of the *Nachträglichkeit* (retroactivity)[24]—at the level of culture. The concept Freud deploys in such effort is that of the relation between generations.

Freud grasped the central dynamics pertaining to the historical reproduction of cultural forms in terms of the relation between generations. "What is meant," he tells us, "is simply that civilization is based on the repressions effected by former generations, and that each fresh generation is required to maintain this civilization by effecting the same repressions."[25] For Freud, history is the history of the struggle between Eros and Death as dramatized concretely in and through the transmission of cultural demands from generation to generation. The history of childhood is the history of the relations between generations. The formation of the superego is concretely mediated in and through such relations. "The superego," Freud tells us in a crucial passage worth quoting at length, is the representative for us of every moral restriction, the advocate of a striving towards perfection. . . . Since it itself goes back to the influence of parents, educators and so on, we learn still more of its significance if we turn to those who are its sources. As a rule parents and authorities analogous to them follow the precepts of their *own* superegos in educating children. Whatever understanding their ego may have come to with their superego, they are severe and exacting in educating children. They have *forgotten the difficulties of their own childhood* and they are glad to be able now to identify themselves fully with their own parents who in the past laid such severe restrictions upon them. Thus *a child's superego is in fact constructed on the model not of its parents but of its parents' superego;* the contents which fill it are the same and it becomes the vehicle of tradition and of all the time-resisting judgments of value which have propagated themselves in this manner from generation to generation. . . . *Mankind never lives entirely in the present.* The past, the tradition of the race and of the people, lives on in the ideologies of the superego, and yields only slowly to the influences of the present and to new changes; and so long as it operates through the superego it plays a powerful part in human life, independently of economic conditions.[26] (emphases added)

This passage recalls Freud's continuous effort to ascertain the specificity of the psychical—as distinct from the economic—in the movements of the history of culture.[27] At the same time, it restates Freud's claim that the restrictiveness of culture is rooted in a striving toward perfection, a repudiation of the imperfect that, as such, cannot help but present and re-present itself as a denial of the helplessness of the human infant.[28] For Freud, the alliance of culture and (self-)destructiveness typified in and through the demands of a punitive and hostile superego preserves itself in and through a deathly ruse that confuses well-being with perfection, happiness with omnipotence—truth with immortality. Freud's conception of our "first duty" as living beings aims at undoing this confusion. The modesty and endurance appropriate to "honest smallholders on this earth" is therefore its only counsel.

To be sure, the fateful conflation of well-being and perfection has its origins not only in the ways in which we treat and mistreat our children, but also, and at the same time, in the biologically rooted propensity to denial that is the only recourse with which our prematurity leaves us. Human beings deny death not only because they are *taught* to do so, but also because they *cannot help* but do so. Yet the very fact that Freud posits the reproduction of culture in terms not only of infantile helplessness but rather also of historically mediated relations between generations is enough to alert us, once again, that this propensity to denial is by no means exhaustive of our capacities.

To grasp the relation between generations as the central concept of Freud's theory of culture is to ascertain that, in Freud's view, the cultural denial of death can and does undergo historical vicissitudes. The 'cunning of death' Freud discerns at the heart of the production and reproduction of cultural forms operates not magically, as it were, but in and through concrete pedagogical practices that give particular content to the historically shifting relations between generations. Freud's insistence to (re)cognize the helplessness of the human infant is informed by his insight that new opportunities embodied by each fresh generation are, though by no means entirely abolished, repeatedly and significantly minimized by way of a momentous forgetfulness on the part of former generations. To say that culture sustains itself in and through forgetfulness is to say that the possible claims of the new are buried, lost behind the veil of infantile amnesia. "Only someone who can feel his way into the minds of children," Freud writes,

> can be capable of educating them; and we grown-up people cannot understand children because we no longer understand our own childhood. Our infantile amnesia proves that we have grown estranged from our childhood.[29]

It is precisely at this point that Freud's pedagogical speculations present themselves as a self-consciously *cultural* effort to minimize the depth of this estrangement. To consider the prospects of a psychoanalytically informed pedagogy is, as Freud permits himself to say of the practice of psychoanalysis, to do a "duty" aiming to "help to strengthen the clamour for the changes in our civilization through which alone we can look for the well-being of future generations."[30]

Freud's speculations are not limited to a denunciation of the pernicious effects of "inopportune and undiscerning *severity* of upbringing." It is true that Freud repeatedly states that "[t]he forcible suppression of strong instincts by external means never has the effect in a child of these instincts being extinguished or brought under control; it leads to repression, which establishes a predisposition to later nervous illness." It is also true that he is constantly mindful of "the price, in loss of efficiency and of capacity for enjoyment, which has to be paid for the normality upon which the educator insists" (emphasis added).[31] Yet Freud's critical analysis of the dynamics of parental love also targets the "attitude of *affectionate* parents towards their children" (emphasis added).[32] At the root of parental love, Freud claims to discern a wish that:

> The child shall have a better time than his parents; he shall not be subject to the necessities which they have recognized as paramount in life. Illness, death, renunciation of enjoyment, restrictions on his own will, shall not touch him; the laws of nature and of society shall be abrogated in his favour; he shall once more really be the centre and core of creation—"His Majesty the Baby," as we once fancied ourselves.[33]

For Freud, this eminently well-intentioned parental wish for the child's bliss is but the return of the parents' own longing for perfection. "The child," Freud tells us, "shall fulfil those wishful dreams of the parents which they never carried out—the boy shall become a great man and a hero in his father's place, and the girl shall marry a prince as a tardy compensation for her mother." The child, in other words, shall achieve a kind of deferred immortality in the parents' name; it shall become the vehicle of the parents' desire:

> At the most touchy point in the narcissistic system, the immortality of the ego, which is so hard pressed by reality, *security is achieved by taking refuge in the child*. Parental love, which is so moving and at bottom so childish, is nothing but the parents' narcissism born again, which, transformed into object-love, unmistakably reveals its former nature.[34] (emphases added)

To forget the difficulties of our own childhood is to seek to forget not only our own but also, and thereby, our *children's* imperfections. It is precisely this parental "compulsion to ascribe every perfection to the child"[35] that facilitates the protracted institution, within the child, of a truly passionate advocate of a striving toward every perfection—a superego whose ambivalent love is, at best, a most ambiguous blessing. In and through the misdirected tenderness of parental love, the birth of every new generation is appropriated by the one preceding it as yet another opportunity to deny its own death. Children appear not as persons in themselves but as objects in and through which the effort to foreclose what we most despise in ourselves gains a new lease on life.

As we noted in chapter 4, *The Future of an Illusion* is premised on a distinction between the ill-fated wish for a "golden age" of human civilization, on the one hand, and the project of an "irreligious education," on the other. This latter project, Freud tells us, is "securely based on the psychological discovery that man is equipped with the most varied instinctual dispositions, whose ultimate course is determined by the experiences of early childhood."[36] In this vein, Freud's *New Introductory Lectures on Psycho-Analysis*—written five years after the publication of *The Future of an Illusion* and two after that of *Civilization and Its Discontents*—insist that the overwhelming weight of childhood experience "carries with it the germ of a hygienic challenge." The question, Freud tells us, is about the possibilities of "inoculation," about the degree to which the intervention of psychoanalysis in the sphere of early childhood might minimize the proclivity to neurosis in later life. To be sure, Freud immediately acknowledges that such a discussion "has only an academic interest at present." The "mere suggestion" of a psychoanalytic intervention, he tells us, "would seem to the great bulk of our contemporaries to be a monstrous outrage, and in view of the attitude towards analysis of most people in a parental position any hope of putting through such an idea must be abandoned for the time being."[37] Thus although a psychoanalytic "prophylaxis" would "probably be very effective," it also presupposes, according to Freud, *a quite other constitution of society.*" Nonetheless, Freud tells us, "I may venture to consider it here" (emphasis added).[38] In fact, it is in and through this tentative consideration that Freud deploys the strategics of a psychoanalytically informed pedagogy.

"Let us make ourselves clear," Freud writes,

> as to what the first task of education is. The child must learn to control his instincts. It is impossible to give him liberty to carry out all his impulses without restriction. To do so would be a very instructive experiment for child-psychologists; but life would be impossible for the parents and the children themselves would suffer grave damage, which would show itself partly at once and partly in later years. Accordingly, education must inhibit, forbid and suppress, and this it has abundantly seen to in all periods of history. But we have learnt from analysis that precisely this suppression of instinct involves the risk of neurotic illness. . . . Thus education has to find its way between the Scylla of non-interference and the Charybdis of frustration.[39]

According to Freud, the complex and difficult cultural task of the educator is "[1] to recognize the child's constitutional individuality, [2] to infer from small indications what is going on in his immature mind," and "[3] to give him the right amount of love and yet to maintain an effective degree of authority." In Freud's view, the maximization of the chances of success in such a task presupposes the sensitivity and openness to childhood experience that is the exclusive hallmark of psychoanalysis. *"The only appropriate preparation for the profession of educator,"* Freud concludes, *"is a thorough psycho-analytic training."*

> It would be best that he [the educator] should have been analyzed himself, for, when all is said and done, it is impossible to assimilate analysis without experiencing it personally. The analysis of teachers and educators seems to be a more efficacious prophylactic measure than the analysis of children themselves, and there are less difficulties in the way of putting it into practice.[40] (emphasis added)

Only the undoing of the educator's own infantile amnesia can hope to seize the possibility of rupturing the cycle of repetition that Freud discerns at the heart of culture. The education of the educator must therefore be located within the terrain of psychoanalysis. No longer as estranged from the difficulties of childhood experience, the "analytic educationalist"[41] is not as unconscious a vehicle of the reproduction of cultural forms. For Freud, the future awaits embedded not in the children themselves, but rather in a transvaluated relation on the part of the educator toward his own parents. Conceived as the upbringing of the next generation, the transformation of culture is itself an act of retroactive resignification. In transforming our relations to our parents, we transform our relations to our children. If a culture is to claim its future, it must alter its past.

Freud's point, to put it otherwise, is that the degree to which a given culture can succeed in its own self-education is the degree to which its living members can manage to place the persistent authority of the dead into question. Since, for Freud, this authority is unconsciously mediated, its questioning is rather a questioning of the unconscious. If psychoanalysis can claim specificity as the hermeneutic of the unconscious *par excellence*, it must of necessity claim a prominent role in the transformation of the culture it criticizes. Fundamentally, this is why Freud grew to regard his discovery of the language of the unconscious as a cultural event of historic proportions.

THE LEGITIMATE FUNCTION OF PSYCHOANALYSIS

Freud's preoccupation with the specificity—and hence the autonomy—of psychoanalysis is evidenced in his brief comments about the "partisan" aims of education:

> It has been said—and no doubt justly—that every education has a partisan aim, that it endeavours to bring the child into line with the established order of society, without considering how valuable or how stable that order may be in itself. If . . . one is convinced of the defects in our present social arrangements, education with a psycho-analytic alignment cannot justifiably be put at their service as well: it must be given another and higher aim, liberated from the prevailing demands of society.[42]

Strangely enough, though certainly "convinced of the defects in our present social arrangements," Freud states that placing psychoanalysis at the service of a "higher aim" oversteps *"the legitimate function of analysis"* (emphasis added).[43] Indeed, he energetically warns us that in speaking of this legitimate function, he is "leaving entirely on one side the fact that psycho-analysis would be refused any influence on education if it admitted to intentions inconsistent with the established social order." Rather than strategic, Freud's concern is that, regardless of how praiseworthy, "[t]his other [higher] aim which it is desired to give to education will also be a partisan one, and *it is not the affair of an analyst to decide between the parties"* (emphases added).⁴⁴ That is, as Jean-Bertrand Pontalis puts it, "[f]or the benefit of those who denounce today's sexual education as excessively normative, it should be added that to avoid that kind of criticism, it is not enough for the teacher simply to change coats."⁴⁵ Like the analyst, the analytic educationalist must rather learn to rest content with "some such role as that of a guide on a difficult mountain climb."⁴⁶ Freud wishes not to engender a new generation subject to new truths, but rather to assume, so to speak, the position of a thoughtful midwife. He seeks not to *teach* but to *enable a child to learn*.

Freud's emphasis upon the legitimate function of analysis is intended to preclude the reduction of the pedagogical situation to the level of a mere transmission of knowledge, of instruction. For regardless of the question of the truth-value—or lack thereof—of the knowledge to be transmitted, instruction cannot in and of itself constitute an adequate mode of communication with the ways of the unconscious. The gulf of infantile amnesia separates not only our adult judgments of value but also—and perhaps more importantly—our *"processes of thought* from those of even normal children"* (emphasis added).⁴⁷ Thus, just as in regard to the psychoanalytic situation itself, Freud warns analysts against merely increasing the analysand's knowledge without altering anything else in him,⁴⁸ so does he insist, in regard to the pedagogical situation, that the psychoanalytic pedagogue not grasp the matter solely at the level of instruction, as an imparting of presumably true, positive knowledge to children. "We can have an analogous experience," Freud writes,

> when we give children sexual enlightenment. *I am far from maintaining that this is a harmful or unnecessary thing to do,* but it is clear that the prophylactic effect of this liberal measure has been greatly over-estimated. After such enlightenment, children know something they did not know before, but they make no use of the new knowledge that has been presented to them. . . . For a long time after they have been given sexual enlightenment they behave like primitive races who have had Christianity thrust upon them and who continue to worship their old idols in secret.⁴⁹ (emphasis added)

Not to instruct but to educate: the task of psychoanalysis is that of a cultural work, a protracted labor upon forces which, though not inaccessible to influence, are at best recalcitrant. Psychoanalysis neither can nor does decide between contending partisan aims of education precisely because it is rooted in the insight that the subordination of the intricacies and subtleties of the pedagogical situation to preestablished truths foreign to a child's psychic functioning is ultimately doomed to failure. When Freud protects the legitimate function of analysis, he is in fact attempting to preclude the forgetfulness of his insights into the unconscious. His respect for resistances at the level of the therapeutic thus appears, at the level of the pedagogic, as respect for the forgotten depths and complexities of a child's universe. His critique of culture targets not only the *goal* but also, and fundamentally, the very *mode* of acculturation.

Thus, rather than a senseless siding with the Scylla of noninterference, Freud's intent is to deploy a particular mode of intervention. Against those he regards as "the adherents of 'the normal person',"[50] Freud wishes to facilitate, pedagogically, communication with that about the subject which the subject itself forecloses. The gift he hopes to offer our descendants is not so much an alternative image of 'normality', as much as an intimation evoking, to borrow a phrase of Moustapha Safouan's, "the pathways that lead to the unconscious."[51] The sole pedagogical task of psychoanalysis is that of catalyzing the preconditions that might enable a subject to place before itself the paradox of a knowledge it does not know it has—a knowledge it simultaneously refuses to tolerate. Its legitimate function is the interminable *cultivation* of the subject's own self-relation as a mode of learning.[52] For Freud, psychoanalysis "itself contains enough revolutionary factors to ensure that no one educated by it will in later life take the side of reaction and suppression."[53] Paradoxically, his refusal to choose between partisan aims is rather a commitment to these revolutionary factors. Freud's hope is to contribute to the construction of a mode of human life that, in questioning and guiding itself, does not do so punitively. Simply put, the cultural revolution Freud claims tentatively to envision aims at a culture that enjoins us to "reflect rather than be angry"— at an undoing of the sociohistorical conflation of morality and punishment that, as Nietzsche well knew, the genealogy of Western culture so painfully exposes.[54]

A GAME OF CHESS

Introducing a paper on psychoanalytic technique, Freud tells us that

> Anyone who hopes to learn the noble game of chess from books will soon discover that only the openings and end-games admit of an exhaustive systematic presentation and that the infinite variety of moves which develop after the opening defy any such description. The gap in instruction can only be filled by a diligent study of games fought out by masters. The rules which can be laid down for the practice of psycho-analytic treatment are subject to similar limitations.[55]

The limitations attendant to a programmatic statement are significantly deepened when the matter at issue is the practical application of psychoanalysis not in treatment but in the field of pedagogy. In fact, Freud explicitly warns us that

> One should not be misled by the statement—incidentally a perfectly true one—that the psycho-analysis of an adult neurotic is equivalent to an after-education. A child, even a wayward and delinquent child, is still not a neurotic; and after-education is something quite different from the education of the immature. The possibility of analytic influence rests on quite definite preconditions which can be summed up under the term 'analytic situation'; it requires the development of certain psychical structures and a particular attitude to the analyst.[56]

To be sure, Freud immediately adds that "if one . . . has learnt analysis by experiencing it on his own person and is in a position of being able to employ it in borderline and mixed cases to assist him in his work, he should obviously be given the right to practice analysis, and narrow-minded motives should not be allowed to try to put obstacles in his way."[57] All the same, Freud's distinction between the pedagogical and the analytic situations is rooted in his awareness that the capacity for judgment that the psychoanalyst seeks to facilitate cannot be presupposed, at least not in the same degree, by the pedagogue. A child cannot be expected to transcend retroactively the helplessness in which he is presently immersed. To expect him to do so is once again to forget that he is a child.

At the heart of Freud's distinction between psychoanalysis and pedagogy is his elaboration of our prematurity, of the helplessness of the human infant. According to Freud, the "immature and feeble ego" of the human child "cannot fend off the emotional storms" it is bound to encounter "in any way except by repression."[58] Thus, Freud tells us unambiguously that "the work of education is something *sui generis:* it is not to be confused with psycho-analytic influence and cannot be replaced by it." When the presuppositions of the analytic situation are lacking, as they necessarily are in the case of children, "something other than analysis must be employed, though something which will be at one with analysis in its *purpose*" (emphasis in original).[59]

Still, the truth of the matter is that there is very little in Freud's *own* work, if anything at all, that can guide us any further. He did not construct a detailed systematic view of what this adaptation of psychoanalysis—and therefore, we might add, of our culture as a whole—to the needs of children might practically entail.[60] He takes his leave not with a programmatic statement but with the recommendation—which, to be sure, we need not underestimate—that the psychoanalytic training of the educator would at least ensure that the object of his efforts, the child, would no longer remain "an inaccessible problem" to him.[61]

What, then, is to be done?
We could do worse than ponder carefully Freud's claim that

> the information gained by psycho-analysis, upon the origin of pathogenic complexes and upon the nucleus of every nervous affection, can claim with justice that it deserves to be regarded by educators as an invaluable guide in their conduct towards children. What practical conclusions may follow from this, and how far experience may justify the application of those conclusions within our present social system, are matters which I leave to the examination and decision of others.[62]

The "fateful question" in terms of which Freud frames the destiny of the human species is staked between the hopes for the future and the intractability of the past, Eros and Death—our longing to live and our equally powerful wish not to have been born. For Freud, the struggle constitutive of human life is a struggle between remembrance and forgetfulness, between modes of experiencing temporality. It is an interminable, deeply practical struggle to define and redefine whence we came, who we are and in what situation we wish to find ourselves in the future. In the end, Freud formulates his question pedagogically, as a question about the upbringing of the next generation.

It goes without saying that I find myself unable—and perhaps unwilling—to venture a response to Freud's question. I can only choose to consider myself satisfied if I have managed to intimate the truth that what we generally (mis)take as Freud's pessimism is rather the emblem of an extraordinary sensitivity to both the dangers and the vulnerabilities of our ordinary, mortal humanity. Freud's theory of culture culminates not in resignation but in a profound invitation to live—to endure life and thus to fulfill our erotic "first duty" as living beings.

NOTES

1. Sigmund Freud, "Two Lies Told by Children," in vol. 12 of *The Standard Edition of the Complete Psychological Works of Sigmund Freud,* ed. and trans. James Strachey et al. (London: Hogarth, 1953–1974), 305.
2. Freud, "Two Lies Told by Children," 307.
3. Freud, "Two Lies Told by Children," 306.
4. Freud, "Two Lies Told by Children," 305.
5. Freud, "Two Lies Told by Children," 305.
6. Freud, "Two Lies Told by Children," 305.
7. Freud, "Two Lies Told by Children," 306.
8. Freud, "Two Lies Told by Children," 307.
9. Sigmund Freud, "The Claims of Psycho-Analysis to Scientific Interest," in vol. 13 of *The Standard Edition,* ed. and trans. James Strachey et al., 190.

10. Sigmund Freud, *The Question of Lay Analysis,* in vol. 20 of *The Standard Edition,* ed. and trans. James Strachey et al., 249.

11. Sigmund Freud, *Civilization and Its Discontents,* in vol. 21 of *The Standard Edition,* ed. and trans. James Strachey et al., 144.

12. Freud, *Civilization and Its Discontents,* 144. In "The Resistances to Psycho-Analysis," Freud writes: "The situation obeyed a simple formula: men in the mass behaved to psycho-analysis in precisely the same way as individual neurotics under treatment for their disorders. . . . The position was at once alarming and consoling: alarming because it was no small thing to have the whole human race as one's patient, and consoling because after all everything was taking place as the hypotheses of psycho-analysis declared it was bound to." Sigmund Freud, "The Resistances to Psycho-Analysis," in vol. 19 of *The Standard Edition,* ed. and trans. James Strachey et al., 221. Similarly, in "The Future Prospects of Psycho-Analytic Therapy," Freud poses the same predicament: "Society will not be in a hurry to grant us authority. It is bound to offer us resistance, for we adopt a critical attitude towards it; we point out to it that it itself plays a great part in causing neuroses. Just as we make an individual our enemy by uncovering what is repressed in him, so society cannot respond with sympathy to a relentless exposure of its injurious effects and deficiencies. Because we destroy illusions we are accused of endangering ideals." Sigmund Freud, "The Future Prospects of Psycho-Analytic Therapy," in vol. 11 of *The Standard Edition,* ed. and trans. James Strachey et al., 147.

13. See chapter 3, "The Critique of the Hypnotist's Authority" and "The Work of Psychoanalysis."

14. Freud, *Civilization and Its Discontents,* 141.

15. Sigmund Freud, *New Introductory Lectures on Psycho-Analysis,* in vol. 22 of *The Standard Edition,* ed. and trans. James Strachey et al., 67.

16. Sigmund Freud, *An Outline of Psycho-Analysis,* in vol. 23 of *The Standard Edition,* ed. and trans. James Strachey et al., 146. See also chapter 3, note 146.

17. Freud, *Civilization and Its Discontents,* 142. "At this point," Freud adds in this same passage, "the two processes, that of the cultural development of the group and that of the cultural development of the individual, are, as it were, always interlocked."

18. Freud, *Civilization and Its Discontents,* 145. Leo Bersani writes: "[. . .] I would suggest that a precondition for such a transformation [of civilized discourse] would be to abandon as a cultural model the great leader's prophetic speech. Freud's ambivalence about that speech and that role in his very performance of it is by no means one of the lesser signs of his extraordinarily moving complexity." Leo Bersani, *The Freudian Body: Psychoanalysis and Art* (New York: Columbia University Press, 1986), 24.

19. Bersani, *The Freudian Body,* 3.

20. Cf. J.-B. Pontalis, "The Illusion Sustained," in *Frontiers in Psychoanalysis: Between the Dream and Psychic Pain,* trans. Catherine and Philip Cullen (London: Hogarth, 1981), 80.

21. Freud, *New Introductory Lectures,* 146.

22. Sigmund Freud, "The Sexual Enlightenment of Children," in vol. 9 of *The Standard Edition,* ed. and trans. James Strachey et al., 139. As noted by the editors of *The Standard Edition,* Freud makes the same observation a year later, in regard

to the practices of marriage and monogamy, in Sigmund Freud, "'Civilized' Sexual Morality and Modern Nervous Illness," in vol. 9 of *The Standard Edition*, ed. and trans. James Strachey et al., 196.

23. See Ernesto Laclau and Chantal Mouffe, *Hegemony and Socialist Strategy: Towards a Radical Democratic Politics*, trans. Winston Moore and Paul Cammack (London: Verso, 1985).

24. I discuss Freud's Nachträglichkeit earlier, in chapter 3, in "From Hypnosis to Psychoanalysis." See also note 53 in chapter 1.

25. Sigmund Freud, *On the History of the Psycho-Analytic Movement*, in vol. 14 of *The Standard Edition*, ed. and trans. James Strachey et al., 57. Elsewhere, in keeping with his conception of culture as an arena of struggle, Freud writes: "Indeed, the whole *progress* of society rests upon the opposition between successive generations" (emphasis added). Sigmund Freud, "Family Romances," in vol. 9 of *The Standard Edition*, ed. and trans. James Strachey et al., 237.

26. Freud, *New Introductory Lectures*, 66–67.

27. See chapter 4, especially "Economics and Psychology" and "Compulsion and Transformation."

28. See chapter 1, especially "Loss and Intersubjectivity"; chapter 3, especially "The Work of Psychoanalysis"; and chapter 4, especially "The Cultural Abandonment of Hypnosis."

29. Freud, "The Claims of Psycho-Analysis," 189.

30. Freud, "Future Prospects," 151.

31. Freud, "The Claims of Psycho-Analysis," 189–90.

32. Sigmund Freud, "On Narcissism: An Introduction," in vol. 14 of *The Standard Edition*, ed. and trans. James Strachey et al., 90.

33. Freud, "On Narcissism," 91.

34. Freud, "On Narcissism," 91.

35. Freud, "On Narcissism," 91.

36. Sigmund Freud, *The Future of an Illusion*, in vol. 21 of *The Standard Edition*, ed. and trans. James Strachey et al., 9.

37. Freud, *New Introductory Lectures*, 148–49. In the very next paragraph, Freud speaks of "an incidental consideration, an indirect way in which the upbringing of children may be helped by analysis and which may with time acquire a greater influence. Parents who have themselves experienced an analysis and owe much to it, including an insight into the faults of their own upbringing, will treat their children with better understanding and will spare them much of what they themselves were not spared" (150).

38. Freud, *New Introductory Lectures*, 148–49.

39. Freud, *New Introductory Lectures*, 149.

40. Freud, *New Introductory Lectures*, 149–50.

41. Freud, *The Question of Lay Analysis*, 249.

42. Freud, *New Introductory Lectures*, 150.

43. Freud, *New Introductory Lectures*, 150.

44. Freud, *New Introductory Lectures*, 151.

45. Pontalis, "Between Knowledge and Fantasy," in *Frontiers*, 97.

46. Freud, *An Outline of Psycho-Analysis*, 174.

47. Freud, "The Claims of Psycho-Analysis," 189.

48. See chapter 3, especially "The Critique of the Hypnotist's Authority."

49. Sigmund Freud, "Analysis Terminable and Interminable," in vol. 23 of *The Standard Edition*, ed. and trans. James Strachey et al., 233–34; quoted by Pontalis, "Knowledge and Fantasy," 97. In the same passage, Pontalis writes: "First of all, notice that the expression 'sexual education' conceals a condensation already present in the term 'to inform' (to give indications and explanations, but also to give form to), which is considerably intensified here: is not the aim *to educate* rather than to instruct? . . . [O]ne must indeed encourage parents and educators not to lie to children, not to answer with 'childish sayings,' in other words with myths concocted by adults for children, but one must not expect such knowledge to replace the unconscious" (emphasis in original).

50. Sigmund Freud, "Analysis of a Phobia in a Five-Year-Old Boy," in vol. 10 of *The Standard Edition*, ed. and trans. James Strachey et al., 141.

51. "Everything else," Safouan adds, "is excess baggage." Moustapha Safouan, "The Apprenticeship of Tilmann Moser," in *Returning to Freud: Clinical Psychoanalysis in the School of Lacan*, trans. and ed. Stuart Schneiderman (New Haven, Conn.: Yale University Press, 1980), 167.

52. Shoshana Felman writes: "But the position of the teacher is itself the position of the one who learns, of the one who teaches nothing other than the way he learns. The subject of teaching is interminably—a student; the subject of teaching is interminably—a learning. This is the most radical, perhaps the most far-reaching insight psychoanalysis can give us into pedagogy." Shoshana Felman, *Jacques Lacan and the Adventure of Insight: Psychoanalysis in Contemporary Culture* (Cambridge, Mass.: Harvard University Press, 1987), 88.

53. Freud, *New Introductory Lectures*, 151.

54. See Friedrich Nietzsche, *On the Genealogy of Morals*, trans. Walter Kaufmann and R. J. Hollingdale (New York: Vintage, 1969).

55. Sigmund Freud, "On Beginning the Treatment (Further Recommendations on the Technique of Psycho-Analysis, I)," in vol. 12 of *The Standard Edition*, ed. and trans. James Strachey et al., 123.

56. Sigmund Freud, "Preface to Aichhorn's *Wayward Youth*," in vol. 19 of *The Standard Edition*, ed. and trans. James Strachey et al., 274.

57. Freud, "Preface," 274–75.

58. Freud, *New Introductory Lectures*, 147.

59. Freud, "Preface," 274.

60. In *New Introductory Lectures*, Freud writes: "I am glad that I am at least able to say that my daughter, Anna Freud, has made this study her lifework and has in that way compensated for my neglect." Freud, *New Introductory Lectures*, 147. See, for example, Anna Freud, *Introduction to Psychoanalysis: Lectures for Child Analysts and Teachers (1922–1935)* (London: Hogarth, 1974).

61. Freud, "Preface," 274.

62. Freud, "Analysis of a Phobia in a Five-Year-Old Boy," 146–47.

Concluding Remarks

The analyst of today, at grips with narcissism, the narcissism of his patients, of his colleagues and himself, sometimes has the feeling that what he perceives of the great clamour of the world, patched up with cement and full of cracks, is but the echo of what he hears in his seemingly padded office. Freud said "I am located on the ground floor or in the basement of the building." We, with less confidence than he had in the powers of the Architect, will say: at the frontier of death and life, a constantly moving frontier which is drawn only to be erased and re-established elsewhere.

—Jean-Bertrand Pontalis

As we have seen, Freud's statement that "to endure life remains, when all is said, the first duty of all living beings" captures epigrammatically his critique of a culture unable to deal adequately with the predicaments of loss and death. In so doing, it presents us with an image—posed in the shape of a "fateful question" about a possible future—of a different culture. Like Freud's "first duty," this future connects the sphere of the ethical, of the superego, not with death but with life. Essentially, Freud's claim is that the chances of Eros are best strengthened in and through an encounter with the irretrievably intersubjective law of death, of mortality. Informed by a pedagogy of loss, a new superego might come to instantiate an ascendancy of the demands of care rather than destructiveness, of Eros rather than Death.

Freud grasps the infant's accession into cultural life not only negatively in terms of the forcefulness of fear but also positively in terms of the formative experiences of loss that catalyze the developmental task of mourning. His concept of culture, then, transcends a merely negative sphere of prohibitions and protections. Beyond the terms of Hobbes's theorization of the relation between individual and society, Freud posits a duty to endure and respect the otherness of the other as constitutive of the very possibility of the self's development. Pedagogically, Freud's "hopes for the future" point toward human beings who are not the *subjects* but rather the *citizens* of culture.

Yet at the same time, Freud insists that the irretrievably relational constitution of the human being does not entail that such relational constitution is exhaustive of human identity. The Freudian work of mourning is radically interminable. It is neither a Hobbesian submission to a feared external authority who represents and instantiates one's own death, nor a Hegelian 'labor of the negative' culminating in a fully sutured reconciliation of particular and universal, individual and society. The work of mourning renders accessible to the subject the field not so much of Reason as of humanized desire. At stake is the possibility not of a self transparent to itself, but of an irremediably fragmented subject whose continuous encounter with the denied cleavages of death is the basis of its accession to the field of temporality. Not transcendence but, in Freud's words, an experience of "longing unaccompanied by despair"[1] is at issue. The discontents of culture can be minimized but not abolished. Nor ought they be. For when positively seized, the sustained endurance of life is simultaneously the continuously renewed cultivation of desire. Freud grasps as the gravest of dangers what Hegel sought as the most desirable of goals. If philosophy were to manage, in Hegel's memorable phrase, to "lay aside the title '*love* of knowing' and be *actual* knowing,"[2] then philosophy would have managed, in Freud's terms, to repress its own Eros.

The specifically political dimension of Freud's pedagogy of mourning is best broached in terms of an examination of the juncture between the denial of death and unquestioned authority, between illusion and domination, that his theory posits at the heart of the culture it criticizes. In Freud's work, this juncture is articulated at two distinct yet complementary levels, the one 'clinical' and the other 'cultural.' Clinically, the origins of psychoanalysis present a critique of a practice—i.e., hypnosis—that by not grounding itself in what it wishes to transform, cannot help but remain either impotent or authoritarian, either unheeded or heeded only as a result of violence. As a therapeutic technique, psychoanalysis must therefore proceed, in its own conflicted way, along the difficult paths of immanent negation.

At the level of the cultural, Freud's critique of the ill-fated trappings of externally imposed authority posits the decline of religion in the modern world as an opportunity to deploy an alternative mode of acculturation.

Freud's daring thematization of the role of the hypnotic in the constitution of social relations and of political authority invites an equally daring extension of the critical principles of psychoanalysis to the sphere of cultural life. For Freud, the political function of religion as a mechanism of social cohesion is as unreliable and as ethically objectionable as a hypnotist's suggestions. Thus, as Freud has it, the "fateful question" modernity poses for itself concerns a redeployment of the fundamental principles holding together the life and work of culture.

For Freud, the historic task of psychoanalysis is to raise this question pedagogically, in terms of the difficult and conflicted terrain of the underestimated and extraordinary weight of early childhood experience. At this juncture, Freud's understanding of the relations between generations as central to the historical production and reproduction of cultural forms opens the way for the consideration of the place of psychoanalysis in an interminable practice of cultural transformation. Freud has in mind not so much a would-be universal therapeutics seeking the psychoanalysis of every member of a given cultural unit, but rather a protracted, attitudinal dissemination of psychoanalytic principles beginning in the sphere of children's pedagogy—of "upbringing" widely conceived. Moreover, since for Freud an alteration of the subject's relation to childhood both posits and presupposes a simultaneous alteration of the subject's own self-relation, this dissemination would overflow onto other spheres of cultural life. However problematic it might be, one can hardly avoid the suspicion that Freud's concerns capture the continuous teaching and cultivation of the 'good life' as crucial to a life-sustaining organization of human existence.

In the most general sense, Freud envisions a culture no longer informed by that deathly ruse whose conflation of well-being with omnipotence, of truth with God, is but an homage to our capacity for self-destructiveness. The paradox he relentlessly explores is that the deepest of repressions obeys a repudiation not of pleasure but of pain, and that, by way of such repudiation, the pleasure-seeking refusal of postponement and negation both enlarges the field of destructiveness and precludes the precarious unfolding of truly human joys. Freud's is an alarmingly simple insight: an insistence to understand, as if against oneself, that the claims of care and pleasure can be cultivated only in and through the inevitable encounter with loss and death.

Thus understood, Freud's theory of culture reopens, in a novel manner, age-old questions about the relation between politics and pedagogy, power and knowledge, rhetoric and reason—relations Freud grasps, in his own terms, as those between hypnosis and analysis. To be sure, not Freud but Nietzsche originally comes to complicate, with epochal forcefulness, the purportedly transparent autonomy of these categories from each other. If not since Machiavelli, certainly since Nietzsche political thought finds itself suspended between a relentless exposure of the workings of power at the heart of every truth-claim and a resulting ambivalence about grounding even its own possibility. It is caught, as it were, between a fascination with the prospects of liberation and a fear that it might surprise itself participating in the "legitimizing plots"[3] it seeks to expose. In Freud's language, post-Nietzschean political thought has discovered the workings of hypnotic suggestion at the heart of the analytic transference, and hence fears for the very possibility of analysis. To discover rhetoric dwelling in the house of reason, war in the heart of culture, is to wonder whether the philosopher is but the most dangerous, most *powerful* of sophists. To put it otherwise, dominant modes of contemporary political thought dramatize a profoundly ironic logic whereby emancipatory concern with the pervasiveness of power loses sight of the category of legitimate authority, thereby obscuring discussion of the problem of tyranny.[4]

Whether—to borrow Nietzsche's terms—our uneasy suspension between God and Nothingness is, as some expect, pregnant with an unborn future, or whether on the contrary, it is, as others nostalgically insist, a symptom of regrettable decline, is a question that, as I stated to begin with, would take us beyond the bounds of what I set out to accomplish. Yet I find myself unable to conclude without recalling that to invoke, with modernity, the claims of democracy, is simultaneously to evoke problems pertaining to the very meaning of both knowledge and authority. As Freud well knew, neither these claims nor those problems can be disposed of in the name of a nostalgic longing for the full positivity of an illusory, lossless Eros that deems itself free from the intrusions of Death. It may well be that, as Leo Bersani has it, the central legacy of Freud's work is to initiate, even if at times against Freud himself, an "ethical-erotic project," born of the awareness of "human beings' extraordinary willingness to kill in order to protect the seriousness of their statements."[5]

Freud's thought does more than simply recall age-old questions. It perhaps also manages to explore anew, to resignify retroactively the very ground from which these questions might be both examined and experienced. For Freud, childhood is this ground—a soil that, fraught with its own difficulties, can by no means do without cultivation, and that presents those who are to tend to it with difficult challenges, temptations to carve the features of their own power. I hope to have shown *not* that age-old questions arise, as it were externally, *out of* an exegesis of Freud's works. Rather, I hope to have shown that those questions belong to the innermost dynamics that animate and reanimate his thought. Amidst our uncertainties, it is certain only that political philosophy affords to ignore Freud's lessons only at the cost of its own impoverishment. It forgoes the effort to envision a culture that promises neither happiness nor consolation, but the modest prospects of enduring the loss of a life truly lived.

NOTES

1. Sigmund Freud, *Inhibitions, Symptoms and Anxiety*, in vol. 20 of *The Standard Edition of the Complete Psychological Works of Sigmund Freud*, ed. and trans. James Strachey et al. (London: Hogarth, 1953–1974), 170.

2. G. W. F. Hegel, *Phenomenology of Spirit*, trans. A. V. Miller (New York: Oxford University Press, 1977), 3.

3. The phrase is Leo Bersani's. See Leo Bersani, *The Culture of Redemption* (Cambridge, Mass.: Harvard University Press, 1990), 4.

4. Cf. Gad Horowitz, "The Foucaultian Impasse: No Sex, No Self, No Revolution," *Political Theory* 15 (February 1987): 61–80. See also Eugene Victor Wolfenstein, *Inside/Outside Nietzche: Psychoanalytic Explorations* (Ithaca, N.Y.: Cornell University Press, 2000). For discussion of the question of post-Nietzschean political theory, see William E. Connolly, *Identity/Difference: Democratic Negotiations of Political Paradox* (Ithaca, N.Y., and London: Cornell University Press, 1991).

5. Bersani, *The Culture of Redemption*, 3–4.

Selected Bibliography

Abramson, Jeffrey. *Liberation and Its Limits: The Moral and Political Thought of Freud.* Boston: Beacon, 1984.

Adamson, Walter L. *Hegemony and Revolution: A Study of Antonio Gramsci's Political and Cultural Theory.* Berkeley: University of California Press, 1980.

Adelman, Howard. "Of Human Bondage: Labour, Bondage and Freedom in the *Phenomenology.*" In *Hegel's Social and Political Thought,* edited by Donald P. Verene, 119–35. Atlantic Highlands, N.J.: Humanities, 1980.

Adorno, Theodor W. "Freudian Theory and the Pattern of Fascist Propaganda." In *The Essential Frankfurt School Reader,* edited by Andrew Arato and Eike Gebhardt, 118–37. New York: Continuum, 1982.

———. "Sociology and Psychology I." *New Left Review* 46 (November/December 1967): 67–80.

———. "Sociology and Psychology II." *New Left Review* 47 (January/February 1968): 79–97.

Adorno, Theodor W., and Max Horkheimer. *Dialectic of Enlightenment,* translated by John Cumming. New York: Continuum, 1982.

Alford, C. Fred. "Freud and Violence." In *Freud 2000,* edited by Anthony Elliot, 61–87. New York: Routledge, 1999.

———. *Narcissism: Socrates, the Frankfurt School, and Psychoanalytic Theory.* New Haven, Conn.: Yale University Press, 1988.

Andreas-Salomé, Lou. *The Freud Journal,* translated by Stanley A. Leavy. New York: Quartet Books, 1964.

Auden, W. H. "In Memory of Sigmund Freud." In *Collected Poems,* edited by Edward Mendelson, 273–76. New York: Vintage International, 1991.

Bacal, Howard A., and Kenneth M. Newman. *Theories of Object Relations: Bridges to Self Psychology.* New York: Columbia University Press, 1990.

Baranger, Madeleine, Willy Baranger, and Jorge Mario Mom. "The Infantile Psychic Trauma from Us to Freud: Pure Trauma, Retroactivity and Reconstruction." *International Journal of Psychoanalysis* 69 (1988): 113–28.

Barret, Michèle. "Psychoanalysis and Feminism: A British Sociologist's View." *Signs: Journal of Women in Culture and Society* 17 (Winter 1992): 455–66.

Bataille, Georges. *Erotism: Death & Sensuality,* translated by Mary Dalwood. San Francisco: City Lights, 1986.

Becker, Ernest. *The Denial of Death.* New York: Free Press, 1973.

Benjamin, Andrew. "Structuring as a Translation." In *Jean Laplanche: Seduction, Translation, Drives,* edited by John Fletcher and Martin Stanton, 137–57. London: Institute Contemporary Arts, 1992.

Benjamin, Jessica. "Authority and the Family Revisited: Or, a World without Fathers?" *New German Critique* 13 (Winter 1978): 35–57.

———. *The Bonds of Love: Psychoanalysis, Feminism and the Problem of Domination.* New York: Pantheon, 1988.

———. "A Desire of One's Own: Psychoanalytic Feminism and Intersubjective Space." In *Feminist Studies—Critical Studies,* edited by Teresa de Lauretis, 78–101. Bloomington: Indiana University Press, 1986.

———. "The End of Internalization: Adorno's Social Psychology." *Telos* 32 (Summer 1977): 42–64.

———. "The Primal Leap of Psychoanalysis, from Body to Speech: Freud, Feminism and the Vicissitudes of the Transference." In *Freud 2000,* edited by Anthony Elliot, 110–38. New York: Routledge, 1999.

Benjamin, Walter. "The Image of Proust." In *Illuminations,* translated by Harry Zohn, edited by Hannah Arendt, 201–15. New York: Schocken, 1969.

———. "On Some Motifs in Baudelaire." In *Illuminations,* translated by Harry Zohn, edited by Hannah Arendt, 155–200. New York: Schocken, 1969.

———. "Theses on the Philosophy of History." In *Illuminations,* translated by Harry Zohn, edited by Hannah Arendt, 253–64. New York: Schocken, 1969.

Bernstein, Richard J. *Freud and the Legacy of Moses.* Cambridge, UK: Cambridge University Press, 1998.

Bersani, Leo. "Erotic Assumptions: Narcissism and Sublimation in Freud." In *The Culture of Redemption,* 29–46. Cambridge, Mass.: Harvard University Press, 1990.

———. *The Freudian Body: Psychoanalysis and Art.* New York: Columbia University Press, 1986.

Bettelheim, Bruno. *Freud and Man's Soul.* New York: Knopf, 1983.

Bloom, Harold. *The Anxiety of Influence: A Theory of Poetry.* 2d ed. Oxford, UK: Oxford University Press, 1997.

Boothby, Richard. *Death and Desire: Psychoanalytic Theory in Lacan's Return to Freud.* New York: Routledge, 1991.

Borch-Jacobsen, Mikkel. *The Emotional Tie: Psychoanalysis, Mimesis and Affect,* translated by Douglas Brick et al. Stanford, Calif.: Stanford University Press, 1992.

———. *The Freudian Subject,* translated by Catherine Porter. Stanford, Calif.: Stanford University Press, 1988.

Bowie, Malcolm. *Lacan.* London: Fontana, 1991.

Bracher, Mark. *Lacan, Discourse, and Social Change: A Psychoanalytic Cultural Criticism.* Ithaca, N.Y.: Cornell University Press, 1993.

Brenner, Charles. *An Elementary Textbook of Psychoanalysis.* New York: Anchor, 1974.

Brown, Joanne, and Barry Richards. "The Humanist Freud." In *Freud 2000,* edited by Anthony Elliot, 235–61. New York: Routledge, 1999.

Brown, Norman O. *Life against Death: The Psychoanalytic Meaning of History.* Middletown, Conn.: Wesleyan University Press, 1959.

———. *Love's Body.* New York: Random House, 1966.

Brunner, José. *Freud and the Politics of Psychoanalysis.* Cambridge, Mass.: Blackwell, 1995.

Butler, Judith. "Gender Trouble, Feminist Theory, and Psychoanalytic Discourse." In *Feminism/Postmodernism,* edited by Linda J. Nicholson, 324–40. New York: Routledge, 1990.

Camus, Albert. *The Myth of Sisyphus,* translated by Justin O'Brien. Middlesex, UK: Penguin, 1975.

———. *The Rebel: An Essay on Man in Revolt,* translated by Anthony Bower. New York: Vintage, 1956.

———. *Resistance, Rebellion and Death,* translated by Justin O'Brien. New York: Knopf, 1961.

Cardinal, Marie. *The Words to Say It,* translated by Pat Goodheart. Cambridge, Mass.: VanVactor & Goodheart, 1983.

Casey, Edward S., and J. Melvin Woody. "Hegel, Heidegger, Lacan: The Dialectic of Desire." In *Interpreting Lacan,* edited by Joseph H. Smith and William Kerrigan, 75–112. New Haven, Conn.: Yale University Press, 1983.

Castoriadis, Cornelius. "Psychoanalysis and Politics." In *Speculations after Freud: Psychoanalysis, Philosophy and Culture,* edited by Sonu Shamdasani and Michael Münchow, 2–12. New York: Routledge, 1994.

Caudill, David S. *Lacan and the Subject of Law: Toward a Psychoanalytic Critical Legal Theory.* Atlantic Highlands, N.J.: Humanities Press, 1997.

Chasseguet-Smirgel, Janine. *Sexuality and Mind: The Role of the Father and the Mother in the Psyche.* New York: New York University Press, 1986.

Chasseguet-Smirgel, Janine, and Béla Grunberger. *Freud or Reich? Psychoanalysis and Illusion,* translated by Claire Pajaczkowska. New Haven, Conn.: Yale University Press, 1986.

Chessick, Richard D. "Prolegomena to the Study of Paul Ricoeur's *Freud and Philosophy.*" *Psychoanalytic Review* 75 (Summer 1988): 299–318.

Chodorow, Nancy J. "Beyond Drive Theory: Object Relations and the Limits of Radical Individualism." In *Feminism and Psychoanalytic Theory,* 114–53. New Haven, Conn.: Yale University Press, 1989.

———. "Freud on Women." In *The Cambridge Companion to Freud,* edited by Jerome Neu, 224–48. Cambridge, UK: Cambridge University Press, 1991.

Christensen, Darrel E. "Hegel's Phenomenological Analysis and Freud's Psychoanalysis." *International Philosophical Quarterly* 8 (September 1968): 356–78.

Church, Jennifer. "Morality and the Internalized Other." In *The Cambridge Companion to Freud,* edited by Jerome Neu, 209–23. Cambridge, UK: Cambridge University Press, 1991.

Comay, Rebecca. "Redeeming Revenge: Nietzsche, Benjamin, Heidegger." In *Nietzsche as Postmodernist: Essays Pro and Contra*, edited by Clayton Koelb, 21–38. Albany: State University of New York Press, 1990.

———. "Mourning Work and Play." *Research in Phenomenology* 23 (1993): 105–30.

Connolly, William E. *Identity/Difference: Democratic Negotiations of Political Paradox.* Ithaca, N.Y., and London: Cornell University Press, 1991.

———. *Political Theory and Modernity.* Ithaca, N.Y., and London: Cornell University Press, 1993.

Cornell, Drucilla, and Adam Thurschwell. "Feminism, Negativity, Intersubjectivity." In *Feminism as Critique,* edited by Seyla Benhabib and Drucilla Cornell, 143–62. Minneapolis: University of Minnesota Press, 1987.

Dallmayr, Fred. "The Discourse of Modernity: Hegel, Nietzsche, Heidegger (and Habermas)." *Praxis International* 8 (January 1989): 377–406.

———. "Freud, Nietzsche, Lacan: A Discourse on Critical Theory." *Politics, Culture and Society* 2 (Summer 1989): 467–92.

Deigh, John. "Freud's Later Theory of Civilization: Changes and Implications." In *The Cambridge Companion to Freud,* edited by Jerome Neu, 287–308. Cambridge, UK: Cambridge University Press, 1991.

de Marneffe, Daphne. "Looking and Listening: The Construction of Clinical Knowledge in Charcot and Freud." *Signs: Journal of Women in Culture and Society* 17 (Autumn 1991): 71–111.

Elliot, Anthony. "Freud, Feminism and Postmodernism." In *Freud 2000,* edited by Anthony Elliot, 88–109. New York: Routledge, 1999.

———. "Introduction." In *Freud 2000,* edited by Anthony Elliot, 1–12. New York: Routledge, 1999.

———. *Social Theory and Psychoanalysis in Transition: Self and Society from Freud to Kristeva.* Oxford, UK: Blackwell, 1992.

Elshtain, Jean B. "Symmetry and Soporifics: A Critique of Feminist Accounts of Gender Development." In *Capitalism and Infancy: Essays on Psychoanalysis and Politics,* edited by Barry Richards, 55–91. London: Free Association Books, 1984.

Erikson, Erik H. *Young Man Luther: A Study in Psychoanalysis and History.* New York: Norton, 1958.

Eskelinen de Folch, Terttu. "Obstacles to Analytic Cure." In *On Freud's "Analysis Terminable and Interminable,"* edited by Joseph Sandler, 93–105. New Haven, Conn.: Yale University Press, 1991.

Felman, Shoshana. *Jacques Lacan and the Adventure of Insight: Psychoanalysis in Contemporary Culture.* Cambridge, Mass.: Harvard University Press, 1987.

Ferrara, Alessandro. "Contemporary Modernity and Its Discontents." In *Modernity and Authenticity: The Social and Ethical Thought of Jean-Jacques Rousseau, 7–28.* Albany: State University of New York Press, 1993.

Flay, Joseph C. "Comment." In *Hegel and the Philosophy of Religion,* edited by Darrel E. Christensen, 142–46. The Hague: Martinus Nijhoff, 1970.

———. *Hegel's Quest for Certainty.* Albany: State University of New York Press, 1984.

Forrester, John. *Dispatches from the Freud Wars: Psychoanalysis and Its Passions.* Cambridge, Mass.: Harvard University Press, 1997.

———. *The Seductions of Psychoanalysis: Freud, Lacan, Derrida.* Cambridge, UK: Cambridge University Press, 1990.

Foucault, Michel. *An Introduction.* Vol. I of *The History of Sexuality,* translated by Robert Hurley. New York: Vintage, 1980.

Freire, Paulo. *Pedagogy of the Oppressed,* translated by Myra Bergman Ramos. New York: Continuum, 1985.

Freud, Anna. *The Ego and the Mechanisms of Defense,* translated by Cecil Baines. New York: International Universities Press, 1966.

———. *Introduction to Psychoanalysis: Lectures for Child Analysts and Teachers (1922–1935).* London: Hogarth, 1974.

Freud, Ernst L., ed. *The Letters of Sigmund Freud & Arnold Zweig,* translated by Elaine and William Robson-Scott. New York: New York University Press, 1970.

Freud, Sigmund. *Analysis of a Phobia in a Five-Year-Old Boy.* In vol. 10 of *The Standard Edition of the Complete Psychological Works of Sigmund Freud,* edited and translated by James Strachey et al., 3–149. London: Hogarth, 1953–1974.

———. "Analysis Terminable and Interminable." In vol. 23 of *The Standard Edition of the Complete Psychological Works of Sigmund Freud,* edited and translated by James Strachey et al., 209–53. London: Hogarth, 1953–1974.

———. *An Autobiographical Study.* In vol. 20 of *The Standard Edition of the Complete Psychological Works of Sigmund Freud,* edited and translated by James Strachey et al., 1–74. London: Hogarth, 1953–1974.

———. *Beyond the Pleasure Principle.* In vol. 18 of *The Standard Edition of the Complete Psychological Works of Sigmund Freud,* edited and translated by James Strachey et al., 1–64. London: Hogarth, 1953–1974.

———. *Civilization and Its Discontents.* In vol. 21 of *The Standard Edition of the Complete Psychological Works of Sigmund Freud,* edited and translated by James Strachey et al., 57–145. London: Hogarth, 1953–1974.

———. "'Civilized' Sexual Morality and Modern Nervous Illness." In vol. 9 of *The Standard Edition of the Complete Psychological Works of Sigmund Freud,* edited and translated by James Strachey et al., 177–204. London: Hogarth, 1953–1974.

———. "The Claims of Psycho-Analysis to Scientific Interest." In vol. 13 of *The Standard Edition of the Complete Psychological Works of Sigmund Freud,* edited and translated by James Strachey et al., 163–90. London: Hogarth, 1953–1974.

———. "Constructions in Analysis." In vol. 23 of *The Standard Edition of the Complete Psychological Works of Sigmund Freud,* edited and translated by James Strachey et al., 255–69. London: Hogarth, 1953–1974.

———. "Creative Writers and Day-Dreaming." In vol. 9 of *The Standard Edition of the Complete Psychological Works of Sigmund Freud,* edited and translated by James Strachey et al., 141–53. London: Hogarth, 1953–1974.

———. "Delusions and Dreams in Jensen's *Gradiva.*" In vol. 9 of *The Standard Edition of the Complete Psychological Works of Sigmund Freud,* edited and translated by James Strachey et al., 1–95. London: Hogarth, 1953–1974.

———. "A Difficulty in the Path of Psycho-Analysis." In vol. 17 of *The Standard Edition of the Complete Psychological Works of Sigmund Freud,* edited and translated by James Strachey et al., 135–44. London: Hogarth, 1953–1974.

———. "The Dissolution of the Oedipus Complex." In vol. 19 of *The Standard Edition of the Complete Psychological Works of Sigmund Freud,* edited and translated by James Strachey et al., 171–79. London: Hogarth, 1953–1974.

———. "A Disturbance of Memory on the Acropolis." In vol. 22 of *The Standard Edition of the Complete Psychological Works of Sigmund Freud*, edited and translated by James Strachey et al., 237–48. London: Hogarth, 1953–1974.

———. "Dostoevsky and Parricide." In vol. 21 of *The Standard Edition of the Complete Psychological Works of Sigmund Freud*, edited and translated by James Strachey et al., 173–94. London: Hogarth, 1953–1974.

———. "The Dynamics of Transference." In vol. 12 of *The Standard Edition of the Complete Psychological Works of Sigmund Freud*, edited and translated by James Strachey et al., 97–108. London: Hogarth, 1953–1974.

———. "The Economic Problem of Masochism." In vol. 19 of *The Standard Edition of the Complete Psychological Works of Sigmund Freud*, edited and translated by James Strachey et al., 155–70. London: Hogarth, 1953–1974.

———. *The Ego and the Id.* In vol. 19 of *The Standard Edition of the Complete Psychological Works of Sigmund Freud*, edited and translated by James Strachey et al., 1–66. London: Hogarth, 1953–1974.

———. "Family Romances." In vol. 9 of *The Standard Edition of the Complete Psychological Works of Sigmund Freud*, edited and translated by James Strachey et al., 235–41. London: Hogarth, 1953–1974.

———. "Fetishism." In vol. 21 of *The Standard Edition of the Complete Psychological Works of Sigmund Freud*, edited and translated by James Strachey et al., 147–57. London: Hogarth, 1953–1974.

———. *Five Lectures on Psycho-Analysis.* In vol. 11 of *The Standard Edition of the Complete Psychological Works of Sigmund Freud*, edited and translated by James Strachey et al., 1–55. London: Hogarth, 1953–1974.

———. "Formulations on the Two Principles of Mental Functioning." In vol. 12 of *The Standard Edition of the Complete Psychological Works of Sigmund Freud*, edited and translated by James Strachey et al., 213–26. London: Hogarth, 1953–1974.

———. *The Future of an Illusion.* In vol. 21 of *The Standard Edition of the Complete Psychological Works of Sigmund Freud*, edited and translated by James Strachey et al., 1–56. London: Hogarth, 1953–1974.

———. "The Future Prospects of Psycho-Analytic Therapy." In vol. 11 of *The Standard Edition of the Complete Psychological Works of Sigmund Freud*, edited and translated by James Strachey et al., 139–51. London: Hogarth, 1953–1974.

———. *Group Psychology and the Analysis of the Ego.* In vol. 18 of *The Standard Edition of the Complete Psychological Works of Sigmund Freud*, edited and translated by James Strachey et al., 65–143. London: Hogarth, 1953–1974.

———. "Humour." In vol. 21 of *The Standard Edition of the Complete Psychological Works of Sigmund Freud*, edited and translated by James Strachey et al., 159–66. London: Hogarth, 1953–1974.

———. *Inhibitions, Symptoms and Anxiety.* In vol. 20 of *The Standard Edition of the Complete Psychological Works of Sigmund Freud*, edited and translated by James Strachey et al., 75–175. London: Hogarth, 1953–1974.

———. "Instincts and Their Vicissitudes." In vol. 14 of *The Standard Edition of the Complete Psychological Works of Sigmund Freud*, edited and translated by James Strachey et al., 136 and 139. London: Hogarth, 1953–1974.

———. *The Interpretation of Dreams.* In vols. 4 and 5 of *The Standard Edition of the Complete Psychological Works of Sigmund Freud,* edited and translated by James Strachey et al. London: Hogarth, 1953–1974.

———. *Introductory Lectures on Psycho-Analysis.* In vols. 15 and 16 of *The Standard Edition of the Complete Psychological Works of Sigmund Freud,* edited and translated by James Strachey et al. London: Hogarth, 1953–1974.

———. *Jokes and Their Relation to the Unconscious.* In vol. 8 of *The Standard Edition of the Complete Psychological Works of Sigmund Freud,* edited and translated by James Strachey et al. London: Hogarth, 1953–1974.

———. "Letter to Frederik van Eeden." In vol. 14 of *The Standard Edition of the Complete Psychological Works of Sigmund Freud,* edited and translated by James Strachey et al., 301–2. London: Hogarth, 1953–1974.

———. "Lines of Advance in Psycho-Analytic Therapy." In vol. 17 of *The Standard Edition of the Complete Psychological Works of Sigmund Freud,* edited and translated by James Strachey et al., 157–68. London: Hogarth, 1953–1974.

———. *Moses and Monotheism: Three Essays.* In vol. 23 of *The Standard Edition of the Complete Psychological Works of Sigmund Freud,* edited and translated by James Strachey et al., 1–137. London: Hogarth, 1953–1974.

———. "Mourning and Melancholia." In vol. 14 of *The Standard Edition of the Complete Psychological Works of Sigmund Freud,* edited and translated by James Strachey et al., 237–58. London: Hogarth, 1953–1974.

———. "Negation." In vol. 19 of *The Standard Edition of the Complete Psychological Works of Sigmund Freud,* edited and translated by James Strachey et al., 233–39. London: Hogarth, 1953–1974.

———. *New Introductory Lectures on Psycho-Analysis.* In vol. 22 of *The Standard Edition of the Complete Psychological Works of Sigmund Freud,* edited and translated by James Strachey et al., 1–182. London: Hogarth, 1953–1974.

———. "A Note on the Unconscious in Psycho-Analysis." In vol. 12 of *The Standard Edition of the Complete Psychological Works of Sigmund Freud,* edited and translated by James Strachey et al., 255–66. London: Hogarth, 1953–1974.

———. "A Note upon the 'Mystic Writing Pad.'" In vol. 19 of *The Standard Edition of the Complete Psychological Works of Sigmund Freud,* edited and translated by James Strachey et al., 225–32. London: Hogarth, 1953–1974.

———. "Observations on Transference-Love (Further Recommendations on the Technique of Psycho-Analysis, III)." In vol. 12 of *The Standard Edition of the Complete Psychological Works of Sigmund Freud,* edited and translated by James Strachey et al., 157–71. London: Hogarth, 1953–1974.

———. "On Beginning the Treatment (Further Recommendations on the Technique of Psycho-Analysis, I)." In vol. 12 of *The Standard Edition of the Complete Psychological Works of Sigmund Freud,* edited and translated by James Strachey et al., 121–44. London: Hogarth, 1953–1974.

———. *On the History of the Psycho-Analytic Movement.* In vol. 14 of *The Standard Edition of the Complete Psychological Works of Sigmund Freud,* edited and translated by James Strachey et al., 1–66. London: Hogarth, 1953–1974.

———. "On Narcissism: An Introduction." In vol. 14 of *The Standard Edition of the Complete Psychological Works of Sigmund Freud,* edited and translated by James Strachey et al., 67–102. London: Hogarth, 1953–1974.

———. "On Psychotherapy." In vol. 7 of *The Standard Edition of the Complete Psychological Works of Sigmund Freud,* edited and translated by James Strachey et al., 255–68. London: Hogarth, 1953–1974.

———. "The Psychotherapy of Hysteria." In vol. 2 of *The Standard Edition of the Complete Psychological Works of Sigmund Freud,* edited and translated by James Strachey et al., 253–305. London: Hogarth, 1953–1974.

———. "On Transience." In vol. 14 of *The Standard Edition of the Complete Psychological Works of Sigmund Freud,* edited and translated by James Strachey et al., 303–7. London: Hogarth, 1953–1974.

———. *An Outline of Psycho-Analysis.* In vol. 23 of *The Standard Edition of the Complete Psychological Works of Sigmund Freud,* edited and translated by James Strachey et al., 139–207. London: Hogarth, 1953–1974.

———. "Preface to Aichhorn's *Wayward Youth.*" In vol. 19 of *The Standard Edition of the Complete Psychological Works of Sigmund Freud,* edited and translated by James Strachey et al., 271–75. London: Hogarth, 1953–1974.

———. *The Question of Lay Analysis.* In vol. 20 of *The Standard Edition of the Complete Psychological Works of Sigmund Freud,* edited and translated by James Strachey et al., 177–258. London: Hogarth, 1953–1974.

———. "Remembering, Repeating and Working-Through (Further Recommendations on the Technique of Psycho-Analysis, II)." In vol. 12 of *The Standard Edition of the Complete Psychological Works of Sigmund Freud,* edited and translated by James Strachey et al., 145–56. London: Hogarth, 1953–1974.

———. "Repression." In vol. 14 of *The Standard Edition of the Complete Psychological Works of Sigmund Freud,* edited and translated by James Strachey et al., 141–58. London: Hogarth, 1953–1974.

———. "The Resistances to Psycho-Analysis." In vol. 19 of *The Standard Edition of the Complete Psychological Works of Sigmund Freud,* edited and translated by James Strachey et al., 211–24. London: Hogarth, 1953–1974.

———. "The Sexual Enlightenment of Children (An Open Letter to Dr. M. Furst)." In vol. 9 of *The Standard Edition of the Complete Psychological Works of Sigmund Freud,* edited and translated by James Strachey et al., 129–39. London: Hogarth, 1953–1974.

———. "A Short Account of Psycho-Analysis." In vol. 19 of *The Standard Edition of the Complete Psychological Works of Sigmund Freud,* edited and translated by James Strachey et al., 189–209. London: Hogarth, 1953–1974.

———. "The Theme of the Three Caskets." In vol. 12 of *The Standard Edition of the Complete Psychological Works of Sigmund Freud,* edited and translated by James Strachey et al., 289–301. London: Hogarth, 1953–1974.

———. "Thoughts for the Times on War and Death." In vol. 14 of *The Standard Edition of the Complete Psychological Works of Sigmund Freud,* edited and translated by James Strachey et al., 273–300. London: Hogarth, 1953–1974.

———. "Thoughts for the Times on War and Death," translated by E. Colburn Mayne. In vol. 4 of Sigmund Freud, *Collected Papers,* translated by Joan Riviere et al., 288–317. Basic, 1959.

———. Three Essays on the Theory of Sexuality. In vol. 7 of *The Standard Edition of the Complete Psychological Works of Sigmund Freud,* edited and translated by James Strachey et al., 123–243. London: Hogarth, 1953–1974.

———. *Totem and Taboo.* In vol. 13 of *The Standard Edition of the Complete Psychological Works of Sigmund Freud,* edited and translated by James Strachey et al., vii–161. London: Hogarth, 1953–1974.

———. "Two Lies Told by Children." In vol. 12 of *The Standard Edition of the Complete Psychological Works of Sigmund Freud,* edited and translated by James Strachey et al., 303–9. London: Hogarth, 1953–1974.

———. "Why War?" In vol. 22 of *The Standard Edition of the Complete Psychological Works of Sigmund Freud,* edited and translated by James Strachey et al., 195–215. London: Hogarth, 1953–1974.

Freud, Sigmund, and Josef Breuer. "On the Psychical Mechanism of Hysterical Phenomena: Preliminary Communication." In vol. 2 of *The Standard Edition of the Complete Psychological Works of Sigmund Freud,* edited and translated by James Strachey et al., 1–17. London: Hogarth, 1953–1974.

———. *Studies on Hysteria.* In vol. 2 of *The Standard Edition of the Complete Psychological Works of Sigmund Freud,* edited and translated by James Strachey et al. London: Hogarth, 1953–1974.

Friedman, R. Zeth. "Kant and Kierkegaard: The Limits of Reason and the Cunning of Faith." *International Journal for Philosophy of Religion* 19 (1986): 3–22.

Fromm, Erich. "A Counter Rebuttal." *Dissent* 3 (Winter 1956): 81–83.

———. "The Human Implications of Instinctivistic 'Radicalism.'" *Dissent* 2 (Autumn 1955): 42–49.

———. *Psychoanalysis and Religion.* New York: Bantam, 1967.

Frosh, Stephen. *Identity Crisis: Modernity, Psychoanalysis and the Self.* London: Macmillan, 1991.

Gabriel, Yiannis. *Freud and Society.* London: Routledge & Kegan Paul, 1983.

Gallop, Jane. *Reading Lacan.* Ithaca, N.Y.: Cornell University Press, 1985.

———. "Reading the Mother Tongue: Psychoanalytic Feminist Criticism." In *The Trial(s) of Psychoanalysis,* edited by Françoise Meltzer, 125–40. Chicago: University of Chicago Press, 1987.

Gardiner, Judith Kegan. "Psychoanalysis and Feminism: An American Humanist's View." *Signs: Journal of Women in Culture and Society* 17 (Winter 1992): 437–54.

Gauthier, David. "The Politics of Redemption." In *Moral Dealing: Contract, Ethics, and Reason,* 77–109. Ithaca, N.Y., and London: Cornell University Press, 1990.

Gay, Peter. *Freud for Historians.* New York: Oxford University Press, 1985.

———. *Freud: A Life for Our Times.* New York: Anchor, 1989.

———. *A Godless Jew: Freud, Atheism, and the Making of Psychoanalysis.* New Haven, Conn.: Yale University Press, 1987.

Goldberg, Steven E. *Two Patterns of Rationality in Freud's Writings.* Tuscaloosa: University of Alabama Press, 1988.

Gramsci, Antonio. *Selections from the Prison Notebooks,* translated and edited by Quintin Hoare and Geoffrey Nowell Smith. New York: International Publishers, 1971.

Green, André. "The Dead Mother." In *On Private Madness,* translated by Katherine Aubertin, 142–73. London: Hogarth, 1986.

———. "Instinct in the Late Works of Freud." In *On Freud's "Analysis Terminable and Interminable,"* edited by Joseph Sandler, 124–41. New Haven, Conn.: Yale University Press, 1991.

———. Introduction to *On Private Madness*, 3–16. London: Hogarth, 1986.

———. "Negation and Contradiction." In *On Private Madness*, translated by Katherine Aubertin, 254–76. London: Hogarth, 1986.

———. "Psychoanalysis and Ordinary Modes of Thought." In *On Private Madness*, translated by Pamela Tyrell, 17–29. London: Hogarth, 1986.

Greenberg, Jay R., and Stephen A. Mitchell. *Object Relations in Psychoanalytic Theory*. Cambridge, Mass.: Harvard University Press, 1983.

Greene, Murray. "Hegel's 'Unhappy Consciousness' and Nietzsche's 'Slave Morality.'" In *Hegel and the Philosophy of Religion: The Wofford Symposium*, edited by Darrel E. Christensen, 125–41. The Hague: Martinus Nijhoff, 1970.

———. "Reply." In *Hegel and the Philosophy of Religion: The Wofford Symposium*, edited by Darrel E. Christensen, 153–35. The Hague: Martinus Nijhoff, 1970.

Grunberger, Béla. "Narcissus and Oedipus." In *New Essays on Narcissism*, translated by David Macey, 15–28. London: Free Association, 1989.

———. "The Oedipal Conflicts of the Analyst." In *New Essays on Narcissism*, translated by David Macey, 29–44. London: Free Association, 1989.

Haaken, Janice. "Beyond Addiction: Recovery Groups and 'Women Who Love Too Much.'" *Free Associations: Psychoanalysis, Groups, Politics, Culture* 3 (1992): 85–109.

Habermas, Jürgen. "The Entry into Postmodernity: Nietzsche as a Turning Point." In *The Philosophical Discourse of Modernity*, translated by Frederick G. Lawrence, 83–105. Cambridge, Mass.: MIT Press, 1990.

———. "The Entwinement of Myth and Enlightenment: Max Horkheimer and Theodor Adorno." In *The Philosophical Discourse of Modernity*, translated by Frederick G. Lawrence, 106–30. Cambridge, Mass.: MIT Press, 1990.

———. "Herbert Marcuse: On Art and Revolution." In *Philosophical-Political Profiles*, translated by F. G. Lawrence, 167–72. Cambridge, Mass.: MIT Press, 1985.

———. *Knowledge and Human Interests*, translated by Jeremy J. Shapiro. Boston: Beacon, 1971.

———. "Psychic Thermidor and the Rebirth of Religious Subjectivity." In *Habermas and Modernity*, edited by Richard J. Bernstein, 67–77. Cambridge, Mass.: MIT Press, 1985.

Hanly, Charles. "Ego Ideal and Ideal Ego." *International Journal of Psychoanalysis* 65 (1984): 253–61.

Harrington, Michael. *The Politics at God's Funeral*. Middlesex, UK: Penguin, 1983.

Harris, Henry S. "The Concept of Recognition in Hegel's Jena Manuscripts." In *Hegel Studien/Beiheft 20*, edited by Klaus Dusing and Dieter Henrich, 229–48. Bonn: Bouvier, 1980.

Hegel, G. W. F. *Phenomenology of Spirit*, translated by A. V. Miller. New York: Oxford University Press, 1981.

———. *Philosophy of Right*, translated by T. M. Knox. Oxford, UK: Oxford University Press, 1967.

Hernández, Max, "Group Formation and Ideology: Text and Context." *International Journal of Psychoanalysis* 69 (1988): 163–70.

Hernández, Max, Moisés Lemlij, Luis Millones, Alberto Péndola, and María Rostworowski. *Entre El Mito y La Historia: Psicoanálisis y Pasado Andino*. Lima: Ediciones Psicoanalíticas Imago, 1987.

Hobbes, Thomas. *Leviathan,* edited by C. B. Macpherson. Middlesex, UK: Penguin, 1985.

Horkheimer, Max. "Authoritarianism and the Family Today." In *The Family: Its Function and Destiny,* edited by Ruth Nanda Anshen, 359–74. New York: Harper, 1949.

———. "Authority and the Family." In *Critical Theory,* translated by Matthew J. O'Connel, 47–128. New York: Continuum, 1972.

———. *The Eclipse of Reason.* New York: Continuum, 1947.

Horowitz, Asher, and Gad Horowitz. *"Everywhere They Are in Chains": Political Theory from Rousseau to Marx.* Scarborough, Ont.: Nelson Canada, 1988.

Horowitz, Gad. "The Foucaultian Impasse: No Sex, No Self, No Revolution." *Political Theory* 15 (February 1987): 61–80.

———. "Psychoanalytic Feminism after Marcuse." Review of *The Bonds of Love,* by Jessica Benjamin. *Telos* 23 (Fall 1990): 176–84.

———. *Repression: Basic and Surplus Repression in Psychoanalytic Theory: Freud, Reich and Marcuse.* Toronto: University of Toronto Press, 1977.

Hyman, Edward J. "Eros and Freedom: The Critical Psychology of Herbert Marcuse." In *Marcuse: Critical Theory and the Promise of Utopia,* edited by Robert Pippin, Andrew Feenberg, and Charles P. Webel, 143–66. Hadley, Mass.: Bergin & Garvey, 1988.

Hyppolite, J. *Genesis and Structure of Hegel's* Phenomenology of Spirit, translated by Samuel Cherniak and John Heckman. Evanston, Ill.: Northwestern University Press, 1974.

———. "Hegel's Phenomenology and Psychoanalysis." In *New Studies in Hegel's Philosophy,* edited by Warren E. Steinkraus, 57–70. New York: Rinehart and Winston, 1971.

———. "A Spoken Commentary on Freud's *Verneinung.*" In *The Seminar of Jacques Lacan: Book I, Papers on Technique, 1953–1954,* translated by John Forrester, edited by Jacques-Alain Miller, 289–97. New York: Norton, 1988.

Isaac, Jeffrey C. "Arendt, Camus, and Postmodern Politics." *Praxis International* 9 (April/July 1989): 48–71.

Izenberg, Gerald N. "Seduced and Abandoned: The Rise and Fall of Freud's Seduction Theory." In *The Cambridge Companion to Freud,* edited by Jerome Neu, 25–43. Cambridge, UK: Cambridge University Press, 1991.

Jacobson, Norman. "Behold *Leviathan!* The Systematic Solace of Thomas Hobbes." In *Pride and Solace: The Function and Limits of Political Theory,* 51–92. New York: Methuen, 1978.

Jacoby, Russell. "Narcissism and the Crisis of Capitalism." *Telos* 48 (Summer 1980): 58–65.

———. *The Repression of Psychoanalysis: Otto Fenichel and the Political Freudians.* New York: Basic, 1983.

———. *Social Amnesia: A Critique of Conformist Psychology from Adler to Laing.* Boston: Beacon, 1975.

———. "Toward a Critique of Automatic Marxism: The Politics of Philosophy from Lukács to the Frankfurt School." *Telos* 10 (Winter 1971): 119–46.

Jameson, Fredric. "Conclusion: The Dialectic of Utopia and Ideology." In *The Political Unconscious: Narrative as a Socially Symbolic Act,* 281–99. Ithaca, N.Y.: Cornell University Press, 1981.

——. "Marcuse and Schiller." In *Marxism and Form,* 83–116. Princeton, N.J.: Princeton University Press, 1971.

Jay, Martin. *The Dialectical Imagination: A History of the Frankfurt School and the Institute of Social Research, 1923–1950.* Boston: Little, Brown, 1973.

——. "Reflections on Marcuse's Theory of Remembrance." In *Marcuse: Critical Theory and the Promise of Utopia,* edited by Robert Pippin, Andrew Feenberg, and Charles P. Webel, 29–44. Hadley, Mass.: Bergin & Garvey, 1988.

Jones, Ernest. *The Life and Work of Sigmund Freud.* 3 vols. London: Hogarth, 1953–1957.

Karme, Laila. "A Mother Dies, A Child Denies: The Reparative Psychoanalytic Process: A Case Study." *Psychoanalytic Review* 75 (Summer 1988): 263–81.

Kelly, George Armstrong. "Notes on Hegel's 'Lordship and Bondage.'" *Review of Metaphysics* 19 (June 1966): 780–802.

Kierkegaard, Søren. *Concluding Unscientific Postscript,* translated by Walter Lowrie and David F. Swenson. Princeton, N.J.: Princeton University Press, 1968.

——. *Fear and Trembling,* translated and edited by Edna H. Hong and Howard V. Hong. Princeton, N.J.: Princeton University Press, 1983.

Koff, Robert. "A Definition of Identification." *International Journal of Psychoanalysis* 42 (1961): 362–70.

Kofman, S. "Baubô: Theological Perversion and Fetishism." In *Nietzsche's New Seas: Explorations in Philosophy, Aesthetics, and Politics,* translated by Tracy Strong, edited by Michael Allen Gillespie and Tracy B. Strong, 175–202. Chicago: University of Chicago Press, 1988.

——. *The Childhood of Art,* translated by Wilfred Woodhull. New York: Columbia University Press, 1988.

——. *The Enigma of Woman: Woman in Freud's Writings,* translated by Catherine Porter. Ithaca, N.Y.: Cornell University Press, 1985.

——. "Metaphor, Symbol, Metamorphosis." In *The New Nietzsche,* edited by David B. Allison, 201–14. New York: Dell, 1977.

Kojève, Alexandre. *Introduction to the Reading of Hegel: Lectures on the* Phenomenology of Spirit, translated by James H. Nichols Jr., edited by Allan Bloom. Ithaca, N.Y.: Cornell University Press, 1969.

Kontos, Alkis. "Between Memory and Dream." In *Thinking about Change,* edited by David P. Shugarman, 53–70. Toronto: University of Toronto Press, 1974.

——. "The Dialectics of Domination: An Interpretation of Friedrich Dürrenmatt's *The Visit.*" In *Powers, Possessions and Freedom: Essays in Honour of C. B. Macpherson,* edited by Alkis Kontos, 153–65. Toronto: University of Toronto Press, 1979.

——. "Metaphor and Political Reality." In *Domination,* edited by Alkis Kontos, 211–28. Toronto: University of Toronto Press, 1975.

——. "Success and Knowledge in Machiavelli." In *The Political Calculus.* Toronto: University of Toronto Press, 1972.

Kovel, Joel. *The Age of Desire: Reflections of a Radical Psychoanalyst.* New York: Pantheon, 1981.

——. "Beyond the Future of an Illusion: Further Reflections on Freud and Religion." *Psychoanalytic Review* 77 (Spring 1990): 69–87.

———. "The Castration Complex Reconsidered." In *Women & Analysis: Dialogues on Psychoanalytic Views of Femininity*, edited by Jean Strouse, 136–43. Boston: Hall, 1985.

———. "Narcissism and the Family." *Telos* 44 (Summer 1980): 88–100.

———. *The Radical Spirit: Essays on Psychoanalysis and Society*. London: Free Association Books, 1988.

———. "Rationalisation and the Family." In *Capitalism and Infancy: Essays on Psychoanalysis and Politics*, edited by Barry Richards, 102–21. London: Free Association Books, 1984.

Lacan, Jacques. *Écrits: A Selection*, translated by Alan Sheridan. New York: Norton, 1977.

———. *The Four Fundamental Concepts of Psycho-Analysis*, translated by Alan Sheridan and edited by Jacques-Alain Miller. New York: Norton, 1978.

———. *The Seminar of Jacques Lacan: Book I, Freud's Papers on Technique, 1953–1954*, translated by John Forrester and edited by Jacques-Alain Miller. New York: Norton, 1988.

———. *The Seminar of Jacques Lacan: Book II, The Ego in Freud's Theory and in the Technique of Psychoanalysis, 1953–1954*, translated by John Forrester and edited by Jacques-Alain Miller. New York: Norton, 1988.

LaCapra, Dominik. "Reflections on Trauma, Absence, and Loss." In *Whose Freud? The Place of Psychoanalysis in Contemporary Culture*, edited by Peter Brooks and Alex Woloch. New Haven, Conn., and London: Yale University Press, 2000.

Laclau, Ernesto. "Psychoanalysis and Marxism." In *The Trial(s) of Psychoanalysis*, edited by Françoise Meltzer, 141–44. Chicago: University of Chicago Press, 1987.

Laclau, Ernesto, and Chantal Mouffe. *Hegemony and Socialist Strategy: Towards a Radical Democratic Politics*, translated by Winston Moore and Paul Cammack. London: Verso, 1985.

Laplanche, Jean. *Life and Death in Psychoanalysis*, translated by Jeffrey Mehlman. Baltimore: Johns Hopkins University Press, 1976.

———. *New Foundations for Psychoanalysis*, translated by David Macey. Oxford, UK: Blackwell, 1989.

———. "Notes on Afterwardsness." In *Jean Laplanche: Seduction, Translation, Drives*, translated by Martin Stanton, edited by John Fletcher and Martin Stanton, 217–23. London: Institute of Contemporary Arts, 1992.

———. "Psychoanalysis, Time and Translation." In *Jean Laplanche: Seduction, Translation, Drives*, translated by Martin Stanton, edited by John Fletcher and Martin Stanton, 161–77. London: Institute of Contemporary Arts, 1992.

Laplanche, Jean, and Jean-Bertrand Pontalis. "Fantasy and the Origins of Sexuality." *International Journal of Psychoanalysis* 49 (1968): 1–18.

———. *The Language of Psycho-Analysis*, translated by Donald Nicholson-Smith. New York: Hogarth, 1973.

Leavy, Stanley A. "The Image and the Word: Further Reflections on Jacques Lacan." In *Interpreting Lacan*, edited by Joseph H. Smith and William Kerrigan, 3–20. New Haven, Conn.: Yale University Press, 1983.

———. *The Psychoanalytic Dialogue*. New Haven, Conn.: Yale University Press, 1980.

Leclaire, Serge. "Jerome, or Death in the Life of the Obsessional." In *Returning to Freud: Clinical Psychoanalysis in the School of Lacan,* translated and edited by Stuart Schneiderman, 94–113. New Haven, Conn.: Yale University Press, 1980.

———. "Philo, or the Obsessional and His Desire." In *Returning to Freud: Clinical Psychoanalysis in the School of Lacan,* translated and edited by Stuart Schneiderman, 114–29. New Haven, Conn.: Yale University Press, 1980.

Levin, David Michael. "The Body Politic: The Embodiment of Praxis in Foucault and Habermas." *Praxis International* 9 (April/July 1989): 112–32.

Lippincott, Mark. *Albert Camus' Theory of Rebellion.* Ph.D. dissertation, Department of Political Science, University of Toronto, 1986.

Loewenberg, Peter. "The Education of a Psychohistorian." In *Decoding the Past: The Psychohistorical Approach,* 43–95. Berkeley: University of California Press, 1969.

Machiavelli, Niccolò di Bernardo. *The Portable Machiavelli,* translated by Peter Bonadella and Mark Musa. Middlesex, UK: Penguin, 1983.

Macpherson, C. B. "Hobbes's Bourgeois Man." In *Democratic Theory: Essays in Retrieval,* 238–50. Oxford, UK: Clarendon, 1973.

———. *The Life and Times of Liberal Democracy.* Oxford, UK: Oxford University Press, 1977.

———. *The Political Theory of Possessive Individualism: From Hobbes to Locke.* Oxford, UK: Oxford University Press, 1962.

———. *The Real World of Democracy.* Toronto: CBC Enterprises, 1965.

Malcolm, Janet. *In the Freud Archives.* New York: Vintage, 1985.

———. *Psychoanalysis: The Impossible Profession.* New York: Vintage Books, 1982.

Mannoni, Octave. *Freud,* translated by Renaud Bruce. New York: Vintage Books, 1971.

———. "Psychoanalysis and the Decolonization of Mankind." In *Freud: The Man, His World, His Influence,* translated by Nicholas Fry, edited by Jonathan Miller, 85–95. London: Weidenfeld and Nicolson, 1972.

Marcus, Donald M. "Aspects of Psychoanalytic Cure." *Psychoanalytic Review* 75 (Summer 1988): 231–43.

Marcus, Steven. *Freud and the Culture of Psychoanalysis.* New York: Norton, 1984.

Marcuse, Herbert. *The Aesthetic Dimension: Toward a Critique of Marxist Aesthetics,* translated by Herbert Marcuse and Erica Sherover. Boston: Beacon, 1978.

———. *Counter-revolution and Revolt.* Boston: Beacon, 1972.

———. *Eros and Civilization: A Philosophical Inquiry into Freud.* Boston: Beacon, 1955.

———. *An Essay on Liberation.* Boston: Beacon, 1968.

———. *Five Lectures: Psychoanalysis, Politics, and Utopia.* Boston: Beacon, 1970.

———. "The Foundation of Historical Materialism." In *From Luther to Popper,* translated by Joris de Bres, 148. London: Verso, 1972.

———. *Negations: Essays in Critical Theory.* Boston: Beacon, 1968.

———. *One-Dimensional Man.* Boston: Beacon, 1964.

———. "A Reply to Erich Fromm." *Dissent* 3 (Winter 1956): 79–81.

Marx, Karl. "Economic and Philosophic Manuscripts of 1844." In *The Marx-Engels Reader,* edited by Robert C. Tucker, 66–125. New York: Norton, 1978.

———. "Theses on Feuerbach." In *The Marx-Engels Reader,* edited by Robert C. Tucker, 143–45. New York: Norton, 1978.

Masson, Jeffrey Moussaieff. *The Assault on Truth: Freud's Suppression of the Seduc-tion Theory*. New York: Farrar, Straus and Giroux, 1984.

McGrawth, William J. *Freud's Discovery of Psychoanalysis: The Politics of Hysteria*. Ithaca, N.Y.: Cornell University Press, 1986.

———. "How Jewish Was Freud?" In *New York Review of Books*, 5 December 199, 127–31.

Mitchell, Juliet. "On Freud and the Distinction between the Sexes." In *Women & Analysis: Dialogues on Psychoanalytic Views of Femininity*, edited by Jean Strose, 27–36. Boston: Hall, 1985.

Merleau-Ponty, Maurice. "Man and Adversity." In *Signs*, translated by Richard C. McCleary, 224–43. Evanston, Ill.: Northwestern University Press, 1964.

Muller, John P. "Negation in 'The Purloined Letter': Hegel, Poe, Lacan." In *The Purloined Poe: Lacan, Derrida and Psychoanalytic Reading*, edited by John P. Muller and William J. Richardson, 343–68. Baltimore: Johns Hopkins University Press, 1988.

Nancy, Jean-Luc, and Philippe Lacoue-Labarthe. *The Title of the Letter: A Reading of Lacan*, translated by François Raffoul and David Pettigrew. Albany: State Uni-versity of New York Press, 1992.

Neu, Jerome. "Freud and Perversion." In *The Cambridge Companion to Freud*, edited by Jerome Neu, 175–208. Cambridge, UK: Cambridge University Press, 1991.

Nietzsche, Friedrich. *The Birth of Tragedy*, translated by Walter Kaufmann. New York: Vintage, 1967.

———. *On the Genealogy of Morals*, translated by Walter Kaufmann. New York: Vin-tage, 1969.

———. "On the Uses and Disadvantages of History for Life." In *Untimely Medita-tions*, translated by R. J. Hollingdale, 57–123. Cambridge, UK: Cambridge Uni-versity Press, 1983.

Nun, José. "Gramsci y El Sentido Común." In *Cultura Política y Democratización*, edited by Norbert Lechner, 199–234. Buenos Aires, Argentina: CLACSO, 1987.

———. "The Rebellion of the Chorus." *Laru Studies* 4 (May 1982): 87–97.

Oakeshott, Michael. "The Moral Life in the Writings of Thomas Hobbes." In *Ra-tionalism in Politics and Other Essays*, 248–300. London: Methuen, 1962.

O'Neill, John. "Critique and Remembrance." In *On Critical Theory*, edited by John O'Neill, 1–11. London: Heinemann, 1976.

———, ed. *Hegel's Dialectic of Desire and Recognition: Texts and Commentary*. Albany: State University of New York Press, 1996.

Paul, Robert A. "Freud's Anthropology: A Reading of the 'Cultural Books.'" In *The Cambridge Companion to Freud*, edited by Jerome Neu, 267–86. Cambridge, UK: Cambridge University Press, 1991.

Pfeiffer, Ernst, ed. *Sigmund Freud and Lou Andreas-Salomé: Letters*, translated by Elaine and William Robson-Scott. London: Hogarth, 1972.

Plato. *Republic*. Translated by Paul Shorey. In *Plato: The Collected Dialogues*, edited by Huntington Cairns and Edith Hamilton. Princeton, N.J.: Princeton Univer-sity Press, 1963, 575–844.

Pontalis, Jean-Bertrand. *Frontiers in Psychoanalysis: Between the Dream and Psy-chic Pain*, translated by Catherine Cullen and Philip Cullen. London: Ho-garth, 1981.

———. "On Death-work." In *Frontiers in Psychoanalysis: Between the Dream and Psychic Pain,* translated by Catherine Cullen and Philip Cullen, 184–93. London: Hogarth, 1981.

———. "Between Freud and Charcot: From One Scene to the Other." In *Frontiers in Psychoanalysis: Between the Dream and Psychic Pain,* translated by Catherine Cullen and Philip Cullen, 17–22. London: Hogarth, 1981.

———. "Between Knowledge and Fantasy." In *Frontiers in Psychoanalysis: Between the Dream and Psychic Pain,* translated by Catherine Cullen and Philip Cullen, 95–111. London: Hogarth, 1981.

———. "The Illusion Sustained." In *Frontiers in Psychoanalysis: Between the Dream and Psychic Pain,* translated by Catherine Cullen and Philip Cullen, 77–83. London: Hogarth, 1981.

———. "On Psychic Pain." In *Frontiers in Psychoanalysis: Between the Dream and Psychic Pain,* translated by Catherine Cullen and Philip Cullen, 194–205. London: Hogarth, 1981.

Poster, Mark. *Critical Theory and Poststructuralism: In Search of a Context.* Ithaca, N.Y.: Cornell University Press, 1989.

Rachlis, Charles. "Marcuse and the Problem of Happiness." *Canadian Journal of Political and Social Theory* 2 (Winter 1978): 63–88.

Richards, Barry. *Images of Freud: Cultural Responses to Psychoanalysis.* London: Dent & Sons, 1989.

Richardson, William J. "Lacan and the Subject of Psychoanalysis." In *Interpreting Lacan,* edited by Joseph H. Smith and William Kerrigan, 51–74. New Haven, Conn.: Yale University Press, 1983.

Richter, Jean Paul, ed. and comp. *The Literary Works of Leonardo da Vinci.* New York: Phaidon, 1970.

Ricoeur, Paul. *Freud and Philosophy: An Essay on Interpretation,* translated by Denis Savage. New Haven, Conn: Yale University Press, 1970.

Rieff, Philip. *Freud: The Mind of the Moralist.* New York: Viking, 1959.

———. "On the Sexual Enlightenment of Children." In *The Feeling Intellect: Selected Writings,* edited by Jonathan B. Imber, 28–32. Chicago: University of Chicago Press, 1990.

Roazen, Paul. *Freud: Political and Social Thought.* New York: Knopf, 1968.

Robert, Marthe. *The Psychoanalytic Revolution: Sigmund Freud's Life and Achievement,* translated by Kenneth Morgan. London: George Allen & Unwin, 1966.

Rorty, Richard. "The Contingency of Selfhood." In *Contingency, Irony, and Solidarity.* Cambridge, UK: Cambridge University Press, 1989.

Rose, Jacqueline. "Femininity and Its Discontents." In *Sexuality: A Reader,* edited by *Feminist Review,* 177–98. London: Virago, 1987.

———. "Why War?" In *Why War?—Psychoanalysis, Politics, and the Return to Melanie Klein,* 15–40. Oxford: Blackwell, 1993.

Roth, Michael S. *Psycho-Analysis as History: Negation and Freedom in Freud.* Ithaca, N.Y.: Cornell University Press, 1987.

Rousseau, Jean-Jacques. *The Social Contract and Discourses,* translated by G. D. H. Cole. London: Everyman, 1973.

Roy, Jean. *Hobbes and Freud,* translated by Thomas G. Osler. Toronto: Canadian Philosophical Monographs, 1984.

Rustin, Margaret, and Michael Rustin. "Relational Preconditions of Socialism." In *Capitalism and Infancy: Essays on Psychoanalysis and Politics,* edited by Barry Richards, 207–25. London: Free Association Books, 1984.

Rycroft, Charles. *A Critical Dictionary of Psychoanalysis.* New York: Penguin, 1983.

———. "Introduction: Causes and Meaning." In *Psychoanalysis Observed,* edited by Charles Rycroft, 7–22. New York: Coward-McCann, 1966.

———. *Psychoanalysis and Beyond.* London: Hogarth, 1985.

———. *Reich.* Glasgow, Scotland: Fontana Paperbacks, 1971.

Sabbadini, Andrea. "Boundaries of Timelessness: Some Thoughts about the Temporal Dimension of the Psychoanalytic Space." *International Journal of Psychoanalysis* 70 (1989): 305–13.

Sagan, Eli. *Freud, Women, and Morality: The Psychology of Good and Evil.* New York: Basic Books, 1988.

Sandler, Joseph. "The Concept of the Representational World." *Psychoanalytic Study of the Child* 17 (1962): 128–45.

———. "The Ego Ideal and the Ideal Self." *Psychoanalytic Study of the Child* 13 (1963): 139–59.

———. "On the Concept of the Superego." *Psychoanalytic Study of the Child* 15 (1960): 128–62.

Safouan, Moustapha. "The Apprenticeship of Tilmann Moser." In *Returning to Freud: Clinical Psychoanalysis in the School of Lacan,* translated and edited by Stuart Schneiderman, 160–67. New Haven, Conn.: Yale University Press, 1980.

Sass, Louis A. "The Self and Its Vicissitudes: An 'Archaeological' Study of the Psycho-Analytic Avant-Garde." *Social Research: An International Quarterly of the Social Sciences* 55 (Winter 1988): 551–607.

Schachtel, Ernest G. "On Memory and Childhood Amnesia." In *A Study of Interpersonal Relations,* edited by Patrick Mullahy, 3–49. New York: Hermitage, 1949.

Schafer, Roy. "Ideals, the Ego Ideal, and the Ideal Self." In *Psychological Issues: Monograph 18/19,* edited by Robert R. Holt, 131–74. New York: International University Press, 1967.

———. "The Loving and Beloved Superego in Freud's Structural Theory." *Psychoanalytic Study of the Child* 15 (1960): 163–88.

———. "Regression in the Service of the Ego: The Relevance of a Psychoanalytic Concept for Personality Assessment." In *Assessment of Human Motives,* edited by Gardner Lindzey, 119–48. New York: Rinehart, 1958.

Schneiderman, Stuart. *Jacques Lacan: The Death of an Intellectual Hero.* Cambridge, Mass.: Harvard University Press, 1983.

———. *Rat Man.* New York: New York University Press, 1986.

Schorske, Carl E. "Freud's Egyptian Dig." *New York Review of Books* 27 (May 1993): 35–40.

———. "Politics and Patricide in Freud's Interpretation of Dreams." *American Historical Review* 78 (April 1973): 328–47.

———. "The Psychoarcheology of Civilizations." In *The Cambridge Companion to Freud,* edited by Jerome Neu, 8–24. Cambridge, UK: Cambridge University Press, 1991.

Schwartz, Joel. "Freud and Freedom of Speech." *American Political Science Review* 80 (December 1986): 1227–48.

Segel, Nathan P. "Narcissism and Adaptation to Indignity." *International Journal of Psychoanalysis* 62 (1981): 465–76.

Sharpe, Ella Freeman. "The Psycho-Analyst." In *Collected Papers on Psycho-Analysis*, edited by Marjorie Brierly, 109–22. London: Hogarth, 1978.

———. "The Technique of Psycho-Analysis: Seven Lectures." In *Collected Papers on Psycho-Analysis*, edited by Marjorie Brierly, 9–106. London: Hogarth, 1978.

Siep, Ludwig. "The Struggle for Recognition: Hegel's Dispute with Hobbes in the Jena Writings." In *Hegel's Dialectic of Desire and Recognition: Texts and Commentary*, edited by John O'Neill, 273–88. Albany: State University of New York Press, 1996.

Smith, Bruce James. "Machiavelli: Remembrance and the Republic." In *Politics and Remembrance: Republican Themes in Machiavelli, Burke, and Tocqueville*, 26–101. Princeton, N.J.: Princeton University Press, 1985.

Smith, Joseph H. "Epilogue: Lacan and the Subject of American Psychoanalysis." In *Interpreting Lacan*, edited by Joseph H. Smith and William Kerrigan, 259–76. New Haven, Conn.: Yale University Press, 1983.

Smith, Steven R. "Hegelianism and the Three Crises of Rationality." *Social Research: An International Quarterly of the Social Sciences* 56 (Winter 1989): 943–73.

Steiner, George. *Nostalgia for the Absolute*. Toronto: CBC Enterprises, 1974.

Stolorow, Robert D. "Transference and the Therapeutic Process." *Psychoanalytic Review* 75 (Summer 1988): 245–54.

Storr, Anthony. *Freud*. Oxford, UK: Oxford University Press, 1989.

Strauss, Leo. *The Political Philosophy of Hobbes*. Chicago: University of Chicago Press, 1952.

Strong, Tracy B. "Nietzsche's Political Aesthetics." In *Nietzsche's New Seas: Explorations in Philosophy, Aesthetics, and Politics*, edited by Michael Allen Gillespie and Tracy B. Strong, 153–74. Chicago: University of Chicago Press, 1988.

———. "Psychoanalysis as a Vocation: Freud, Politics and the Heroic." *Political Theory* 12 (February 1984): 51–79.

Suarez-Orozco, Marcelo. "The Heritage of Enduring a 'Dirty War': Psychosocial Aspects of Terror in Argentina, 1976–1988." *Journal of Psychohistory* 18 (Spring 1991): 469–505.

Taylor, Charles. "Atomism." In *Powers, Possessions and Freedom: Essays in Honour of C. B. Macpherson*, edited by Alkis Kontos, 39–61. Toronto: University of Toronto Press, 1979.

———. *Hegel*. Cambridge, UK: Cambridge University Press, 1979.

Tracy, David. "Mystics, Prophets, Rhetorics: Religion and Psychoanalysis." In *The Trial(s) of Psychoanalysis*, edited by Françoise Meltzer, 259–72. Chicago: University of Chicago Press, 1987.

Trilling, Lionel. *Sincerity and Authenticity*. Cambridge, Mass.: Harvard University Press, 1971.

Turkle, Sherry. *Psychoanalytic Politics: Freud's French Revolution*. New York: Basic, 1978.

Ver Eecke, Wilfred. "Hegel as Lacan's Source for Necessity in Psychoanalytic Theory." In *Interpreting Lacan*, edited by Joseph H. Smith and William Kerrigan, 113–38. New Haven, Conn.: Yale University Press, 1983.

Waelder, Robert. *Basic Theory of Psychoanalysis*. New York: Schocken, 1964.

Walzer, Michael. *Exodus and Revolution.* New York: Basic, 1985.

Wartenberg, Thomas E. "Social Movements and Individual Identity: A Critique of Freud on the Psychology of Groups." *Philosophical Forum* 22 (Summer 1991): 362–82.

Wellmer, Albrecht. "Reason, Utopia and the *Dialectic of Enlightenment.*" In *Habermas and Modernity,* edited by Richard J. Bernstein, 35–66. Cambridge, Mass.: MIT Press, 1985.

Wexler, Laura, and Elizabeth Young-Bruehl. "On 'Psychoanalysis and Feminism.'" *Social Research: An International Quarterly of the Social Sciences* 59 (Summer 1992): 453–83.

Whitebook, Joel. "Intersubjectivity and the Monadic Core of the Psyche: Habermas and Castoriadis on the Unconscious." *Praxis International* 9 (January 1990): 347–64.

———. *Perversion and Utopia: A Study in Psychoanalysis and Critical Theory.* Cambridge, Mass.: MIT Press, 1995.

———. "Reason and Happiness: Some Psychoanalytic Themes in Critical Theory." In *Habermas and Modernity,* edited by Richard J. Bernstein, 140–60. Cambridge, Mass.: MIT Press, 1985.

———. "Reconciling the Irreconcilable? Utopianism after Habermas." *Praxis International* 8 (April 1988): 73–90.

Wolfenstein, Eugene Victor. *Inside/Outside Nietzsche: Psychoanalytic Explorations.* Ithaca, N.Y.: Cornell University Press, 2000.

———. "Michel Foucault and Psychoanalytic-Marxism." *South Atlantic Quarterly* 97 (Spring 1998): 361–89.

———. "Psychoanalysis in Political Theory." *Political Theory* 24 (November 1996): 706–28.

———. "Reply to Curtis and Kalyvas." *Political Theory* 26 (December 1998): 825–29.

Wollheim, Richard. *Sigmund Freud.* Cambridge, UK: Cambridge University Press, 1971.

Yalom, Irvin D. *Love's Executioner and Other Tales of Psychotherapy.* New York: Basic, 1989.

———. *When Nietzsche Wept: A Novel of Obsession.* New York: Basic, 1992.

Index

About the Author

Abraham Drassinower is an assistant professor in the Faculty of Law at the University of Toronto. His teaching and research interests include property, intellectual property, legal and political philosophy, critical theory, and psychoanalysis.